THE IMPOSSIBLE JEW

£12.99

6c   J

14

The Impossible Jew

Identity and the Reconstruction of
Jewish American Literary History

Benjamin Schreier

NEW YORK UNIVERSITY PRESS
New York and London

NEW YORK UNIVERSITY PRESS
New York and London
www.nyupress.org

Cover art © Estate of Larry Rivers / Licensed by VAGA, New York, NY

References to Internet websites (URLs) were accurate at the time of writing.
Neither the author nor New York University Press is responsible for URLs
that may have expired or changed since the manuscript was prepared

LIBRARY OF CONGRESS CATALOGING-IN-PUBLICATION DATA
Schreier, Benjamin.
The impossible Jew : identity and the reconstruction of Jewish American
literary history / Benjamin Schreier.
pages cm   Includes bibliographical references and index.
ISBN 978-1-4798-6868-1 (cl : alk. paper)
ISBN 978-1-4798-9584-7 (pb : alk. paper)
1. Jewish literature—United States—History and criticism. 2. Jews—Identity.
3. Cahan, Abraham, 1860–1951—Criticism and interpretation. 4. Roth, Philip—
Criticism and interpretation. 5. Foer, Jonathan Safran, 1977– —Criticism and
interpretation. I. Title.
PS153.J4S37   2015
810.9'3529924—dc23   2014044422

New York University Press books are printed on acid-free paper,
and their binding materials are chosen for strength and durability.
We strive to use environmentally responsible suppliers and materials
to the greatest extent possible in publishing our books.

Manufactured in the United States of America

10 9 8 7 6 5 4 3 2 1

Also available as an ebook

To my mother and father, for teaching me that
there's no good way to be a Jew

CONTENTS

ACKNOWLEDGMENTS

Thanks first of all to Dean Franco, an extraordinary friend who helped me find my feet in academia and who lit the path when I started figuring out I wanted to write about Jewish American literature. I still seek him out, even when I know I'm headed for another misstep regardless of what he says; it's good to know there's a better way, if only for accounting purposes. Thanks also to Eric Hayot, who helped me work out, or through, or maybe just on, some of this book's key ideas when it in fact started looking like a book. He's been a weird, but great, mentor, despite being born the same year I was. Chris Castiglia at least had the decency to be older than I am in taking on the role of mentor. At Penn State, Jon Abel, Robin Becker, Kevin Bell, Hester Blum, Robert Caserio, Rich Doyle, Jonathan Eburne, Charlotte Eubanks, Kit Hume, Julia Kasdorf, Tony Kaye, Brian Lennon, Jonathan Marks, Aldon Nielsen, Daniel Purdy, Christopher Reed, Scott Smith, Susan Squier, and Lisa Sternlieb all, alphabetically, helped me in one way or another—sometimes both— as I worked on this book. Some graduate students here—exceptional intellects and responsible scholars—have also left their traces on this book: Abe Foley, Denise Grollmus, Ryan Marks, Emily Robins Sharpe, Matt Weber, and Susan Weeber.

I got into Jewish literature obliquely, having received no "proper" training or acculturation in the Jewish studies world; nonetheless, some phenomenal scholars have been nothing but encouraging as I clawed (and continue to claw) my way in: thanks (also alphabetically) to Jeremy Dauber, Jonathan Freedman, Michael P. Kramer, Adam Zachary Newton, Laurence Roth, Sarah Stein, and Hana Wirth-Nesher. I'd be remiss not to acknowledge also Rona Sheramy, who always seems to find five minutes or so in her busy schedule to hear me complain annually about the AJS. Pieces of this book saw light originally in a variety of places; thanks to Tom Beebee, Ezra Cappell, John Duvall, Rachel Gordan, Lori Harrison-Kahan, Sarah Imhoff, Josh Lambert, Jessica Lang, Holli

Levitsky, Dan Walden (z"l), Gary Weissman, and Steven Zipperstein, even if in at least one of those cases the person probably wants absolutely nothing to do with this book, for welcoming my contributions and urging me on. Daniel O'Hara has been tirelessly encouraging and an incredibly good reader—for years now. Thanks also to others: Paul Bové, David Deutsch, Nathaniel Deutsch, Marc Epstein, Caren Irr, Daniel Itzkovitz, Brett Kaplan, Hartley Lachter, Shaul Magid, Jeff Melnick, and Rob Tally.

Thanks to Sarah, Ava, and Reuben for so often suffering my neglect as I wrote. My dear friends David Greven and Alex Beecroft have provided me nothing but love and support for what is approaching twenty years. I can't express how much they mean to me; I could trot out some cliché, but it would sound like bullshit. So I'll let this impossibility stand as my acknowledgment. Thanks to my parents (see above). Thanks to my brother, Josh, and sister-in-law, Lise, who try not to roll on Shabbos; from the bris to this, they can't miss. And lastly, from the Wailing Wall to the social hall to all y'all, thanks to the Jews—well, at least some of them.

* * *

An early version of chapter 2 appeared as "Against the Dialectic of Nation: Abraham Cahan and Desire's Spectral Jew," *MFS Modern Fiction Studies* 57.2 (2011): 276–299. A small piece—like, no more than a fifth or a quarter—of chapter 3 appeared in a much earlier version as "New York Intellectual/Neocon/Jewish; or, How I Learned to Stop Worrying and Ignore Ruth Wisse," *Studies in American Jewish Literature* 31.1 (2012): 97–108. And I have adapted some discussions from "The Failure of Identity: Toward a New Literary History of Philip Roth's Unrecognizable Jew," *Jewish Social Studies* 17.2 (2011): 101–135, in various places throughout this book but in no place extensively, and the total is no more than a handful of pages. Finally, a generous grant from Penn State's Institute for the Arts and Humanities helped me write chapter 4.

Introduction

The School of Criticism I Wouldn't Be Caught Dead In:
A Polemic on Theorizing the Field

First things first: the take-away. In the interest of figuring out how a category of identity is critically put to work by Jewish literary study, this book tries to make it more difficult to assume that the study of Jewish literature is necessarily part of a larger study of The Jews as a population (or linked group of populations)—itself a concept or entity that must ultimately be taken for granted, at least in its categorical legibility, if it is going to mean anything at all. That is, we can make all kinds of noise about different kinds of Jewish populations and different modes of Jewish identification, but the problem this book addresses is the pernicious nationalism of thinking that relies on population—on the compelling security provided by a concept of population—to stabilize and underwrite the categorical identity of an archive of work. Alternatively, I suppose I could say that this book is part of a project to resituate Jewish studies in order to make room for a critical study of Jewish identity or Jewish identification, or of the ascription or detection or relevance of Jewish categoricalness, that is not grounded in the more or less ethnographically or anthropologically coded study of Jews and what they do and how they do it. Such a project would reconceptualize Jewish studies as operating precisely as the *displacement* of the assumption that Jewish studies is the study of Jews. But in fact I do not really want to put it this way, at least not primarily, because another thing I want this book to do is help break down the walls of the ghetto in which Jewish literary study these days so often seems to be contained, a ghetto instantiated simultaneously along three professionally powerful axes: on the one hand in the sometime seeming unwillingness on the part of fields such as comparative ethnicity studies, American studies, and multicultural literary studies to welcome Jewishness into the fold of privileged identities; on the other hand in the unwillingness of Jewish studies (that is, as a hegemonic bloc) either to accept critical literary studies as a legitimate part of its project or to pursue a sustained critique of identity, which would likely include opening itself to thinking its counterethnic other; and, amazingly, on a third hand in Jewish American literary study's fairly consistent aversion to sustained theorization and self-critique. But the problem I am really focused on in this book is the way in which Jewish American literary study has isolated itself. While American studies and ethnic American literary formations have been busy putting themselves through rigorous processes of self-criticism over the past forty years or so, the field of Jewish American literary history has, in a word, not. Only very recently, in the last generation, have we seen any kind of sustained push among critics in Jewish American literary history toward self-theorizing work, and even then this kind of scholarship has represented a pretty small minority. Thus, if Jewish American literary study has been excluded from the institutionally validated embrace of academic ethnicity- and American studies–based formations, we can also read this exclusion as symptomatic; in any case, though there is certainly work to pursue on the comparative and ethnic studies side of things, this book proceeds as a critique of the compensations of Jewish American literary study's self-imposed ghetto, of its own separatist and nationalist biases, more than anything else. Thus my problem here: I am criticizing precisely the people I want to convince. In a ridiculous perversion of the Groucho Marx joke, I am trying to become a member of the club I cannot stop complaining about.[1]

Even while this book is often polemical, one of its central goals is to emphasize the lines of relation and mutuality between Jewish American literary study and those institutional establishments from which it persists in alienation, such as American studies, multicultural and multiethnic studies, critical theory, and Jewish studies. But the path toward cooperation that *The Impossible Jew* takes is not one charted by comparativist methodologies. The critical future of Jewish American literary study lies in a nonidentitarian concept of identity that theorizes how the desire for historiographic reference overdetermines and disrupts the seductive coordination of identity and normalization that so often erects barriers of ostensible historical self-evidence between readily recognizable groups—and between the professional formations that invest them; Jewish American literary study's model of identification cannot be reduced to the representational historicism authorizing the humanities' recognitive obsession with anthropologistic reference. A generation ago, Jonathan Rutherford argued, in describing the evolution of his own thinking about identity and difference, "Most writing on the cultural politics of difference has been formulated from marginal positions—those places that my own ethnic, sexual and class location has constructed as the Other";[2] the dominant paradigms through which the academy customarily thinks about difference indeed frequently take the form of minoritarian-coded practices inflected in some way by a concern with resistance. *The Impossible Jew* on the other hand aims to interrupt those reifying procedures that precognitively situate the thinking of difference in often nationalistically, and almost always positivistically, legible populations. Jewish American literary study can sustain a critique of how a concept of identity functions as a police form in the ethnographically limned historicist study of identifiable groups—and therefore opens itself up to an array of critical identity projects situated in other recognizable ethnic, multicultural, comparative, and/or theoretical fields. Thus though my focus is pretty much exclusively on Jewish American literary studies and the habits through which its practitioners operate in what sometimes looks very much like a golden ghetto, I hope this book can operate as a kind of goodwill gesture to the future of the critique of identity more generally.

The Impossible Jew begins with a category problem. Because it is difficult to imagine identity-based literary history without a concept of identity, those of us working in the field of Jewish American literature specifically and Jewish studies more generally need to account for the Jewishness that anchors the field—much as our friends in other identity-based fields have had to do with their field-defining concepts. Now I should say at the outset (as I hope will not be a surprise) that I am perfectly willing—even happy—to allow claims to the effect that Jewish American writers do not have to be read as Jewish American writers— according to the same logic that suggests that African American writers do not have to be read only in African American literature classes, that LGBT writers do not have to be read only in queer studies classes, that male and/or female writers do not have to be read only in gender studies classes, and so on. I still remember an anonymous reader's report that recommended rejection for an article I had submitted to a reputable scholarly journal some years ago (a recommendation that was heeded, I should add). The reader, imagining him- or herself (I myself imagine) unsettling the grounds of my argument (which had to do with the terms in which it is possible and/or desirable to talk about the Jewishness of literature by and about Jews), insisted that Jewish writers will be valued on the basis of the quality, not of the Jewishness, of their writing (the exact words were "Jewish American literature won't survive because of its Judaic sources, its Jewishness so-to-speak, but solely through its literature"; I still have the letter). Though I think that is debatable, at least insofar as *Kaaterskill Falls* and *The Chosen* are still in print, I of course concede the point that the reader was trying to make. That said, this reviewer punted precisely the problem he or she positioned him- or herself to address, which is the problem of categories and categoricalness: once one employs a category like "Jewish American literature" and expects it to do any work whatsoever, one takes on a responsibility for that category, which involves, at the very least, theorizing it. Confident (and sometimes sanctimonious) talk about an alternative between literary value and its putative others often serves as a smokescreen or diversion rooted in the purported positivity of literary work, a distraction from focusing on the habits and procedures that govern the production, circulation, and legibility of literary judgments. For the time being, at least, there are culturally viable, institutionally legible, and professionally compensated methods and practices for categorizing, reading, teaching, interpreting, and indeed publishing on Jewish literature, and it is under the aegis of these methods that a lot of writing by Jewish authors is read and discussed. It was certainly under the aegis of such methods that I had submitted the article in question for publication. That said, for a critic to recognize his or her situation within a dominant professional order does not have to be the same thing as embracing or assenting to the reproduction of this order's institutional claim of self-evidence. The problem I start with is therefore a choice that must be perpetually confronted and reconfronted: By what right and through what procedures is the Jewishness that orients the field of Jewish American literary study anchored? Are we going to contest the Jewishness under the rubric of which Jewish American literature is professionally given—that is, as a field, as it is encountered, read, studied, cognized, taught, known, and/or analyzed—or are we going to naturalize it by taking it for granted? Are we going to use this contestation to forge alliances with other critical projects, or are we going to take advantage of an institutional security grounded in the identity category's legibility?

It is one thing to start with a canon of texts already certified as "Jewish" and analyze them as such, which likely participates, even tacitly, in an effort to inventory some set of elements common to those texts and to link that inventory to a claim about the texts' Jewishness. This kind of professionalized literary historical labor, while useful, naturalizes the Jewish identity of Jewish literature and assumes the critic's ability to recognize it; moreover, it usually links into a project to secure the coherence of a specifically Jewish subject formation that unifies all historical expressions of Jewish culture—in large part by taking that subject for granted. It is another thing entirely, however, to begin by imagining how a criticism invested in the concept of Jewish identity takes up literary practices—that is, practices that span "literature," "literary history," and "literary criticism"[3]—in the interest of analyzing the modes in which they contest how texts can come to be recognized as Jewish; in this case, the burden of identity-based criticism shifts to the literary critical apparatus itself in its bearing toward texts whose categorical legibility—as Jewish—cannot be taken for granted. Such a realignment would call for a reconceptualization of the fundamental identity-based literary historical question: not What can we say about this Jewish text? but How does this text enable an identitarian literary historical practice or agency? The former question inevitably sees a legitimated historical narrative as a canon's representational foundation: Jewish literature furnishes access to a Jewish history that we do not doubt our ability to recognize. The second question, however, arises in the absence of that kind of methodological and historiographic—and anthropological or ethnographic—confidence and therefore cannot consider the literary historical problem of identity as essentially delineated by already-legitimated regions of identitarian self-evidence (such as "ethnicity" or "population"); uncertain what Jews look like, literary criticism in this mode seeks to devise vocabularies for a discourse of Jewyness.[4] Such a critical discourse would begin by not conceptualizing identity in literature primarily in terms of reference, representation, or proper-ty,[5] and certainly not in the name of a unity or totality organized under the banner of nationalism, and would instead investigate how knowledge of identity is produced, an investigation that necessarily locates itself not where individuals and groups are identifiable but rather at the limits of processes of identification and classification.

Jewish American literary study cannot ground itself in an assumption that Jews call out from the texts of history to be recognized; we must consider the categorically disruptive possibility that the act of literary historical identification is conditioned by our critical practices. Despite a recent surge in critical work on Jewish American literature, too much scholarship remains dominated by the historicist expectation of an identifiable historical subject of which literature is presumed to constitute part of the record. It is a mistake for Jewish American literary study to understand the literature ultimately by way of an identifiable and/or legible, which is at some level to say coherent, Jewish people, however pluralized such a fundamentally biologistic concept might be—usually via one or more legitimated narratives of Jewish American social or cultural history (such as assimilation, a political shift rightward, changing relations with African Americans, secularization, or post-Holocaust Zionism). By doing so, it inevitably conceives of itself as an arm of a larger, multidisciplinary narrative of The Jew that depends on a kind of nationalist logic as it confidently looks for traces of a recognizable Jewish subject. As much as the general historiographic project often articulated under the umbrella of Jewish studies (no matter a particular endeavor's disciplinary home) may attend to the transformation and/or multiplicity of its "Jewish" object matter, it largely retains a prescriptive identitarian confidence that this object stably persists in being "Jewish."

As I signposted at the outset, the Jewish American literary field seems now to be paying the price for such nationalist insularity, in the form of insiderism, trivialization, and ghettoization. But it is a complex process of ghettoization, with multiple and often discontinuous histories and agents accounting for it; I will take up this problem in a more sustained manner in chapter 1. Part of the problem is certainly that other fields that one might expect to concern themselves with Jewish or Jewish American identity and the machinery of Jewish identification, or that under other circumstances might so concern themselves, continue to avoid the field; thus Jewish studies is only rarely made (or thought to be) a part of academic ethnicity studies formations, and Jewish American literature is not always included in the welter of identity groups privileged by the academic study of American multicultural literature. Anecdotes undoubtedly abound, but here is some (selective) evidence: the words "Jew" and "Judaic" and their variants show up only a handful of times in Abdul JanMohamed and David Lloyd's important collection *The Nature and Context of Minority Discourse*, for example, many simply as quotations from Deleuze and Guattari's Kafka book and a few others in the context of Israeli Hebrew-language writing about the Israel-Palestine conflict; "Jewish" shows up only three times in David Palumbo-Liu's 1995 *The Ethnic Canon*, and never as a serious focus, for another well-remarked example; and the word appears another handful of times in Michael Omi and Howard Winant's *Racial Formation in the United States*, mostly merely in lists of various ethnicities.[6] Christopher Douglas's *A Genealogy of Literary Multiculturalism*, more firmly anchored in establishment English-department-based multiculturalist Americanism than these other books, explicitly eschews analysis of Jewish literature because American Jews are not a group "whose members continue to be racialized";[7] this clearly amounts to a kind of evasion of Jewish American literary study's problematic status. Jewish American literature obviously carries little of the prestige or capital of ethnic literature anchors such as Latina/o, Asian American, and Native American literatures, and I wonder how many search committees advertising for jobs in broadly defined "US multiethnic lit" have Jewish literature in mind. A second contributing factor in the ongoing ghettoization of Jewish American literary study, however, is that Jewish studies as an institutional formation continues to look with suspicion on the methodologies, practices, and even archives of literary history and criticism. While disciplines such as philology remain esteemed by, and retain their capital in, the Jewish studies complex, modern literature and literary studies, particularly as taking shape in texts written in America, in texts written in languages other than the identitarian fetish languages Yiddish or Hebrew, and in texts written since 1900, continues to be undervalued—especially when this literature is taken as an object of literary studies rather than of historiography.[8] And a third root of this ghettoization, finally, is that until fairly recently, the bulk of Jewish American literary historiography has been content to pursue an undertheorized practice. Mark Shechner has recently discussed how Jewish American literary studies so frequently seems to lack the dynamism and self-theorization that characterize the other "ethnic" American literature fields: while many other "studies" fields consistently criticize their own methodologies and archives, Jewish American literary study frequently seems more or less fixed and complacent, even antitheoretical.[9] According to Shechner, however, it is not that Jewish American literary studies lacks a theory of itself; it in fact has embraced one—immigration—but has so naturalized and normalized it that no one ever thinks of analyzing or mentioning it, lacking the professional will or sometimes even capacity to make it an object of thought or criticism. As will become abundantly clear (if indeed it is not obvious already), I am in *The Impossible Jew* fairly sympathetic to this argument, though I expand from Shechner's specific focus on immigration to look at the restrictive effect of the field's precognitive historicism more generally.

Even close to four decades since Philip Roth's Nathan Zuckerman began mercilessly parodying the literary professional search for an extraliterary Jewish referent, too many scholars still presume that a more or less uncritical representational historicism is the best way to coordinate (I resist calling this practice "reading") Jewish American literature's Jew. But what happens to identity-based literary study if we no longer take for granted the location, fact, and accounting of Jewish American identification? What if the structure of the literary historical triangulation of author, text, and recognizable identity or identifiable historical subject were not taken to be self-evident, and what if we thought about Jewish American literary criticism as emerging out of a text's resistance to categorical confidence about Jews? I argue here that what we possibly still too easily call Jewish American literature continues to be pressingly relevant as a countertext to—decisively *not*, that is, a positive escape from—a historicist literary historical paradigm, ascendant at least since the 1960s and '70s, that takes identity for granted as a secure literary historical position.[10] One of my central arguments in *The Impossible Jew* is that if the institution of Jewish American literary study allows us to argue that Jewish identification is a relentless theme throughout Jewish American literature—and we have to admit at the very least that it certainly can be seen to be—then such identification in fact mostly only uncertainly and dubiously erupts in these texts. As Michael Kramer's critique of literary history's romance with "metonymic ethnicity" can help illuminate, Jewish American literary scholarship must attend more rigorously to the destabilizing confrontation between its own desire for Jewish identity and the literature's depiction of a miscarried Jewish identification.[11]

To restage my encounter with the unsatisfied reviewer, therefore, we might say that the field of Jewish American literary study cannot take for granted how—but really even that—Jewish literature is Jewish. If we do not need to read writers born with a touch of the Torah brush for their texts' "Jewishness," then if we *are* interested in a literary historical concept of Jewish identity, we need to admit that the field of Jewish American literary study inheres at least partly, but undeniably and necessarily, in the often professionalized, and always institutionally situated, activity of treating literature as "Jewish"—I am not sure why or how else we would maintain the field. We do not have to maintain the field, certainly, but if we do find it important enough to maintain—and university courses, academic programs, professional conferences, and journals and publishers' lists at the very least certainly suggest that an infrastructure persists for maintaining it—we do so by choosing to read texts as Jewish, enabling the field precisely in this choice. The categorically "Jewish" subject that Jewish American literary study—and more widely Jewish studies in general—identifies in "Jewish" texts is in fact, at least in part, consolidated by the constitutive practices through which we read, teach, and write about those texts. Jewish identity and identification are at once the field-organizing ideals of Jewish American literary study and the spectral strategic location of Jewish American literary study. But if this is a constitutive problem for the field of Jewish American literature, it also provides a site at which Jewish American literary study can contest its alienation from other fields, insofar as it is a problem that is largely shared with any "Jewish studies" work broadly pursued under the Jewish identity rubric and, more widely, by other marginal, minority, and/or ethnic studies formations.

Even as I say this, however, I must also admit that this is a realization that is belated in Jewish American literary study, as it is in Jewish studies more generally. The fact is that many other fields of ethnic study have for some time been exploring the critical ruptures that open out of this awareness. Particularly helpful to my project in *The Impossible Jew* have been Kandice Chuh's argument for the "subjectlessness" of Asian

American discourse and Ramón Saldívar's elaboration of what he calls a "postracial" aesthetics. Chuh's attempt to displace debates about Asian American subjectivity that ultimately depend on some version of ethnographic identity for intelligibility is pressingly relevant to Jewish American literary studies; the point is not to construct yet another positive formulation of Jewish difference but rather to prioritize the negativity of difference by insisting that a subject only becomes recognizable and can act as such by conforming to certain regulatory matrices. Subjectlessness for Chuh is a "conceptual tool" for a "strategic anti-essentialism"; if we imagine a field (such as Asian American studies or Jewish studies) as subjectless, then rather than looking to complete the identitarian category (whether Asian American or Jewish American or anything else), to actualize it through methods such as inventorying its characteristics or enumerating the various components of its differences, critics would be positioned to contest the institutional effects of the "various configurations of power and knowledge," both inside and outside the academy, "through which the term comes to have meaning." As a method, subjectlessness produces the subject as "always also an epistemological object."[12] Saldívar's term "postrace" lays some of the groundwork for how I put that project to work in *The Impossible Jew*. As he explains, "the term 'postrace' does not mean that we are *beyond* race; the prefix 'post' here does not mean a chronological 'superseding,' a triumphant posteriority. Rather, the term entails a conceptual shift to the question of what meaning the *idea* of 'race' carries in our own times. The *post* of postrace is not like the *post* of post-structuralism; it is more like the *post* of postcolonial, that is, a term designating not a chronological but a conceptual frame." For Saldívar, the postrace aesthetic performs how "race in the twenty-first century still matters, not as a line to be crossed or as the substance of difference . . . but as a real effect of imaginary patterns of behavior."[13]

Jewish literary study needs to build on this kind of critical work that addresses the representational problems of identity and identification. To be sure, there has been work in what has become known as Jewish cultural studies that aims to complicate the representation of identity and its history—one thinks, for example, of such works as Jonathan Boyarin's *Thinking in Jewish*; Ann Pellegrini's *Performance Anxieties*; Jonathan and Daniel Boyarin's *Critical Inquiry* essay "Diaspora: Generation and the Ground of Jewish Identity" and their edited volume *Jews and Other Differences*; David Biale, Michael Galchinsky, and Susannah Heschel's edited volume *Insider/Outsider*; Sander Gilman's *Jewish Frontiers*; Daniel Boyarin, Daniel Itzkovitz, and Ann Pellegrini's edited volume *Queer Theory and the Jewish Question*; Caryn Aviv and David Shneer's *New Jews*; Vincent Brook's edited volume *You Should See Yourself: Jewish Identity in Postmodern American Culture*; and Jonathan Freedman's *Klezmer America*.[14] But such works as these remain a small offshoot in a much larger and dominant archive of identitarian Jewish studies work that too often eschews critical interrogation of its constitutive terms. Moreover, works such as these, coming out in the 1990s and the first decade of this century, were emerging in the wake of an intense academic investment in identity studies programs—a sustained professional response to a multilateral critique of essentialism across the humanities that, when taken up by the institutional bureaucracies necessary to put it to work in mounting departments, programs, and faculty positions in the various identity studies fields, had the perverse effect of contributing to the very structures of Balkanization that the lessons of antiessentialism ostensibly warned against.[15] I am arguing neither that this historical fact evacuates these works of critical potential nor that my own work is insulated from it. But a critical Jewish studies has to work very hard to contest this inherent gravitational fall back toward identitarianism.

Critics working in the Jewish American literary field need therefore to appreciate a disruption at the heart of our enterprise: representation cannot be thought to *organize* our field—that is, we cannot take for granted that Jews, Jewish identity, and/or Jewish history are represented in Jewish literature—because the possibility of representation is in fact *organized by* the constitutive activity of the field, because much of what we can actually point to as being categorically represented in a given text is a spectral product of our interpretive desire. We can call this a hegemonic institutional formation: beginning in the authorizing expectation that already-legitimated Jewish texts necessarily link to a Jewish subject or history ensures that representation represents primarily the hegemonic critic's own historical imagination, insofar as the already-legible narratives of Jewish history that Jewish literary history mobilizes to resolve Jewish literature are themselves the products of interpretive will. Once the decision is made to treat a text as Jewish, the Jewish signified overdetermines the textual signifier, making the text representative of "its" Jewish identity. The Jewish unity or identity of a text is not a datum or textual attribute; it is a project, produced in the institutionally bound activity of reading and deferred through an assemblage of metonymic recognitions. Thus a text's Jewishness can never be finally fixed or positively located; to begin analytic investigation in the assumption that Jewish "difference" is a positivity that anchors or guides historical inquiry can never amount to anything other than an instantiation of the critic's compensated and legitimated penchant for recognizing the totalizing identity he or she wants to recognize. This is why historicism is a banal, self-confirming dead end for identity-based literary study. A critical Jewish American literary study needs to approach texts obliquely, remaining open to the resistance of interminable parodic or simulacral traces of its own interpretive desire.

Showing how an unstable anxiety about identity in writing by American Jews gets reinscribed by a professional-institutional desire—taking form in literary historical practice—to recognize Jews, *The Impossible Jew* seeks to liberate Jewish American literary study from a normalizing historicist project oriented around the expected recognition of a nationalistically coherent Jewish substance or population, however pluralized it may be, a project that imagines itself subservient to the historiography of a subject it does not ultimately call into question. I am tempted to call this kind of criticism "essentialist," insofar as it normatively predicates itself on the existence of a historical Jewish "essence"—even if only assumed and not even explicitly so at that—that unifies the variety of historical manifestations of Jewish culture and being, no matter how much these manifestations shift or change over time or how this "essence" is defined. But this term is so overloaded by now with institutionally bound meanings, past debates, and academic canards—and so dismissible—as to be more obfuscating than clarifying. David Biale, for example, in his early essay "Confessions of an Historian of Jewish Culture," voiced a reasonable suspicion that most Jewish studies scholars do not have much interest in or use for "a monolithic definition of Judaism" but instead operate in the context of an interest in a much "wider set of practices," namely, a deessentialized "horizon of Jewish culture." Hoping to expose the "hegemonic" construction of the "fiction" of an "autonomous" religious concept of Judaism, Biale advocated a "counter-historical" historiography that would function "to subvert established myths from the past and thus open up new possibilities for Jewish self-definition today"—such as by pointing out "the tensions and interactions between texts and contexts, between intellectual elites and the broader culture of which they are a part." Jewish studies scholars would presumably thus be less interested in policing the boundaries of some fictively unified and "authoritative" set of religious practices than in exploring the variety of all those populations that self-define as "Jewish."[16] Amos Funkenstein made a parallel argument grounded in the same fundamental logic in his essay "The Dialectics of Assimilation."[17] And yet this gesture toward liberal expansiveness underlying such broad-gauge cultural studies approaches—or rather the structure of the theoretical move that sanctions it—betrays a fundamental identitarianism precisely in ostensibly moving beyond one. Such arguments as Biale's and Funkenstein's, and as have been reproduced across a mainstream of liberal/left Jewish studies scholarship that they have authorized, in fact appeal to historical diversity and the interpenetration of text and context only insofar as they rely on a structuring concept of identity that works precisely by controverting any epiphenomenal diversity. If Biale wants us to doubt the organized coherence of "Judaism," he calls on us to recognize the organized coherence of "Jewish culture"—and indeed to reinscribe the authority of its categorical unity. The stuff of Jewish studies analysis here may be continually in flux, revising and reinventing itself, even unfixed and inessentially constructed, but the categorical identity—that is, as *Jewish*—of the legibly Jewish entity continually resolving into an object of scholarly regard in such work is never in any way disrupted; below all the flux and revision and reinvention, an identitarian foundation remains quite stably and always already recognizably Jewish. Such ostensibly antiessentialist arguments for historical contingency are in fact grounded in the primordial act of taking for granted an identifiable Jewish subject. So instead of using a term like "essentialist," as I have already tipped my hand, I am using the possibly even more polemical term "nationalist," which is also overloaded, though I hope less securely so.

The reductio ad absurdum of the kind of historicist scholarship I am challenging here is Ruth Wisse, insofar as she illustrates the dangerous surveillance—what William Spanos describes as a process of "overseeing"[18]—inscribed by historicism's fall toward identitarianism. Wisse is an interesting figure of institutional power insofar as her influence is attested even in much of the work that challenges her. An indication of her leading or hegemonic role can be found in the frequency with which the phrase "brilliant but flawed" and its ideological cognates can be found in reference to her work.[19] It is a notable gesture, a kind of heterodox obeisance: whereby scholars reaffirm her claim to the field even in marking their own revisionist stance in relation to it, thereby reinscribing her masterful position or leading function. In any case, I turn here to her work because it so starkly illuminates the theoretical and political investments of historicist scholarship. Wisse begins her gate-keeping defense of a modern Jewish canon by admitting a putative problem of canon definition, at least one as buttressed by concepts of nation and state as hers is: essentially, the fact of modern Jewish multilingualism and even multiculturalism. But she quickly belies any apparent anxiety by betraying her fundamental axiom—that "there exists a modern Jewish people" that anchors the identity of, insofar as it is "reflected" in, even the most "centrifugal"-seeming set of modern Jewish literature.[20] Wisse opposes her mission to an apathetic or pessimistic— certainly superficial—perception of a "centrifugal" modern Jewry, marked by "the decline of religious faith, the disintegration of cohesive communities, the weakening of ethnic ties": "Yet just as there exists a modern Jewish people, so too does a modern Jewish literature exist, and I hope to show that the difficulty of defining them does not lessen their actuality" (xv). It is as if the very grammar of that final sentence testifies to Wisse's project: syntactically, one expects those final two pronouns— "them" and "their"—to refer to "literature," but really, she is only interested in "modern Jewish literature" as evidence of, dependent on, and ancillary to the "modern Jewish people" that is the real subject of her nationalist project. As she succinctly puts it a few pages later, "Modern Jewish literature is the repository of modern Jewish experience. It is the most complete way of knowing the inner life of Jews" (4).

My objection to this kind of literary historical project is twofold.[21] First, Wisse offers no theoretical account of how her "people" is "reflected" in her "literature," mostly, I imagine, because she does not think she needs to; how does the identity or "inner life" of the "modern

Jewish people" make its way into, and therefore guarantee the categorical definition of, "modern Jewish literature"? This question is an unavoidable one for any critical Jewish literary study, but Wisse seemingly does not address it; or at least she does not find it necessary to theorize the concept of representation underlying her approach. My guess, incidentally, is that she relies on something like liberal nationalism's culturally generative notion of race to do the job. Second, I object to the police function that Wisse ascribes to her Jewish literary canon; even as it "reflects" a unified Jewish historical body, Wisse's category of "Jewish literature" in fact consolidates dispersed Jewry by dint of its very categorical coherence: "the works I feature derive so powerfully from a particular cultural community that they make a special claim on the members of that community to be reabsorbed by them in a cycle of creative renewal" (5). This surveilling move is an unpardonable sin for any truly critical Jewish literary study, but Wisse's work is seemingly reducible to it. For Wisse, the history of Jewish literature and the historical Jewish subject metonymically reinforce, by testifying to, each other: though it is difficult to pin down the antecedent of her final "them," in her clause "reabsorbed by them" (another troubling and powerful pronoun), for her it hardly matters. On this score, I am tempted to double down and call the statist normativity of Wisse's work "Zionist," insofar as this literary historical police function repeats the nationalist ingathering of the Diaspora that Zionist ideology promotes—a repetition or parallel notable in normalizing identitarian terms such as "reabsorb" and "renewal." That said, I will admit that I hesitate in appealing to the term "Zionism" insofar as I do not want my work to be sucked into the intellectual vacuum that is the academic alternation between, on the one hand, the reactionary lunacy of those who equate any criticism of Israel with anti-Semitism and, on the other, untempered doltish denunciation of any scholarly privileging of Jewish identity as tarnished by an association with Israeli oppression.[22] In any case, Wisse's police function reproduces, more generally, a form of legibility determined and contained by the logic of the state form.

Having said this, I should point out that the effort to compile and justify an archive constitutes necessary work for critical Jewish literary study. But it is not sufficient work. And the project as Wisse conceptualizes and articulates it—that is, as, at a fundamental level, militantly nationalist labor—is undertheorized, anticritical, and bullying, and it suppresses the analytical ability to contest the givenness of Jewish identity that Wisse so desperately wants professional scholarship to take for granted. Thus the real problem that I am trying to address here is ultimately not, as some readers might anticipate, the gate-keeping modality of this kind of scholarship, its desire to police who gets to count as Jewish and who does not, who is allowed into the Jewish canon and who is not; there is already a healthy body of Jewish studies work that undertakes just this critique, and many of my readers who might be tempted to respond to the preceding with a healthy "What the hell are you even bothering talking about Ruth Wisse for?" are to varying degrees likely in accord with it. The more fundamental problem—and the one *The Impossible Jew* aims primarily to challenge—is the identitarian logic that not only is fundamental to Wisse's polemic but lies at the foundation of so much Jewish-studies-sponsored scholarship: the anthropological expectation that a legibly Jewish population (or populations) stands as the final representational guarantor of a body of literature. This is a nationalist operation that even much scholarship otherwise explicitly hostile to Wisse's nationalist project, I think, may in fact share. My point is not that historicism is necessarily a scholarly parochialism; it is that nationalist habits of thought are the inevitable concomitant of the representative methodologies in which historicism inheres.

The Impossible Jew asks what happens for Jewish American literary study "after" identity. Following efforts to chart a "postracial" or "subjectless" criticism, the book works toward a postidentitarian concept of identity, one that grounds a literary critical practice that recognizes that we need a concept of identity for literary study not in order to normalize what we might call, following recent elaborations of the concept of biopolitics, a biologistic humanities practice grounded in the legibility of a historical population that today we have little choice but to understand via racialist conceptual habits structured by a concept of heritability, but precisely insofar as it enables us to critically think about the normative power of identity as an organizing principle, about the relay points whereby epistemological practices and administrative practices cross each other.[23] Foucault's argument that the "point of departure for the organizational line of a 'biopolitics'" is the "doubling" wherein the political concept of the subject of right appears as a "population a government must manage" provides a powerful critical tool for analyzing the ways in which population as a historical-biological phenomenon and population as a historiographic-normative phenomenon can be considered not simply relevant to each other but necessary to each other.[24] Biopolitics' emphasis on how a population recognized as a set of living beings falls under specific forms of knowledge and techniques that are themselves rationalized according to the demands of the management of state forces helps to illuminate or model the administrative power and knowledge practices organized by what I am calling the biologistic concept of identity in Jewish studies. Any predication of identity—as "Jewish" or ethnic or anything else—carries with it a series of critical questions about its own possibility and the practices it underwrites, including questions about what such predication allows critics to do, about the desirability of a vocabulary of identity, about the ethics of identification, about the constitution of canons, about professional habits and institutional practices, and so on. I mean the "after" in "after identity" to point toward a reimagining of what "identity" means for literary practice. Taking work such as Saldívar's and Chuh's as a launching-off point, I am interested in resolving critical practices potentially capable of disrupting the biologism of current representational-historicist habits of thinking about and around ethnicized identity. My goal is to show how identity does not have to circulate exclusively as the effect of a biologization that prevents analysis of its function as a form of criticism.[25] *The Impossible Jew* charts the possible contours of a Jewish American literary study that neither embraces the self-evidence of identitarian markers nor believes that we simply are beyond or have superseded them but rather is dedicated to questioning the meaning and efficaciousness of the idea of identity. *The Impossible Jew* argues for reading "Jewish" for the historiographic, affective, institutional, and professional desires that invest the term and that in turn invest the field of the term's application, rather than for a population to which the term ultimately, presumably, refers. Judith Butler describes a site of contestation as "the point of departure for a set of historical reflections and futural imaginings" and as such "never fully owned, but always only redeployed, twisted, queered from a prior usage and in the direction of urgent and expanding political purposes";[26] following this definition, this book contests the ineluctable relay between representation and identity for the practices that constitute Jewish literary study, Jewish studies more broadly, and the humanities in general.

The Impossible Jew employs a literary critical concept of Jewishness not to render a Jewish population or Jewish writers as an object of historical analysis but to explore the history, meaning, and power—simultaneously and contradictorily cultural, social, political, intellectual, institutional, and religious—of Jewish identity. I want at least to begin the process of rendering the act of ascribing Jewish identity—in my specific case, the literary critical act of ascribing Jewish identity—as an object of analysis. In alliance with José David Saldívar's project in *Trans-Americanity*, I have in a sense tried to turn the adjectives "Jewish" and "Jewish American" into nouns, approaching these identifying concepts, thought processes, and practices of ascription and categorization as the simultaneous vehicles and objects of Jewish American literary study—as the objects of a critical Jewish American literary practice *precisely insofar* as they operate as its vehicles.[27] Doing so, scholars, critics, and readers can release the interpretive desire for categorical predication and even communal belonging from the nationalist documentary orbit in which it so frequently restrictively circulates. When we redirect our analysis away from an identifiable Jewish subject assumed to representationally underwrite a canon of Jewish American literature and toward an anxiety about Jewish identification that is as much a characteristic of our critical practice as it is a phenomenon in the texts we take to be proper to that practice, we reimagine too the temporality of Jewish identity: no longer anchored in the stable coherence of an ethnographically or biologistically secure Jewish past, identity-based literary criticism can derive its sanction from an as-yet-undiscerned future of Jewish identifiability. *The Impossible Jew* hopes to open space for an alternate critical discourse about Jewish identity that would examine the desire for identification as a critical criterion for the examination of texts. In the process, I range over well-trod textual ground in my close reading of Jewish American texts, but always in order to show how that ground has suffered the imposition of a reductive nationalist[28] cartography. Rather, and more significantly, than helping us understand Jews, Jewish literature can help us understand how we structure our thinking about Jews—how, as Jonathan Boyarin might put it, we "think in Jewish."[29]

* * *

One final note on how I proceed in this book. *The Impossible Jew* is precisely not the kind of book that reads Jewish American literature for a particular representative characteristic or function of Jewish American literature, and it does not try to make historiographically representative claims about Jewish American texts or more or less sociological or ethnographic claims about the Jews who wrote them. I do not try to instrumentalize or impose on a sanctioned set of Jewish American texts a methodological rubric or trope or specific lens, nor do I try to recover for the field of literary study the virtues of some set of heretofore unrecognized texts. Instead, I have tried to read established texts—that is, largely uncontroversial texts considered exemplary or representative of a Jewish American canon—against the professionalizing machine of their historicist canonicity. As such, the chapters to follow appear not as episodes in a historical narrative about Jewish American literature but rather as moments in the successive elaboration of a critical counternarrative of Jewish canonicity. The book does not articulate a theoretical rubric in its first chapter and then "apply" it across a set of representative texts in the following chapters so much as it is organized around a problem about Jewish identification arising in the encounter between habitualized ways of thinking about literature and professional literary practice on the one hand and an institutionally legible canon of Jewish American literature on the other.

After chapter 1's genealogy of the nationalist identitarianism underwriting the current academic isolation of the historicist mainstream of Jewish American literary practice, four chapters follow that proceed chronologically according to the texts standing as their analytical occasion but that try to rebuild a critical Jewish American literary study step by step. Across all four of these chapters, the book articulates a concept of particularity for the study of identity that is neither positivistically opposed to some ontological concept of universality nor grounded in what is inevitably nationalized and biologized ethnic self-evidence. Through a close reading of Abraham Cahan's turn-of-the-century novella "The Imported Bridegroom," chapter 2 begins this process by imagining what an identity-based literary critical practice would look like that seeks its authorization from a future of identification about which it necessarily remains uncertain rather than from a recognizable identitarian past about which it cannot but be confident. Thus liberated from an arboreal paradigm of identity-based literary history, chapter 3 takes as its focus the ways in which a main current in scholarship on the New York intellectuals has, by preconceiving these critics as representative of the experience of a Jewish American subject, cleared ground for a racialist-nationalist biographical project that reads the rise of Zionist neoconservatism from the belly of the New York intellectuals as a natural or inevitable emergence overseen by a concept of responsibility to Jewish polity; in this chapter, I show how a biologistic interpretive framework displaces the possibility of critical interrogation of the ways in which Jewishness becomes legible. If chapters 2 and 3 focus on the habits of thought in which historicist identitarianism polices a biologist nationalism in the understanding of identity-based literature, combining to displace the self-evidence of a Jewish historical subject that might serve as the presumed object of Jewish American literary study, then chapters 4 and 5 pivot to chart literary practices that reinscribe the possibility of counternormative Jewish identification outside the secure markers of a biologistically self-evident Jewish history. Focusing on Philip Roth's 1986 novel *The Counterlife*, which stands near the middle of Roth's nearly-thirty-year-long chronicle of writer Nathan Zuckerman, chapter 4 takes its cue from Zuckerman's claim at the end of the novel that he can only be a Jew where there are no other Jews to argue that Roth's Zuckerman books critically illuminate the desire for Jewish self-evidence, showing that the discourse of "The Jew" demands a necessary critical text to supplement it; Roth is important to Jewish American literary study because his work stages the fundamental polemical labor of a Jewish literary history. Chapter 5, finally, argues that Jonathan Safran Foer's 9/11 book *Extremely Loud and Incredibly Close* forces us to admit that its Jewishness is completely dependent on our desire to find it; the book positions us to think of identity not primarily as something represented in narrative but more fundamentally as a specter haunting the narrative place where it is desired. In figuring precisely this literary historical desire for identity, Foer's book points us toward a responsible way to retain Jewish identity as a critical term.

Over the years I wrote this book, I toyed (of course) with the phrase "The State of Jewish American Literary Studies" or something similarly clever. The idea was a double entendre—deadpan turn to the camera—suggesting that in taking a look at the current situation in the field, I am also analyzing a predominant statism in professional thinking about Jewish American literature. Though better sense prevailed, even a cursory look through the book insists on the importance of a critique of statism. Sometimes this is obvious, as in my discussion of the reactionary Zionism through which an autobiographical neoconservative narrative has reinscribed the legacy of the New York intellectuals. But everywhere this book aims to destabilize and denaturalize the hegemonic gravity by which literary historical thinking about identity is pulled toward historicist structures, procedures, and habits that conform with the logic of state. This includes the tendency to think of literature in terms of documentarity, representativity, and positivism and to think of identity in a cluster with nation, body, population, and subject.

1

Toward a Critical Semitism

On Not Answering the Jewish Question in Literary Studies

I wrote this book because the professional study of Jewish American literature has repeatedly raised two questions for me: first, Why has Jewish studies had such a difficult and unsatisfying relationship with multiculturalism, with critical identity studies, and with critical theory more generally? and second, Why does literary study in general, but especially Jewish American literary study, so often seem the neglected stepchild in the Jewish studies world? Theorizing a way past these institutional impasses through analysis of the professional interpretive and historical habits by which Jewish American literature has been canonized, *The Impossible Jew* argues for reimagining identity as an active cultural medium—that is, in which both "literature" and "criticism" operate—rather than simply as the categorical name for a coherent representational object of historicist knowledge. Identity stands not as an ethnographic positivity to be transcoded by critical practice—whether by analyzing texts' representational or documentary procedures or through other, related, analytical activities—in other words, but as the catalyst for imagining texts whose force and relevance can never be reduced to an anthropological narrative. Jewish literary study can therefore be understood in terms of a history of the desire for a representational concept of The Jew rather than as part of the history of the representation of Jews.

Once we decide that the field of Jewish American literary studies at its most general inheres at least partly in the ability to treat literature as "Jewish" (and "American") or in examining the relevance to professional literary practice of some concept of categorical "Jewishness" (whether biographical, historical, religious, or otherwise), and maybe more specifically in analyzing how a categorical Jewish subject is constituted in literature or how the discipline of literature can help the humanities understand the constitution and legibility of such a subject, then a future for it lies in not taking for granted how, or really even that, Jewish literature is about Jews. That is, Jewish American literary study—as part of an effort undertaken by a critical Jewish studies more generally—still needs to theorize itself. There are significant theoretical, disciplinary, institutional, and ethical differences between categorically identifying Jewish literature with the history of a recognizable Jewish subject coherent enough across its historical diversity to administer a continuous Jewish legibility—that is, an understanding of Jewish literary study as essentially a humanist or anthropological historicism, as allied at some level to elementary forms of ethnography and/or autoethnography—and conceptualizing the category of Jewish literature as offering us the analytical means to critically reimagine, to contest the givenness of, the representation of Jewishness in the first place. *The Impossible Jew* proposes that we displace the historicist confidence of the former in order to critically imagine for the present the political, professional, and institutional position of Jewish identification allowed by the latter.

I take this as the important lesson that Foucault's genealogy holds for identity-based literary criticism, and if it is one to which other ethnic studies fields have been receptive, it is belated in Jewish studies; and it is what I pursue in this book—not just for the sake of Jewish studies on its own but so that Jewish studies can more productively join a larger critical project. Far from pretending to solve the problem of identity in literature, far from providing a "corrected" account of Jewish identity for literary study, my point is precisely that we need to approach identity as in fact *a problem*—a problem around which Jewish literary study needs to deliberately and critically organize itself.[1] In order to analyze the constitution of a subject within a historical framework, we cannot assume the existence of this subject—certainly not in the readily available sociologically, ethnographically, or otherwise historiographically instrumental humanist vocabularies. This is the fundamental error of identitarianism that *The Impossible Jew* challenges. A critically minded Jewish American literary practice, like the critical Jewish studies of which it would be a part, instead of anthropologically imagining the Jewish history it inhabits as positively cohering around a recognizable Jewish subject as its record, expression, or representation, should rather account for the constitution of knowledges, discourses, object domains, and vocabularies wherein "Jewish" identification accrues signification and legitimacy—but without making reference to a subject precognitively expected already to organize or otherwise authorize this field, either by standing in transcendental relation to, or by persisting more or less continuously as the agent of the history considered proper to, the field.[2]

Indeed, this would have to the itinerary of *any* identity-based scholarly enterprise that imagines itself as critical and not simply historical; and it is precisely on this point, at this site or juncture, that a critical Jewish studies will necessarily make common cause with other critical identity programs. Jewish studies will link with legitimated academic multiculturalism formations not simply because Jewish identity joins the ranks of the other privileged identities in the multiculturalism club but because it participates in a multivalent, multiply-sited, and discontinuous critique of the identitarian habits of thought and institutional practices that allow multiculturalism to take for granted the historical and biological self-evidence of various identity groups or populations. A wide-ranging effort began in a number of disciplines in the early 1990s to outline a Jewish cultural studies that tries precisely to integrate Jewish studies with multiculturalism—scholars such as Sander Gilman, Daniel and Jonathan Boyarin, and David Biale set the tone, and texts such as the Boyarins' edited volume *Jews and Other Differences* and *Insider/Outsider: American Jews and Multiculturalism*, edited by Biale, Michael Galchinsky, and Susannah Heschel, were early field anchors[3]—but even if they took aim at an epiphenomenal identity politics, these efforts too infrequently targeted the fundamental identitarian habits of thought that stand as the real agent of Jewish studies' woeful isolation or gilded hermeticism, depending on how one looks at it. To argue along with Sara R. Horowitz, for example, whose essay in the Biale et al. collection has accrued a great deal of field prestige, that Jewish texts "constitute our record and map—our packable, portable culture—our tracks across time and space, through cultures, histories, and languages" and that therefore "in reading them, in reading ourselves in them and against them, we enact the multicultural" does more than instantiate the error (indeed, the libel), with its domineering first-person-plural confidence, that Jewish studies is an exclusive, coterie affair dismissible by anyone not in the circle of Jews doing Jewish studies; it perpetuates a pernicious historicist exceptionalism—and this in the name of advocating for a cosmopolitan Jewish studies more invested in crossing borders than in controlling them! Despite an effort to account for the "paradoxical" status of Jewish studies, whereby it is not really accorded the same importance as other multicultural formations in an academic culture that supposedly values "difference," Horowitz insists on reinscribing precisely the Jewish exception—through such figures as the "outsider" and the "marginal Jew"—that underwrites this neglect: "Jewish Studies is the study of Jews in their (and our) own terms. It recognizes that Jewish culture has been subordinate in Western Culture, marginalized, translated, and appropriated. While Western thought has been notably occupied with the figure of 'the Jew' and with the 'Jewish question,' the internal perspectives of Jews have been largely invisible."[4] Such cultural studies approaches will need to work more diligently to subvert the compulsion to resolve the existential status of the Jewish subject if they are going to participate in any serious critique of identity. The job of a critical Jewish American literary study cannot be, as an arm of a larger ethnographic or historicist enterprise, to produce or refine verified knowledge of an already legible and already professionally legitimized Jewish subject—necessarily a project that engages nationalistic itineraries and procedures of thought—but rather needs to study the processes, practices, and institutional settings in which such a categorical subject becomes recognizable enough to bear verifiable statements in the first place. The job of a critical Jewish American literary practice must be to displace the consideration of Jewish American literature from its normalized representational link to a self-evident Jewish subject, to practice a labor of negation in opposing the national normalization of Jewish identity.

To be clear at the outset, what I *do not* mean is simply that Jewish literary study right now reifies a unitary Jew or that it participates in the production of a unitary concept of Jewish identity. Nor am I interested in debates about whether Jewish studies too restrictively guards what gets to count as "Jewish." Certainly since the advent of the Jewish cultural studies movement, no work in Jewish studies worth reading advances such positions. Rather, in theorizing the field of Jewish literary study, I more generally want to open up professional space for scholarship that does not imagine itself part of a broadly historicist project, that resists the anthropological impulse to conceptualize the category of "Jewish literature" as a way to resolve, focus on, or otherwise get at "Jews," at least insofar as that abstraction functions in academic literary studies and beyond as an ultimately self-evident generative, culturalist and/or biologistic, anchor. This kind of identitarian historicist scholarship— I wonder if it goes without saying that this is by far the predominant mode of scholarship in the professional Jewish studies field—should be challenged for its reliance (that is, in the last instance) on a nationalistic concept of peoplehood and for the totalizing interpretive structure it inhabits, which in foregrounding the production and refinement of documentary knowledge of Jewish history in all its facets, emphasizes recuperative recognizability and coherence as intellectual values at the expense of critical analysis of its own professional and institutional position and conditions of existence and of the role of the literary or humanist intellectual in occupying that position. As a theory of totality, it necessarily takes for granted the identity it purports to analyze: the abstract Jewish subject that oversees the field is inevitably discoverable in all the objects and phenomena that the field comprises, and the scholar trained in the field demonstrates legitimacy to the extent that he or she finds this identity. The critical Jewish American literary study I envision will attempt to displace what Paul Bové has called the authorizing ideal of mastery that administers such historicist literary scholarship, which is organized around and takes for granted "representative systems of power." Mastery becomes the "device" that "slides critics back within" a "servility" to a unified and coherent representational scheme that "establishes the identity of meaning with history."[5] The masterful historicist critic reads history as the totalized field of meaningful representation of the subject already established and preordained as properly organizing that history: historicist criticism ends where it begins.

These two tendencies—the nationalist impulse and the totalizing one—can combine with nasty results in the case of Jewish studies. As the multidisciplinary study of Jews, contemporary Jewish studies (certainly in the US), with its significant nationalist inheritance derived (at least conceptually but also historically) from its origins in *Wissenschaft des Judentums*, displays its administrative alliance with an organizing appeal to mastery in its historicist anthropological biases. I fear that any broadly ethnographically or historiographically grounded anthropologistic scholarship, regardless of how it pictures itself, insofar as it organizes itself around an appeal to mastering the representational history of a generative subject, relies ultimately on a racialist or biologist criterion, inherited from nineteenth-century thinking about nationalism and developed in the crucible of twentieth-century academic thinking about culture, in applying or talking about the "Jewish" category. At the very least, not much energy has been devoted to a search for, and not much legitimacy has been granted to, alternative organizational criteria for the logical consistency and coherent self-relation of a Jewish studies that counts among its proper objects of inquiry, and does not seriously contest the continuity between, social-science-based analysis of Sephardic women in Morocco, religious analysis of the writings of the early Rabbinic period, historical analysis of Polish Jewish refugees in the Soviet Union during the Holocaust, institutional analysis of Yiddish language movements, and literary historical analysis of Cynthia Ozick, for a few arbitrary examples. In the future that I envision for Jewish literary criticism, a rejection of the field's current representational-historicist biases would render such a normalization of a generative Jewish subject's anthropological self-evidence impossible and thereby open up space for a far-reaching critique of how the humanities instantiates itself in the categories it deploys. The Jewish literary criticism that I envision will need to displace the biologistic triangulation of representation-field-subject, overseen by an ideal of mastery, that has hegemonically organized Jewish studies thinking. I am all for holding on to the academic category of Jewish literature and to academic programs in Jewish studies, and I am not trying to say that categories are bad; after all, if we are going to retain categories such as Jewish literature or Jewish literary studies—and the current state of academic and trade publishing certainly seems to suggest that they are part of a popular and compelling bloc of categorical markers—some degree of conceptual unity is necessary. But it is the responsibility of criticism to denaturalize and denationalize how we use them, not to reproduce their institutional self-evidence.

It sometimes looks like literary scholars do not have many choices in the post–Culture Wars university, since the mass swerve away from "Theory." In English departments, where a whole lot of literary scholarship is now produced, conventional interpretive wisdom often takes the form of either a general dismissal of criticism, one that would have us believe that language is a stable medium of communication and/or that literary practice has no place for sustained reflection on its own productive and analytical capacities, or, more frequently, a generalized historicism, one that would have us instrumentally render literature as an inevitably second-tier historiographic tool, valued to the extent that it can tell us about phenomena, transformations, or subjects that we already want to recognize and whose significance we already take for granted. In this situation, identity-based or "studies"-based literary analysis can be easily reduced to a form of critically denatured recognition-administered documentarianism, linked to an instrumental narrative about minoritarian presence in the university and overseen by a primary question about what a particular category of literature tells us about a particular category of people.[6] To avoid this constraining and reactionary alternative in Jewish literary studies, we need to articulate a way of thinking about Jewish literature that does something other than assume that the literary Jews we find in the texts we read—and that categorically authorize our literary historical practice—re-present the historical Jews whom we already know wandered in the Sinai or made meal offerings at the *Beis HaMikdash* or stayed in Babylon after the Decree of Cyrus or were kicked out of Spain or died at Kishinev or paid dues to the International Ladies' Garment Workers' Union or went to the gas chambers of Treblinka or made Hollywood or wrote for *Commentary* or drove tanks into Ramallah in 1967 or created Jordache Jeans or produced a bunch of low- to middle-budget films in the '80s with B-list actors like Chuck Norris and Charles Bronson. Such historicism, beyond failing to articulate its critical justification through a theorization of literary representation (how, exactly, does "literature" "represent" "Jews"?), legitimizes literature largely to the extent that it devalues literature—and to the extent that it delegitimizes specifically literary criticism: dependent literary value becomes a lens to focus independent historical value.[7] What is worse, it is premised on a fundamentally nationalistic or biologistic logic that, while paying lip service to the social divergence, historical change, and/or ontological disjunction that separate, say, Jacob's sons from the brothers Nakash or, perhaps alternatively, Emma Lazarus from the Moses or David of her poems or Bernard Malamud from Morris Bober is in fact predicated on subordinating those differences in a categorical assertion of the shared, if abstract, but coherent, concrete, and historically continuous Jewish identity or peoplehood recognizably shared by (or at least asserted of) both.

Because of literary criticism's disciplinary focus on the machinery of representation, it can help guide an effort to relocate the "Jew" of Jewish studies off the self-evident generative ground of a normalized and nationalized historicism. Criticism should trace the ways in which literature and the professionalized languages of literary history have, in synchronization with other disciplines, taken for granted a Jewish subject constituted not only as an object of humanities-based scholarship but also, as in the widespread coordination of institutionalized academic Jewish studies with professionalized philanthropic and governmental discussions of Israel and Zionism, of Jewish social formations, and of Jewish demography, as an object of the languages of political institutions, population control, and state policy. Rather than expecting nationalized Jewish meaning in Jewish literature—for example, whereby Cold War Jewish American literary practices and Cold War Jewish American demography are understood to share a self-evident organizing subject—we should be interrogating how the knowledge of Jewishness we derive from literature is consolidated and regulated by professionalized languages of Jewish identity. This is a general problem for identity-based scholarship, to be sure; but insofar as other identity-based formations have been critically interrogating this administrative problem for at least a generation already, it constitutes another in a series of sites where Jewish studies can be seen to isolate itself. The future of Jewish American literary study that I am interested in lies not in a historicist question about how Jewish literature represents Jews or in an ontological question about how it is Jewish or in a performative question about how it enacts Jewishness but instead in a critical question about how Jewish literature contests Jewish identity.

Rather than beginning from the assumption that the institutional or disciplinary category of Jewish literature derives its legibility and justification from a self-evident Jewish subject of history, scholarship on Jewish American literature can reclaim from its subjection to historicism the possibility—and critique—of aesthetics, which Jacques Rancière describes as "a delimitation of spaces and times, of the visible and the invisible, of speech and noise, that simultaneously determines the place and the stakes of politics as a form of experience," the "distribution of spaces, times, and forms of activity that determines the very manner in which something in common lends itself to participation and in what way various individuals have a part in this distribution."[8] Reconceptualizing the recognition of Jewishness as an aesthetic rather than historiographic operation reemphasizes the political quality of the processes whereby and the practices in which an identity is recognized as something in common, insofar as it restores to analytical thinking attention to the fact that what governs the ability to categorically recognize a group is not simply or only a positivistic characteristic shared by the constituent members of the group. If the historicist or anthropological register emphasizes the *what* of recognition—to poach off Scotty's exclamation toward the end of *Star Trek IV: The Voyage Home*, "Capt'n, thar be Jews here!"—the aesthetic or political emphasizes the *how* of recognition, refusing to employ the tools of categorical recognition without at the same time genealogically questioning their institutional ascendance and availability, remaining everywhere attentive to the difference any act of recognition makes—or, to poach off an unnamed helmsman's report at the beginning of *Star Trek VI: The Undiscovered Country*, "I can confirm the location of [Jewish literary] Praxis, but I can no longer confirm the existence of [Jewish literary] Praxis." The context of this "aesthetic" analysis, which is without a doubt about Jewish identity, is not primarily in the secure mapping of a categorically legible Jewish literature onto a categorically legible Jewish subject but more significantly in the dynamic critical interchange between "Jewish literary scholarship" and "Jewishness"—where no recognition is not a displacement and every inscription is also a reinscription.

Rancière's term "distribution" usefully displaces a concept of categorical identity as a fixed positive quality of a coherent group. If we want to avoid the nationalist trap into which insufficiently critical identity-based literary study threatens to fall, we need to explore the possibility of articulating and working with a nongenerative account of identity in literature. *The Impossible Jew* argues for developing literary practices that do not simply reproduce the legitimized identity of an already-recognized people or group that either wrote a body of literature or are represented in it. Rather than begin by assuming an anthropological source of the Jewishness of Jewish literature and Jewish literary study, I suggest we begin with the overdetermination of identity, in an assertion that wherever and however we engage a text, we need to confront—and contest—the already-recognizable categorical givenness of identity.[9] To begin with the normalization of ready-to-hand generative concepts of Jewish identity—whether cultural, biographical, religious, or the like—is to risk falling into the racialism that Michael Kramer diagnosed more than a decade ago; indeed, as a field, we have not adequately dealt with Kramer's admonition that the concept of identity that so often supports historicist scholarship is itself buttressed by a generative racialism linking author and text, that even when Jewish literary study does not deliberately or explicitly theorize the identity of literature, it begins with a de facto racialist theorization of this identity. As Kramer diagnoses the state of the field, regardless of how much critics emphasize Jewish "culture" or "history" or "religion" and so on, these metonyms still rely on an albeit often-suppressed concept of Jewish race for their categorical force.[10] There seem to me to be two possible responses to Kramer. One is to not be bothered by, and in effect to ignore, this latent racialism by means of a reactionary defense of the institutional prerogatives of professionalized literary practice; this certainly seems a common, at least de facto, response. One can look, for example, to the five responses to Kramer published along with his essay in *Prooftexts*, which seem to have set the tone for the field's overwhelming neglect of Kramer's admonitory critique. To a one, they suppress the contradiction that Kramer illuminates in a defense of the legitimacy of their normalized critical stance, challenging, in four of the five cases with self-righteous hostility, Kramer's suggestion that a concept of race underlies the coherence of the category of Jewish literature. The seemingly unobjectionable secular notion of an identifiable Jewish group or "people" that these five indignant respondents uphold in their shared outrage at Kramer's term "race" has no theoretical foundation, paradoxically, other than the nationalistic concept of race (a concept that Jonathan Freedman valuably traces back to fifteenth-century Spain but that really came into its own in the eighteenth and nineteenth centuries). That this is precisely Kramer's point I suppose adds a note of black humor to a consideration of a sadly uncritical major current of Jewish literary studies, which allows these critics to enjoy the self-satisfaction of decrying the term "race" even as they rely on the pernicious inheritance of its categorical power.[11] The alternative response to Kramer would be to articulate a way of critically thinking about the identity of literature that is not generative. Jewish American literary scholarship needs to comprehensively theorize the identity of Jewish American literature, which involves at minimum articulating the stakes of its investment in the concept of identity.[12]

We must begin to think the identity of Jewish literature as not defined primarily by the identity of the contexts of its authorship, by the identifiable metonyms the literature represents, or by the identified practical work it does, all of which align with the policed historicist recognition of an anchoring historical subject already marked or identified as "The Jew" whose legibility reproduces a racialist structure of literary-cultural generativity. Rather, a concept of identity should be important to literary study to the extent that it aids our critical understanding of the productive and directive labor—that is, the hegemony—of categories in humanistic inquiry. Jewish literary study should articulate itself in an analytical vector that aims to secure Jewishness as a legible object of scrutiny and practice alike, a vector I call "semitism" precisely for the echoes it sounds with its precursor, "anti-Semitism": for its powerfully contested crossing of recognition, the presumption of collective being, and the erotics of agency. I hope my term's displacement of its ancestor signals its foundation in the same intellectual operation that made its forerunner so compelling in and for history. "Semitic" Jewish literary study approaches literature as productive of a kind of legibility, as manufacturing for the present the possibility of marking a categorically Jewish subject. As such, a vital element of literary critical semitism is a genealogy of the historicism of currently ascendant professional languages of identity; we need to understand how identity has come to be authoritatively talked about and how the institutional practices that normalize that talk developed—not in order to index readings of literature to them, for such historicist interpretive common sense is precisely the object of semitism's counterhegemonic project, but to critically disrupt their enabling nationalism.

The Jewish Problem as the Problem of "Jewishness"

In what sense does the Jewish identity that underwrites our practice exist? Important recent work in literary studies has troubled the clarity and self-evidence of the conceptual boundaries of Jewishness, and by now no responsible scholar of Jewish American literature can pursue his or her work without denormalizing the look, status, and availability of the practice's discursive anchor, The Jew. In fact, the past decade or so has witnessed a small surge in work devoted to a theoretically sophisticated criticism of Jewish American literature. Coming easily to mind as having charted paths for this critical hesitation is the scholarship of critics working both in specifically Jewish American literary studies, such as Kramer, Adam Zachary Newton, Hana Wirth-Nesher, and Jonathan Freedman, and in more broadly inter- or multiethnic American literature, such as Caroline Rody, Dean Franco, and Joshua Miller, after which it is now difficult to take for granted either the object of Jewish American literary analysis or our critical investments in such a project.[13] Adding to this emerging critique, I am asking a more primary question here about how we employ the category of Jewish American literature. Freedman's great book *Klezmer America*, which has emerged as one of the most influential recent works in Jewish literary studies (and as a lightning rod for many critics) in channeling much of the power of the revolution in Jewish cultural studies, offers an important illustration of where *The Impossible Jew* makes its critical turn. Freedman's valuable move is to attend not simply to Jews but to the knowledge practices that grasp them, to the "shifting *figure* of the Jew."[14] If "The Jew" has been and continues to be a powerful signifier in the West, its meaning is ambiguous in the wake of a "category confusion" instigated as much by those who are inscribed and defined by that category as it is influenced from outside the borders enforced by that category. Freedman is on firm footing when he argues that any historically minded analysis of Jewish identity has to begin in an appreciation that our very ability to imagine and identify the field is the result of a syncretic contestation enacted in and around both gentile and Jewish culture, a disputation that transformed (and continues to transform) the ways in which Jewish identity—to say nothing of otherness more generally—is imagined in America. But it also seems at times that Freedman wants to have it both ways. I worry that the syncretism and "definitional hybridity" he discovers in his "klezmerical" reading of Jewishness are valuable for their ability to retain something conceptually coherent and essentially Jewish even as they purport to define that term nonessentially as hybridity. In other words, Freedman's work may still take for granted an anchoring historical subject that is unambiguously Jewish, despite gestures to the contrary. It is telling in this regard that he ends the book with a potentially essentializing reinscription of Jews as a kind of model minority for cultural interpretation (and this after he devotes quite a bit of time, rightly, to attacking the reactionary trope of the model minority): though the "ethnoracial future" may belong to "other Others" than Jews, "the narrative frames in which their alterity will be imagined, circumscribed, accommodated, the shapes into which they will revise those definitions and, in responding, trace new arcs of identity and culture for themselves and the nation at large—all these will continue to be shaped, for better or worse, by the discourses and experiences of those people who have historically served as the very emblem of otherness and whose greatest and most distinctive contribution to the national culture may well prove to have been to give that otherness a local habitation and a name."[15] As valuable as is Freedman's attempt to deal with Jewishness as a discursive rather than positive entity—and I should say that I am able to make these criticisms only as a result of his trailblazing work—I worry that his argument reestablishes the historical self-evidence of an abstract Jewish subject. Because he begins his cultural-studies-situated work with and depends on a continuously legible, even if abstract, historical Jew, his analysis ultimately leaves intact the generative Jew of historicist scholarship. I would like to pursue Freedman's otherwise-destabilizing trajectory further and develop a critical vocabulary capable of liberating Jewish American literary study from the historicist criterion.

However, even as we seek to legitimate a nonhistoricist and counter-generative critical vocabulary for talking about identity, we cannot minimize the extent to which the means of doing so have been made practically and professionally unavailable—and therefore the difficulty of our task. As Kramer's critique suggests, it is exceedingly easy these days to think and talk about identity in academic contexts; but only insofar as identity talk takes form in a limited set of specific gestures and postures does it garner scholarly or professional legitimacy. Identity as we currently think about it has a curious academic history. Even as poststructuralism and postcolonialism were discovering how difference undermines the Western bourgeois subject's pretensions to ahistorical and universal primacy in the humanities, "minority identity" has come to occupy a privileged position that appears to have evaded the poststructuralist critique—indeed, often by claiming the mantle of this critique. But this displacement could proceed only through a general institutional suppression of the negative labor of difference. We now privilege a thoroughly positivized normalization of difference, as "diversity," as a field of equally legible positions and of a simple readiness for the endless proliferation of new readings of authorized acts of recognition. If these days we protest the coherence of a generalized "Western" subject's representation in language, literature, and culture, we seem a lot less concerned about talking about the special minority identity claims of, for example, women, African Americans, queer culture, Latinos, Native Americans, immigrants, Asian Americans, and Jews. We underwrite the coherence of these special identity groups by assuming their significance—in course titles, general education requirements, academic programs, funding streams, Modern Language Association divisions and discussion groups, and publishers' lists. The universal subject has been banished from humanities-based criticism, but in his place has proliferated professionalized interest in multicultural identity groups, the literatures they write, and the cultures in which we find them represented.

This state of affairs, beginning with what Dean Franco has called the "new vogue of difference" in scholarly, cultural, and political worlds beginning in the Vietnam era, obviously has a history; Franco traces a "dominant politics of recognition that emerged in the sixties" and the "subsequent emergence of minority authors into the publishing mainstream, combined with the academic valorization of multiculturalism and ethnicity, [which] would render the study of the 'other' a near-moral imperative."[16] But this elevation of difference was not univalent or unchallenged, and what now looks like an antagonistic structure has contributed the keywords and basic lineaments of the current self-evidence of ascendant thinking about identity. For at the same time, even by the early sixties, cultural fault lines had become apparent between this ideology of ethnic nationalism on the one hand and a defense of liberal individualism on the other.[17] Even as the former was underwriting the claims of so many post-civil-rights and post-colonial-cultural movements and "progressive social and academic policies on ethnicity, culture, and race" oriented around the belief that "the individual can only be free through the freedoms gained on behalf of the group" and that "freedom of consciousness for [a] group's citizens" could best be gained through "arts that promoted group identity," the latter was articulating itself with a dissenting belief that "the freedom of the individual to express his or her culture" could only be grounded in a "clear defense of liberalism against group-based claims for rights" and that it was the individual, not the group, that "underwrites culture and ethics."[18] But now, a couple of generations later, we have witnessed a curious convergence. On the one hand, the multiculturalist elevation of an ideal of diversity explicitly defines itself against an individualistic abstention from group-based identity claims. On the other hand, however, it can look a lot like these two opposing interpretive wills have lost much of their antagonism and in fact seem far more frequently to complement each other than not; group consciousness or even ethnic nationalism no longer seems to exist in tension with individualistic emphases, which rather seem to exert themselves now precisely in terms of recognizable affiliations. Indeed, if one still hears grumbling on the right about affirmative action and "quotas," such complaints are often justified in large part through an appeal to just this sort of collective affiliation—"I belong to such-and-such a group and didn't need special treatment," or "preferential treatment is un-American," or "normal white Christians are being discriminated against in multiculturalism's expanding infatuation with minority rights claims," and so on—even as cultural or group claims are often articulated in individualistic terms, of either obligation or right.

The tone of dominant social, cultural, and academic debate about identity has shifted: if cultural clashes in the '60s and '70s often took the form of violent confrontations (on campus and off) over recognition, by the '90s a dominant multiculturalism no longer emphasized this struggle and now often takes form in a commodified celebration of already-legible "difference"—often conceptualized as various positivities—as but one more consumable in a pervasive identity market. In a variety of academic, political, and literary-cultural contexts, individuals are incited through a network of institutional compensations to adopt recognizable positions and gestures coded according to definite professional postures allied or otherwise linked to identifiable groups. This is precisely a process of commodification, which invests legible positivities made possible through processes of difference.[19] Cultural pluralism has followed a wild course from Horace Kallen's progressive advocacy of statist cultural harmony in the face of the nativist threat— an advocacy that, according to Mark McGurl, "attempted to have it both ways, assimilating ethnic individuals to the mainstream *as other*"[20]—to the often-separatist ethnic nationalist movements of the Vietnam era and their simultaneous refraction through a reactionary liberal individualism as an insistence that, in Franco's words, "an individual's cultural practices are his or her own business . . . and can be a basis for neither discrimination nor special treatment" and on to our current version of multiculturalism, again in Franco's words, as "the banal celebration of differentiated generative cultures."[21]

We need to look at the intersection of two professional transformations in order to understand how the availability of alternatives to the generative nationalism that dominates current thinking about identity has been restricted. On the one hand is the way in which, initially, cultural pluralism as it developed at the beginning of the twentieth century and, subsequently (and derivatively), multiculturalism as it came into its own during the Vietnam era reified a racialized subject in order to talk coherently about representative culture. On the other hand is the way in which recent professional criticism has increasingly positivized the poststructuralist interest in the "minor" and the "marginal" via a process that functions as an academic translation of commodification.

Walter Benn Michaels has argued since the early 1990s for jettisoning appeals to ethnic or "cultural" identity because as they take form in multiculturalism, they cannot hold water without the help of an ultimately biologically determinist (and illegitimate) concept of race—a concept that is uncritically reproduced and reinscribed by slack-witted claims about the supposed "social construction" of race, claims that allow uncritical intellectuals to have their concept of race even as they pat themselves on the back for ostensibly undermining it.[22] Operating on ground prepared by Michaels, Christopher Douglas has more recently argued that multiculturalism's powerful innovation was in forging a racially based relativistic understanding of identity that derives sanction at once from nativist racialism and from a Cold War national identity disarticulated from any particularist description of a specific group, differentiating himself from his dynastic predecessor's argument that multiculturalism's concept of identity is continuous with the modernist nativism of the 1920s. Thus a multiculturalist concept of identity for the humanities that could categorically unify differences between real historical groups only emerged in an early Cold War context in which writers were responding to "a political milieu increasingly pressed to define national character." This new concept of identity functions as a kind of "supplement" to the pluralist anthropological description of culture, initially formulated by Franz Boas, that Douglas locates at the beginning of his genealogy of literary multiculturalism; capable of unifying vastly divergent cultural practices, it "perform[s] a labor that mere cultural description fails to do." The "group ontology" that multiculturalism borrowed from the Cold War project of national identity worked to provide a way of thinking about a group "without necessary reference to what the group actually did or believed," a way of thinking that begins with a recognition that the group cannot be defined solely through a description of "its current and historical experiences, its values, its practices." Thus multiculturalism can think such "group ontology" without the crutch of explicit racialism—for example, in the context of an Americanism that can define its difference from nationalism—even as its concept of identity is a "way of retaining racial technology as a guarantor" and administrator of cultural belonging. While Douglas argues that "multicultural literary studies has more or less ignored his [i.e., Michaels's] most important theoretical challenge, that our current notions of culture and identity depend theoretically (and for historical reasons) on an unacknowledged turn to race," he also wants to put some daylight between himself and Michaels. Douglas insists that culture has "not always been (and need not be) grounded in a race or turned into an identity" and that Cold War patriotism, rather than modernist racialism, was in fact the context in which a strong concept of identity was introduced into thinking about multiculturalism, allowing multicultural writers since the 1960s to, in effect, reessentialize our dominant thinking about cultural difference. Douglas is particularly concerned with how this unfortunate racialist essentialism has persisted and now fuels our current politically banal form of literary multiculturalism. Thus the "achievements of multiculturalism have been pluralism, tolerance, antiracism, and the dethroning of Western cultures as universal ones. But to the extent that multiculturalism has turned pluralism into the celebration of difference as such" and "is committed to identity and not description," the real problem is that it expends itself only in investing available identities but goes no further, justifying this commitment only by "ground[ing] . . . culture in race," by which maneuver "it reinstalls the disturbing (and faulty) thinking that social being is inherited."²³

Certainly since Werner Sollors's pathbreaking work on ethnic literary study dating from the early to mid-'80s, it has been possible—and almost always correct—to complain that a concept of "ethnicity" too easily ends up as a simple placeholder for an unverifiable and unsavory concept of race. But the response does not have to be the neopositivist path taken by Michaels, who would abandon talk of "identity" in favor of the more materially valid term "class." Michaels is persuasive in his critique of the racialist heritage of currently ascendant ideas about culture and ethnicity, but he does not allow for legitimate ways to acknowledge the critical, productive, and governmental or administrative power that is in fact wielded by the concept of identity. And Michaels's disciple Douglas, who makes noises about trying to leverage a critical concept of identity, relies on an overly simplistic neopragmatist notion of authorial agency, reducing the problem of identity, in the last instance, to a stance adopted by an author—as indeed Michaels before him has done. We need a more critically sophisticated way of talking about identity. (I might add, moreover, that these two critics avoid questions of specifically Jewish identity.)²⁴ In any case, a racialist conception of culture alone does not sufficiently explain how we got to our present scholarly position; a discontinuous development in humanities-based critical theory was also necessary to prime academic multiculturalism's banal nationalism pump.

Ironically, Deleuze and Guattari likely occupy an important place in this institutionalized shift toward an inert and commodified sense of difference. Their concept of "minor literature"—what "a minority constructs within a major language," that is, rather than how a hegemonic identity represents itself in its own, proper language—can open up space for nongenerative and counterrepresentational thinking about identity insofar as it "oppose[s] a purely intensive usage of language to all symbolic or even significant or simply signifying usages of it."²⁵ Yet we find these days that the "nomad" or "immigrant" or "gypsy" that the "minor" writer becomes "in relation to one's own language"—namely, a figure who can "tear literature away from its own language, allowing it to challenge the language and making it follow a sober revolutionary path"[26]—has in a lot of humanistic scholarly discourse been largely reified into a self-evident, certainly a privileged, representational subject in its own right. If we no longer care to hear about how literature speaks for humanity at large, we are more than happy to certify the proper, representational power of identity claims attested by marginal figures in minor literatures. The minor nomad is now as privileged as the sovereign subject ever was; just as we once presumed that the universal subject was represented in literature, we now want to hear what the nomads, immigrants, and gypsies have to say for themselves. Thus—and though I cannot imagine this was their goal, it certainly does illustrate their claim that no intensity can be transcendentally deterritorializing[27]— Deleuze and Guattari's counternormative moves now often function as the means through which identity formation has been renormalized and rearticulated.

Indeed, now—after more than a generation of scholarly appropriation—Deleuze and Guattari's characteristic language can be seen to have been indicative: they begin with a counternormative, antiessentialist gesture but then use what can easily be seen as more or less normalizing, essentializing terms to reinscribe its intensities, suturing them into an organized, representational, and above all proper form in which the minor speaks his own self:

> The three characteristics of minor literature are the deterritorialization of language, the connection of the individual to a political immediacy, and the collective assemblage of enunciation. We might as well say that minor no longer designates specific literatures but the revolutionary condition for every literature within the heart of what is called great (or established) literature. Even he who has the misfortune of being born in the country of a great literature must write in its language, just as a Czech Jew writes in German, or an Ouzbekian writes in Russian. Writing like a dog digging a hole, a rat digging its burrow. And to do that, finding his own point of underdevelopment, his own *patois*, his own third world, his own desert.[28]

Though the emphasis on intensities and holes ostensibly destabilizes a hegemonic literary historical paradigm that presumes the generative representational identification of subject and literature, Deleuze and Guattari's language allows for its own normalizing reterritorialization: "Only in this way can literature really become a collective machine of expression and really be able to treat and develop its contents,"[29] the possessiveness of "its" carrying the potential to completely undo the "minor" critique of proper-ty. Thus can identity be reinscribed as the representational, proper key to identity-based and minority canons. A reifying reading of Deleuze and Guattari's idea of the minor, therefore, seems partly responsible for the hegemonic rise of an essentializing anthropological form of historicist literary interpretation, as their challenge to a hegemony of representation has become one of the dominant modes through which literary criticism imagines itself mastering the arts of self-representation.

A good example of how this kind of hegemonic reappropriation or reinscription proceeds, drawn indeed from one of the field-defining texts of Jewish cultural studies, is Chana Kronfeld's appeal for the study of Hebrew and Yiddish modernism "in the age of privileged difference." Though "modernism is famous for its affinity for the marginal, the exile, the 'other,' . . . the representative examples of this marginality typically are those writers who have become the most canonical high modernists." The problem is that scholarly inquiry into modernism has traditionally constructed the marginal zones that so attract it in terms of a canonical center that is determinative in the last instance; Kronfeld wants to dispute this dominant theorization of modernism and try to construct the major or center through the minor or marginal. Thus she asks, "How to search out and counterpose an alternative tradition and alternative theory of marginal modernisms without universalizing them out of existence?" But she looks suspiciously like she is reifying the marginal when she speaks in such terms or, as later, in the vocabulary of "liminal modernism."[30] Her "marginal" or "minor" or "periphery" or "alternative"—at least as her syntax presents these terms—seem to claim as much self-evidence as does the major tradition whose hegemonic appeal to universalism she hopes to historicize into instability. I may be splitting hairs, but does Kronfeld's argument not essentially boil down to a bureaucratic advocacy for Hebrew and Yiddish modernism's inclusion in the category of "minor literature," an inclusion that Kronfeld worries Deleuze and Guattari's insistence that minor literature be written in a major language denies? The impulse underlying this advocacy strikes me as precisely the kind of normalization of which a key critique is the great legacy of Deleuze and Guattari's work. If I am wrong, I will be happy to be corrected, but it looks to me like the ultimate issue for Kronfeld is not the question of language; it is showing that Jews had their own voice—and that their marginal acts of self-representation manifested a kind of resistance to canonical dominance. This is what happens when critics invest too much a priori significance in concepts of "marginality" or "the margin," which is of course ironic in Kronfeld's case, because her argument started from what looked like precisely an assertion of this claim.[31] Again, my point here is simply that we need to sustain a critical investment in the theorization of identity.

All this is to say that we now find ourselves in a position in which it is exceedingly difficult to conceive of identity in nonrepresentational, nonanthropological, and nonnationalistic ways. My aim is not to say that we should not be able to talk about the Jewishness of Jewish American literature or that identity is an illegitimate concept for literary studies. Rather, I want to question the identitarian discourse or project that almost always frames talk about the Jewishness of Jewish American literature, and I want to begin the effort of imagining new ways of thinking that do not rely on the heritage of nationalistic (and racialist) logic that currently circumscribes normalized academic, political, and public discussion of identity. How we think about this problem determines how we think about the address that Jewish literature makes—to its readers, certainly, but more specifically to the field of Jewish literary study. That is, the urgent task for a critical identity-based literary study is to render conspicuous not just how we understand but how we *want to* understand the terms in which "minority" literature is or asks to be read. One way to understand the still-dominant academic banalization of multiculturalism is that its identitarian infrastructure represents the victory of a homogenizing discourse of universalism; a paradox, of course, is that this is precisely the formation that multiculturalism purportedly aimed to topple. All these differences we celebrate are indelibly insistent in proportion to the degree to which they are inscribed by an imperial process of commodification that takes form in their ability to express their value in the single currency of an obsessive desire for "difference," which really means legibly differentiated positivity; the recognition of diversified identity is the way the culture market invests its capital. But this institutional recognition has been decoupled from a sustained critique of its history, from any sense of the theoretical and professional struggles, tensions, wills, and conflicts that have rendered it viable and operative; testifying only to the self-evident logic of the commodity, it naturalizes an anthropological nationalism. Thus scholarly articles, university courses, and publishers' lists about identifiable literatures provide a marketplace for academic consumption and the means by which academic capital reproduces itself; on this exchange, positivized and nationalized difference—in the form of a legible and more or less coherent concept of an identifiable "people," be it Jewish, Chicano, Asian American, African American, Native American, or the like, however paradoxically or even absurdly inscribed—exists primarily as vehicle for the production of academic work, only to be counted as "different." Mark McGurl has written eloquently on this process, in explaining his preference for the term "cultural pluralism," a term "historically associated with figures like Randolph Bourne, Alain Locke, and especially Horace Kallen," over "the more recent and essentially synonymous 'multiculturalism' for the way it helps to return us to first principles unburdened by accretions from the so-called 'culture wars' of the 1980s and 90s, in which the mass media took a brief interest in the 'scandal' of differentiation, making hay with what was in fact the orderly appearance of new subfields in the humanities, new writers on the syllabus, and so forth." As he continues, it is "no wonder, then, that cultural pluralism and the multiversity have coupled so nicely. Both are driven by the logic of expansion and differentiation, and the continual birth of new scientific subdisciplines is echoed, on the other side of campus, in the emergence of Ethnic and Women's and Cultural Studies, and, within English departments, in the demarcated study of alternative literary canons."[32]

Alain Badiou has shown how identitarian practices in the humanities and the empty universalism of homogenizing commodification are "entwined"; they mirror and maintain each other, as identities serve primarily as "figures" for "investment by the market" but "never demand anything but the right to be exposed in the same way as others to the uniform prerogatives of the market. The capitalist logic of the general equivalent and the identitarian and cultural logic of communities or minorities form an articulated whole."[33] As the institutionalization of academic multiculturalism reveals, what Badiou calls the "identitarian or minoritarian logic" that grounds this "culturalist" practice inevitably takes form in the humanities as a historicist "relativism" that can approach and analyze knowledge and the apparatuses that house it most persuasively through the particular history of a recognizable group or "subset of humanity"—often, Badiou points out, as a history of victimization.[34] Indeed, a strong current running through academic multiculturalism and ethnicity studies fairly consistently since their ascendency in the late '60s justifies them through a humanist articulation of group ontology and resistance and/or via a general structure of redress or affirmative action. Abdul JanMohamed and David Lloyd contend in the introduction to their important collection that "minority discourse" discloses patterns of domination common to the suppression of all minority groups in hegemonic systems; more than a decade later, David Palumbo-Liu emphasizes the policy work a critical, international multiculturalism can do and holds it up as a keystone of post-9/11 opposition to neoliberal nationalist thinking: "if we could each, when thinking multiculturally, think of subnational, national, and regional cultures beyond our borders and even continents, and how these cultures have been produced historically, ideologically, materially, and in interaction with each other, we will have made some small move away from the mystification of civilizations, on both sides."[35] I hope to suggest neither that these two formulations amount to the same thing nor that they represent the only modes in which academic multiculturalism has expressed itself; rather, the institutional formations in which multiculturalism often manifests itself in the academy—represented here by two professionally prestigious formulations separated by more than a decade of significant transformation in the field—have for the most part not been willing or able to validate themselves without appeal to a culturalist history that demands to be read according to humanist protocols aligning with nationalist patterns of legibility. The point is precisely that no viable alternative to this identitarian culturalism has been able to present itself in academically legible terms.

For Badiou, the "real unifying factor" behind the minoritarian proliferation of institutional formations given over to the proper representation of identity groups is the absolute sovereignty of the globalized market's abstract homogenization, where "everything that circulates falls under the unity of a count, while inversely, only what lets itself be counted in this way can circulate."[36] Identity-based literary criticism can thus easily become banal because it reduces itself to declaring or reproducing what Daniel O'Hara calls a recognizable group's "identity-theme" or "brandlike" "cultural affiliation," to essentially counting what has already been counted. But its claim of relevance is also contradictory, really only what O'Hara calls "an ersatz façade of universalism":[37] each multicultural group's claim to representation is an identical assertion of categorical self-evidence. We know how to recognize these identity claims, but our conceptualization of them essentially ends, because it begins, in this recognition. Thus an undergraduate at a comprehensive college or university is probably given an opportunity to take courses in Jewish American literature, African American literature, Latino literature, Asian American literature, and Native American literature, for example, but the public and institutional role these courses play can often suppress critical questions about the institutional-political history of this identitarian opportunity. To talk of Jewish literature under this banner is to be pretty confident about the existence and categorical security of Jews and about the literature's relationship to these Jews, but it is unclear what we are supposed to do other than reproduce this already-available nationalist confidence—that is, by demonstrating how the literature expresses or asserts its Jewishness or more generally its relevance to a scholarly, cultural, or political interest in identity, but without criticizing the expectation that it should or the project allowing us to show that it does. Understood under this interpretive regime, literature cannot do much more than illustrate a historical narrative that the critic already takes for granted as an object of scholarly desire. For example, see all the scholarship since the mid-'90s that reads Jewish American literature for transformations in Jews' fraught relationship with African Americans or that reads Jewish American literature for transformations in Jews' fraught relationship with Israel and Zionism or that reads Jewish American literature for transformations in Jews' fraught relationship with American political institutions and discourse or that reads Jewish American literature for transformations in Jews' fraught relationship with Judaism, and so on. Because this dominant identitarian multiculturalism precognitively articulates the aesthetic concept of identity proper to an academic field with the social concept of identity proper to the historical field, it often ends up justifying itself via a narrowly professionalized, positivized, and more or less simply and ghettoizably representational concept of culture—as Badiou argues, a culture "conceived as culture of the group, as the subjective or representative glue for the group's existence, a culture that addresses only itself and remains potentially nonuniversalizable."[38] There is no question that we want to defend some concept of universality for the study of ethnicity and identity in literature, at least insofar as I cannot imagine another means of articulating the claims we make about them (or the reason someone else might possibly want to read what we write); but it does not have to take form under the auspices of nationalistic historicism's leveling commodification.[39]

Even if established academic Jewish studies formations have been slow to focus on these institutional tendencies as an object of criticism, an emerging body of critical ethnicity studies constitutes a resource for a critical Jewish studies interested in theorizing its own power. Mark Chiang's critique of Asian American studies' investment of identitarian cultural capital through the displacement of the conflict between community and scholarly representation, for example, offers one such productive avenue of interrogation. Examining the institutionalization of Asian American studies, and mindful of precisely this identitarian problem, Chiang argues that "the history and subsequent development of Asian American studies as an academic field cannot be fully grasped in terms of identity or its theoretical technique. Rather, in order to advance beyond some of the theoretical cul-de-sacs to which the anti-identitarian critique has led, political work in Asian American studies (as well as in other fields) needs to investigate the conceptual and institutional structures of representation constituting one of the links between the academic field and the political field in liberal democracy." Alluding to Kandice Chuh's advocacy for a strategically antiessentialist or "subjectless" discourse of Asian American studies—another important asset for a multilateral critique of identity—Chiang argues for decoupling Asian American studies from the humanist history of a political subject, suggesting that the object of efforts to construct a "nonrestrictive and nonessentialist" account of the group should be "not a community or a people but, first, a category and, second and more important, a field."[40] A similar theoretical repositioning away from a self-evident nationalistic ground is desperately needed in Jewish studies—a repositioning that will necessarily abandon the de facto policy of self-segregation and consider making common cause with the critique of identity in and across other "ethnic" fields. Rather than tallying recognizable characteristics under the sign of historicist correspondence and competence, identity-based literary criticism can be reimagined as analyzing how texts distribute the means to make an identification, producing the terms in which a future recognition can take place. Legible ethnic or historical differences are not the identitarian warrant from which literary historical practices draw their legitimacy; they are rather the objects to which the negative labor of literary critical practices must be addressed, what must be, in Badiou's terms, "traversed" if we are going to understand not just how a text participates in and articulates itself with the constitution of an identifiable subject but also why, in the interest of what sort of political project, it can ask to be so identified. Badiou's significance for a rethinking of identity in literary studies beyond the banal dictates of identitarianism lies in this inversion of the temporality of subjectivity—grounding it in a future recognition to come instead of a self-evidently recognizable generative past. We can return a concern with the universality of differencing to literary critical scholarship about identity—suggested in the institutional history of contention suppressed in our current celebration of diversity—by understanding difference not as the positivized "ethnic" end that authorizes recognitive historicist analysis but as a critical beginning, the contested space in which any kind of categorical thinking about identity will have had to have taken place.

The Impossible Jew asks that we reconceptualize Jewish American literary study as taking place where differential practices demand critical labor by irrupting into unaccountability rather than where differentiated practices bear recognizable interpretations by growing out of the available accountability of already-legitimated nationalized narratives. Criticism must take the form of a reimagination of difference that would contest the inscription of closed-off identities by the abstract homogenization of the market, which inevitably amounts to taking for granted that the identity of literature representationally follows the identity of a recognized historical subject. A critical Jewish literary study will attempt to imagine how literature renders "Jewishness" analytically and interpretively available, emphasizing its own activity and deemphasizing a now-hegemonic historicist positivism. Trying to think about Jewish literary history outside a mimetic or metonymic historicist paradigm that at the end of the day relies on a more or less stable Jewish historical subject would involve conceptualizing categorical group identity not as a secure, filial given but as a coordination of archives, beliefs, traditions, and attractions actively organized as much as they are presumed to be given, what Edward Said might have called an affiliative project that analyzes that "constant re-experiencing of beginning and beginning-again whose force is neither to give rise to authority nor to promote orthodoxy but to stimulate self-conscious and situated activity, activity with aims non-coercive and communal."[41] Scholars interested in the representation of Jewish identity should admit the activity of these administrative procedures in order to open them up for analysis and imagine categorical group identity as a project in which author and reader both participate through the agency of the text, in a process in which texts, characters, plots, authors, and readers equally participate in a predication of Jewishness in contexts where it is already professionally, culturally, institutionally, or politically given. The "Jew" of this literary history attempts to name itself; this Jew-ish claim of identity aspires to universality in a context in which "Jews" are not necessarily immediately recognizable and "Jewish" cannot necessarily be employed with any certainty. This claim is unfinished and contested, the farthest thing from self-evident. Here, identity is not unequivocal on national or ethnic or doctrinal grounds, and it is not a transparent generative machine.[42] The identity of this Jewish American literary history only gains its referent after the fact of the literature's production of a vocabulary that makes it available, and the practice or activity of "Jewish American literature" as a field emerges in the space between this prospective identification and the retrospective temporality of representation.

The Institutionalization of Jewish Categoricalness

But such a critical practice cannot hope to justify itself in an institutional framework that continues to value identity primarily in generative terms as an anthropological anchor. Beyond the more general problem of how the humanities have normalized identity, the specific academic history of Jews and their studies—including the often institutionally marginal position of Jewish literature in English departments—illustrates another mode in which identitarianism has functioned as an obstacle to a critical theorization of the identity of Jewish American literature. The institutional emergence of Jewish studies and, on a smaller scale, Jewish literary studies in the American academy, though more or less contemporaneous with the arrival of other ethnic studies programs, has a very different history from those other identity-based academic units. The professionalization of academic multiculturalism in the '60s and '70s was intimately coupled with a number of institutional developments that increased "minority" presence—in the form of both bodies and scholarly attention—in the academy. Whether ethnic literature and "studies" programs—with their curricula and faculty positions—were negotiated after, and as a result of, sit-ins and strikes or established to prevent struggles within the academy from boiling over in the first place, the institutional mandate and function remained essentially the same. The publishing industry has also driven a lot of the growth of academic ethnic studies, quite apart from any direct campus activism. Many schools or departments may have ended up hiring in ethnic literature to diversify their faculties, but many others could do so because the subject accrued prestige and became fashionable, supported by an infrastructure of professional incitement oriented around field-defining questions and narratives, emergent canons, the fame of scholarly "masters" in the field, and so on—and not necessarily to ameliorate local activism or contention. However we look at, and whatever history we read this emergence into, the struggle over ethnic canons that racked universities in the Vietnam era was broadly legitimated under the banner of identity politics, as a kind of representational advocacy, and it could be easily linked by any number of parties to what was going on outside the academy.[43] This history provides some explanation for why critics operating under the multiculturalism and multiethnic literary study rubrics so persistently find it easy to coordinate aesthetic and political concepts of representation.

But by this time, Jews had already achieved a significant academic presence, gained outside the revisionist identitarian program of institutional identity politics that accompanied the later ethnic studies movements; as a lot of scholarship has attested, Jews entered the academy largely by acceding to the dominant professional academic values already in place.[44] Unlike the Vietnam-era influx that was coordinated in part with the ethnic studies movements to follow, Jews' large-scale entrance into the academy was decoupled from the articulation or normalization—in any discipline—of a recognizably "Jewish" canon of texts. So even if US Jewish studies programs—to which the teaching of Jewish American literature in English departments is often allied these days insofar as the identitarianism of Jewish studies now more often than not furnishes the umbrella institutional justification for developing, circulating, and studying Jewish canons (just as multiculturalist identitarianism, what Kandice Chuh has called "arguably the dominating paradigm of U.S. academic culture today," furnishes such institutional justification in other "ethnic" contexts)[45]—started popping up at about the same time as other ethnic studies programs, they developed once Jews were already largely assimilated into the academy. And if the movement for ethnic rights and representation in the academy quickly institutionalized itself via tenure lines, budgets, and publishing trends, Jewish studies programs benefited from a very different process of professional normalization, owing a good part of their theoretical infrastructure to Jewish studies' philological roots in relatively hermetic nineteenth-century bourgeois nationalist historicism, which differed significantly in tone and tenor from the assertive revisionism of postwar ethnic nationalism. As a result, Jewish studies developed in a kind of confident institutional isolation from the fraught political and critical fixation on identity that was going on ethnically around it—even if it ultimately found an academic and professional home that is justified, limned, and delineated by the same institutional logic that supported (and continues to support) the ethnic and identity studies bloc. The identity basket into which institutional Jews put their professional eggs was initially very different from that into which institutional African Americans, Chicanos, Asian Americans, and Native Americans, for example, put theirs. By Vietnam (to resort to some shorthand), Jews were already part of the academic establishment, teaching The Canon—rather than, for example, a *Jewish* canon—and thus part of the problem as far as other others were concerned. There has been a lot of recent work that tries to explain this difference between the academic presence of Jews and other others via the ostensible fact of race—that is, Jews assimilated and achieved professional access by becoming white, a privilege not accorded other groups—but I am unconvinced by much of this work for a number of reasons, primary among which is that the explanation that Jews were able to assert their whiteness when other groups could not relies on a host of other assumptions that are not always subjected to criticism in this kind of scholarship. In any case, the ethnic and racial identity-based academic programs that developed in the generation after Jews made their large-scale academic debut often grounded their institutional mandate in an aggressive assertion of nationalized difference charged with the delicate task of normalizing the frequently violent antiestablishmentarian struggle that got them there. Insofar as the study of multicultural literature primarily serves the goal of representing and recognizing "minorities" in the academy, as an institutional apparatus it does not encompass Jews because they were part of the reason that the academy did *not* include African Americans, Latinos, Asians, Native Americans, and the like.

It pays also to consider the Six-Day War for its role in an identitarian realignment during this intensifying period of Cold War imperial tension and anti- and postcolonial resistance movements: with increasingly assimilated (and white) postwar American Jews hitching their collective identity to an increasingly first-world Israeli star (itself attracting interest among political elites in the US as a potential bulwark to be deployed against Soviet influence among some of its Arab neighbor states), it became increasingly possible to think about Jewish identity—particularly after the occupation—in terms of a hegemonic opposition between an American/Israeli/white/first-world constellation and a non-American/Palestinian/nonwhite/third-world constellation, a logic administering the legibility of position simultaneously on both sides of the boundary it inscribes. While I doubt this opposition is simply determinative of a very complex and multivalent American discourse on Jewish identity, it likely plays a role after Israel takes on the burden of the territories, certainly for those to whom Israel is relevant to an accounting of American Jewish identity and given the broader emergence of a hegemonic Zionism in the US more generally. Caryn Aviv and David Shneer offer a quick genealogy of the hegemonic place of Zionism in Jewish thinking and the thinking of Jews in America: it is not only that "the destruction of the vibrant socialist circles and many religious Jewish communities of Eastern Europe" left Zionism "the dominant political ideology. . . . The discursive and power relationships that shaped global Jewish communities changed dramatically. After the [Second World] war, the majority of American Jews moved out of the working classes and into the suburbs. They lost their tangible connection to Eastern Europe, where many formerly Jewish towns had been decimated, and in its place began creating the mythic Eastern Europe that haunts American Jews today. As American Jewish identities, practices, and communal affiliations increasingly became options, and as more Jews married non-Jews, Israel became a convenient focal point around which to rally in solidarity." That is, it is not so much that Israel grounded a specifically *aliyah*- or immigration-oriented Zionism but that a "support for Israel as a civic religion" became the center "around which to build a modern secular Jewish identity" in America.[46] Benedict Anderson's concept of "long-distance nationalism" seems helpful here. And on the subject of Israel—and especially in the context of the post-'67 redeployment of Holocaust victimhood charted by Norman Finkelstein in *The Holocaust Industry*—I could add that the Holocaust almost certainly offers another, traumatic, paradigm to explore in the articulation of Israel with Jewish studies discourse. Israel's self-justifying link to the Holocaust, and through it to an American exceptionalist justification of the US as freedom's savior that was impressively burnished after World War II, proved fertile ground in which the US-Israeli bond could grow and flourish during the Cold War transformation of this exceptionalist discourse.[47] This triangulation between Israel, the US, and American Jews, mutually articulated with the hegemonic development of a self-evident American Jewish Zionism, offered further institutional incitement for Jewish studies discourse to elaborate a concept of Jewishness insulated from the critical itineraries of other ethnic studies areas.

If a lot of Jewish literary scholarship envisions itself as part of the multidisciplinary academic study of an ultimately historically self-evident "Jewish" people, this professional mandate therefore has a specific history exacerbated by the peculiar institutional isolation of Jewish studies programs. As Jonathan Boyarin points out, other ethnic and identity studies programs' broad ties to demands for affirmative action and diversification as a general mandate for universities often position them to receive subsidization through governments or general university budgets, but Jewish studies programs are at least as commonly funded by wealthy alumni and sometimes even by local Jewish communities or national Jewish organizations. Boyarin also emphasizes Jewish studies' philological roots and its institutional history of "isolation" from "the other 'minority' or 'ethnic' studies establishments and would-be establishments," which also accounts for the sad fact that "unlike such fields as gay and lesbian studies or cultural studies . . . Jewish studies is not a predominantly critical discipline": Jewish studies is often critical neither in establishing the horizon of legibility of its discursive field nor in imagining itself as fundamentally oppositional—it simply never had to do either.[48] There are obvious exceptions to this predominance; but as a rule, it can be difficult to exorcise from Jewish studies work an institutional expectation that analysis *of* Jews should function also *for* "the Jews," which is to say in the interest of an ideologically productive image of Jewry. Thus, as Boyarin puts it, "*Jews* are not marginal in American academic institutions, but Jewish criticism is at home neither in cultural studies nor in Jewish studies."[49] Boyarin's response, as many Jewish studies intellectuals know, is to dispense with a stable discourse of nationality or home, certainly one that coordinates with a coherent, positivized concept of identity, and to replace it with a discourse of what he calls "*critical post-Judaism*," by which, invoking Levinas, he means

a way of being Jewish "otherwise than Being." . . . This kind of identity formation is not enabled solely through its own intellectual passion and inventiveness, but on the contrary, only within or at the margins of academic institutions and academic culture (and even then generally outside the disciplinary boundaries of "Jewish studies"), and certainly at the margins of Jewish institutional life in the United States. As a post-Judaism, it is marginal to the would-be "Jewish community" monolith. As criticism, it is subject to centrifugal pressures. It finds its creative tension in an unstable mixture of accommodation and resistance to the centrifugal spin toward the margins, and it need not be its members' only Jewish world.[50]

In this dedication to criticism lies a promising future for Jewish American literary studies.

David Biale, Michael Galchinsky, and Susannah Heschel also point to the discontinuous formation of Jewish studies and other ethnic studies programs in American universities, but, following a different heading than Boyarin's deterritorializing criticism, they help illustrate how historicist criticism can be seduced by the normalizing temptations of ethnographic self-accounting and self-justification. "Emerging at about the same time, the late 1960s and early 1970s, these disciplines owe their origins to very different circumstances. Jewish studies in America developed precisely at the moment when Jews felt themselves fully integrated and the field became a vehicle for establishing their right to be considered part of the Western canon. Ethnic studies often took the opposite track, criticizing the Western canon for its exclusionary practices and promoting ethnic and racial particularism. Jewish studies typically subscribed to an Enlightenment vision of the university while ethnic studies often challenged this vision." Thus Jews are "anomalous": they are "insiders who are outsiders and outsiders who are insiders," making for a "special ambivalence" with which Jews face their condition within the multicultural occasion. Jews—that is, both inside and outside the academy, and I think this elision helps to spotlight the problem—are caught between divergent allegiances, wanting to "rigorously articulate what makes Jews distinct while showing the ways in which Jewish history and thought contribute to the humanities at large."[51] It pays to pause over their conspicuous term "discipline," which suggests a uniform field, a relatively coherent and stable articulation of doctrine, methodology, and proper content; because if there is one thing Jewish studies, with its potpourri of archaeology, cultural studies, theology, philology, linguistics, history, and so on, is *not* it is a single discipline. Telegraphed by this term "discipline," Biale, Galchinsky, and Heschel aim to leverage the "special ambivalence" they mark. "Instead of bemoaning the Jews' anomalous status, we have sought to turn it into a productive virtue . . . [with which to] challenge the conventional polar opposition of a majority 'monoculture' and a marginalized 'multiculture.' Precisely because we believe that the Jews constitute a liminal border case, neither inside nor outside—or, better, both inside and outside—they have the capacity to open up multicultural theory in new and interesting ways."[52]

The difference between these two (more or less recent) analyses of the Jewish studies problem illustrates the difficulty facing the study of Jewish American literature that I have been trying to analyze here. Biale, Galchinsky, and Heschel stake their claim in a positivization of Jewish identity: it may not be without contradiction—an outsider on the inside, their Jew is always too much of an insider to be claimed by the outsiders—but the picture they draw of the modern Jew, their romanticized reification of Jewish liminality, is powerfully stable. They reward the liminal or minor with representational capacities, as if it denoted the very categorical coherence that the concept is proclaimed to displace. Their "anomalous" looks a lot like Americanism's American "exceptional": their secure Jewish subject, adumbrated by their elision of "Jews" and "Jewish studies," is precisely where they ground a set of "productive" practices that render an expected Jewishness legible. Paying lip service to an ostensible postmodern disruption of identity politics, they in fact expect to reaffirm a consolidated minoritarian representational politics that takes for granted the generative category of The Jew as the anthropological ground of an identitarian Jewish studies: "In a variety of ways, then, to be a Jew, especially at this historical juncture, means to lack a single essence, to live with multiple identities. Perhaps the Jews are even emblematic of the postmodern condition as a whole."[53] "Emblematic," their Jew has a strategically normalized shape and history that they take for granted as verifiable. In this sense, their image of responsible Jewish studies work looks like a relatively less critical version of Freedman's argument that any American thinking of identity is ultimately grounded in the complicated history of culture work that went into defining "The Jew." Boyarin, by contrast, begins precisely by troubling the priority and proper-ty of Jew and Jewish studies; unstable, untenable, and never transparent, beginning from what is recognizably given but disrupting the given's claims to generative self-evidence, criticism may be the only place[54] available to locate a legitimate analysis of our modern discourse of the Jew.

In diagnosing the desire to establish a historicist foundation on which to coordinate interpretations of Jewish American literature, my aim here has been to identify the institutional transformations that have made such historicist readings so seductive to literary critics and so dominant in literary scholarship, that have made sustained literary criticism so rare in institutional Jewish studies, and that have made Jewish studies a kind of black sheep in the multicultural landscape of the post-Vietnam academy. I hope thereby to critically illuminate the possibility of critical alternatives for the study of Jewish identity that do not take root in the nationalism that is this historicism's necessary logical concomitant. So long as Jewish literary study limits itself to a nationalistically inscribed, identitarian historicism that expects generative representation—so long, that is, as it grounds itself in the expected recovery of a legible "Jewish" subject that presumably spans the period of "Jewish" history (and that is often assumed to align with territorial Zionism)[55]—it alone, really, bears much of the blame for its institutional and methodological isolation. We need to reorient our interpretive practice away from historicist recognition, anchoring Jewish literary study not in a presumptive positive, nationalistic entity identifiable as "The Jew" but in an analytical activity that captures[56] Jewishness as a legible object of scrutiny, critically negating the ways in which identity is overdetermined as a recognizable category. Taking form in this critical activity, a vector I call "semitism," Jewish studies cannot have a proper—which is to say its own—field.

Semitism

A "semitic" literary criticism would privilege in its readings analysis of the way texts render Jewishness as an attractor or focus, of how texts deconstruct the givenness of Jewish identity. Thus in figuring Jewish identity as an object at once of theorization, historicization, desire, and practice, "Jewish" literary texts destabilize and displace what "Jewish" might possibly refer to. The result is a disarticulation of all the markers or registers that might otherwise have been organized to signify the generative authority of "Jewish"—histories, languages, populations, values, traditions, doctrines, ethics, filial inheritances, geographies, theories, institutions, mythologies, and so on. Jewish categoricalness persists not in recognizing a determining historical subject or people but in the power or compulsion or will to trace the itinerary of this antinormalizing disarticulation, at the site of the counterrecognition of an identity that is never where it is properly legible. One of my arguments in this book is that Jewish American literary history—manifested both in the canonical texts and narratives it has invested and in the historical narratives, critical debates, and institutional formations in which it has instantiated itself—has always and everywhere anchored itself in questions about Jewish identification and about what gets to count as Jewish. This I do not think is a particularly controversial claim. What I find sad and surprising, however, is how often Jewish literary study has coordinated the analysis of these questions with a positivist narrative project to document and stabilize a coherent Jewish historical subject that we now lack an ability to grasp without a nationalist conceptual infrastructure. Thus the semitic inquiry I gesture toward here is designed to reorient Jewish literary criticism through a displacement of the recovery or description of a Jewish subject and toward the critical analysis of the modes in which we have understood and can understand Jewish identification. Indeed, we should not be surprised that it is often in just those most easily identifiable texts in which canonical literary history has professionalized itself that the potential and modes of semitic criticism are most conspicuous and productive.

Bernard Malamud's 1957 book *The Assistant*, which locates Jewishness in a matrix of desire even as it so strikingly wants to take it for granted as an origin, offers an instructive engagement with such semitic inquiry—for precisely the reasons that have since its publication fueled the temptation to read the text into readily available extra- or nonliterary narratives of assimilation. Approached from the perspective of a critical semitism, the novel's reinscription of Jewishness in a Christian symbolic vocabulary need not be understood primarily in terms of a reductive historicist judgment about Malamud's place in an already-legible narrative of the development of Jewish American literature or of Jewish American literature's place in an already-legible narrative of Jewish experience in America or in modernity—a banal labor at the stable site where the already expected is recognized—and can instead be approached as an opportunity to critically examine how and where and why "Jewish" accrues reference and exerts a power to organize and administer the production of meaning or how and where and why referents accrue Jewish identification—a critical labor at the unstable site where the categorical crosses the recognizable. Exploring how Jewish-ness becomes an object of attraction in the book allows us to explore how Jewishness becomes an object of attraction for our critical prac-tice. Such an approach to Jewish literature would not necessarily ignore historiographic questions about narratives of, say, social assimilation or cultural divergence, but it would prevent literary interpretation from being reduced to banal reiterations of these narratives.

About Italian American Frank Alpine redeeming himself out of criminality and anti-Semitic abjection on the back of long-suffering Morris Bober and becoming a Jew in the process, the book destabilizes the ground on which categorical identity can claim generative or essen-tialist self-evidence. While the initially anti-Semitic Frank insists on dif-ferentiating Jews, distinguishing them from others, Morris, the Jewish shopkeeper whom he initially held up at gunpoint but then returned to work for in an act of repentance,[57] is equally adamant about describ-ing his Jewishness in terms that do not necessarily exclude gentiles—he essentially boils it down to doing good. Figuring just the problem of Jewish literary history that I am discussing here, the book situates its exploration of Jewish identification in a space carved out by a rheto-ric of boundaries and desire: Frank begins questioning Morris about Judaism only a page or two after Morris's daughter, Helen (whose Hel-lenized name already inaugurates a question about legitimate modes of Jewish legibility), rebuffs Frank's advances while they are out on a date with a sententious "Don't forget I'm Jewish."[58] But Helen's ease of identification here is displaced by a much larger failure of self-evidence in the text (evinced not least in the fact that Helen's "Jewish"-ness is expressed almost nowhere else). Frank and Morris's discussion about identity begins with Frank's thwarted tendentiousness: "Say, Morris, suppose somebody asked you what do Jews believe in, what would you tell them?" (123). Frank's assumption that Jews are identifiable (and dif-ferentiated) by a coherent set of beliefs and practices—the "what" that "Jews believe in"—is linked here to his own inability to identify him-self; his desire to know is projected onto an anonymous and dislocated "somebody" he can no more than "suppose" the existence of.[59] Interest-ingly, Morris stumbles before this hypothesis of Jewish differentiation; he is "unable at once to reply." Responding to Morris's failure, Frank asks a new question, replacing a presumption of praxis with one of ontology: "What I like to know is what is a Jew anyway?" (123).

Mirroring Frank's initial eschewal of responsibility for his question in "suppos[ing] somebody [else]" to ask it, Morris similarly answers in a voice other than his own, as, presumably, he feels "ashamed of his meager education": "My father used to say to be a Jew all you need is a good heart." Pushed by Frank to state what he himself believes, Morris asserts, "The important thing is the Torah. This is the Law—a Jew must believe in the Law." But then Frank, having noticed that Morris never goes to *shul*, does not keep a kosher store, does not himself follow the rules of *kashrus*, and does not pray or wear a skullcap, asks whether Morris considers himself a "real Jew." Though he closes the store on Yom Kippur, Morris insists, "sometimes . . . to have to eat, you must keep open on holidays." *Kashrus*, he claims, is "old-fashioned": "What I worry about is the Jewish Law." Frank's objection is understandable: "But all those things are the Law, aren't they? And don't the Law say you can't eat any pig, but I have seen you taste ham." Morris's appeal to a kind of radical virtue ethics is conspicuous:

> This is not important to me if I taste pig or if I don't. To some Jews is this important but not to me. Nobody will tell me that I am not Jewish because I put in my mouth once in a while, when my tongue is dry, a piece ham. But they will tell me, and I will believe them, if I forget the Law. This means to do what is right, to be honest, to be good. This means to other people. Our life is hard enough. Why should we hurt somebody else? For everybody should be the best, not only for you or me. We ain't animals. This is why we need the Law. This is what a Jew believes. (124)

Possibly frustrated, Frank rightly points out that such a definition fails to categorically differentiate Judaism, that "other religions have those ideas too," and then he tries a different tack: "But tell me why it is that Jews suffer so damn much, Morris?" If Frank, acting as a kind of multi-culturalist,[60] assigns Jews positivistic historical particularity in thinking that they suffer because "they like to suffer" (that is, on the assumption that it is easiest for one to do what one culturally is), Morris eschews any such simple differential logic: "If you live, you suffer. Some people suffer more, but not because they want. But I think if a Jew don't suffer for the Law, he will suffer for nothing." Frank, already having shown himself suspicious of Morris's dedication to the "Law," asks the shopkeeper, "What do you suffer for, Morris?" If Morris's answer is fascinating— "I suffer for you"—his clarification, for which Frank asks, is mindboggling: "I mean you suffer for me." Frank is willing to let it go at that, but Morris reiterates his theme: "If a Jew forgets the Law, he is not a good Jew, and not a good man" (125). At least as Morris lays it out here, and contrary to what Frank thought, Jewish suffering redeems *all* the Jews involved—even those who are not Jews. Frank's final conversion to Judaism appears redundant, therefore, in the face of this universalist assertion that (if I will be allowed to poach off Sartre) Jews are other people, given that Morris has already consigned him a Jew—a label now only dubiously or incompletely referred to a material and/or heritable "ethnic" history—for choosing to return to the store to do penance, according to "the Law," for earlier robbing it.

But Morris's devaluation of ethnic particularity does not function as the novel's final court of identification. It is Frank, avatar of identitarian particularism, and not Morris, spokesman for ethical—ethnical?— universalism, in whom identification aspires to universality as the traversal of its own defining difference. It is by now a scholarly commonplace to point out that Morris here offers a salient gloss on Malamud's infamous suggestion that "every man is a Jew though he may not know it,"[61] which positions Judaism as a generally available figure for *all* human suffering; as he explained in a later interview, "It's a symbolic way of showing how history, sooner or later, treats us all."[62] Incidentally, Malamud made his "every man is a Jew" claim in 1968, two years after Robert Alter wrote disapprovingly (in *Commentary*, American Jewry's house journal for disapproval) that for Malamud, Jewishness is frustratingly "symbolic" rather than material, a "metaphor" for "all men's inevitable exposure to the caprice of circumstance and the insidious snarl of history: all people are in this way 'chosen,' Jews only more transparently than others."[63] Thus, it is also fair to say that *The Assistant* on this score undermines an easy categorization of Jewishness; the book ends with Christian Frank Alpine's learning to suffer for the redemptive benefit of others and converting to Judaism through a very Christ-like rebirth. After falling into the grave of the dead Jew Morris, he rises to take on

Morris's historically specific Ashkenazi traits—such as a proficiency in conversational Yiddish (he also takes over Morris's place in the grocery, which Alter labels "the symbolic locus of being a Jew" in the novel)[64]— and gets circumcised ("after Passover," we are told, which is close enough to Easter for this tendentious critic [246]). This Italian Catholic may become a Jew—indeed, the novel's only viable Jew, a Jew with a future—but only by becoming Christ. In this book, Jewish generativity administered by race or ethnicity or biology, that is, heredity, is a dead end (pretty literally), but then again, a securely policed set of Kramer's impugned ethnic metonyms does not fare much better; the future of Jewish identification opens into discursive uncertainty, the only legible articulation of which identification is not only metaphoric but spectral. Jewishness remains available in *The Assistant*, but only as a desire circulating through a Christian metaphorology, as a ghost lacking its own proper, self-sufficient substance.

Leslie Fiedler famously—infamously to many people—maligned similar Jewish literary phenomena and processes as "Jewish Christolatry"[65] and saw it rendering Jewishness vestigial. I think we can more compellingly look at it in a different way. *The Assistant*'s Christolatry exposes Jewishness more as a region of desire, energizing aspirational energies, than as a historically self-evident "ethnic" given (Morris could in this sense be faulted for not being able to articulate the terms of his Jewish identification). Or rather, paradoxically, Jewishness is given only to the extent that it has already become an object of desire. Jewish identity is not so much a fantasy as a kind of infrastructure to house fantasy, allowing Frank to affiliate with and name his relationship to a practical cultural archive that, as sanctioned by Morris but only as so sanctioned, is categorical. A generative Jewish identification may survive here, but only in its own deconstructive displacement, thoroughly circumscribed by the futurity of desire. Far from being disappointed with Malamud, pace Alter, for making Jewishness too metaphorical or symbolic or, pace Fiedler, for Christianizing it, we might instead take Malamud seriously, in the name of critical thinking rather than anxious ethnography, for producing a work that offers a fantastic opportunity to think about how Jewish literary studies can develop a compelling way to talk about a pervasive desire for Jewish identification that does not reduce or fix it via historicist or anthropological metonymy.

Fiedler cites two "paradoxes" associated with the rise of Jewish American literature to (what he calls) its "dominant position in the culture of the modern world."[66] The first is that this rise occurred (starting in the '40s and '50s) "at a moment when the Jewishness of the Jewish-American community had become problematical." The majority of Jewish Americans coming of age during the twentieth century could access their religious heritage (when they did) only at "secondhand." Acquired at firsthand were "images and stereotypes" proper to Jews' "acculturation in a Christian society." Thus Fiedler's second paradox: when these Jewish American writers did move into "traditional provinces of religion and mysticism, from which the Enlightenment presumably delivered them," it was more often than not "to Christian mythology and theology that they turned in quest of images and themes."[67] Fiedler cites Malamud's *The Natural* (1952), which replays the Grail legend; Henry Roth's *Call It Sleep* (1934), in which David Shearl reenacts an *"imitatio Christi"*[68] in emerging from his sacrificial-baptismal-resurrectional electrocution at the train tracks to redeem an immigrant past (as the figure of fallen humanity) for an American future; and Nathanael West's *Miss Lonelyhearts* (1933), with its eponymous protagonist's obsession with Christ's redemption of human suffering. Along with *The Assistant*, another book that comes to mind that we might add to this list is Mike Gold's *Jews without Money* (1930), for its use of innocent Joey Cohen's sacrificial death and narrative resurrection. The possibility of recognizing or naming Jewish identity in these famously "Christological" Jewish texts depends on a Christian index: difference is irresolvably attested in the supposedly universalizing move to displace it.

In Henry Roth's case, according to Fiedler—this narrative is now familiar—the Marxism and high modernism he learned at City College (at the feet, famously, of Eda Lou Walton, his teacher, mentor, and lover—and *Call It Sleep*'s gentile dedicatee) provided Henry the discursive means to revolt against not only the vestigial Orthodox Judaism and emergent crass bourgeois aspiration of his parents' generation but also the genteel Victorian values that influenced the teaching and analysis of literature. Conspicuously legible to us critics today, an identification affect oversees Fiedler's argument: he describes a "process of cultural assimilation that began for us long before we reached the university," lessons starting in grade school and even before in how to "pass," in a "life-style utterly alien to that of my ancestors." Fiedler's polemical word is "brainwashing": what began with Dick and Jane ended with "literature classes aimed at persuading [him] that [he] was the cultural heir of Longfellow, Whittier, and Holmes, Shakespeare and Milton, Wordsworth and Dickens." Fiedler's American Jews suffered the imposition of a tradition to which their own Jewishness could not be more than ancillary; when they came to take possession of that heritage, "they assimilated, adapted, and introjected myths deeply rooted in a religion utterly alien and indeed hostile to that of their own forbears." As a result, they came to "identify their most sympathetic characters, the surrogates for their essential selves, with archetypal terminal 'good Jews'"—that is, those birthright Jews who escaped the bondage, the fate and destiny, of their premodern heritage; and they identified those who rejected their modernism and experimental art—"including their own kin," Fiedler significantly adds—with "bad Jews," Jews condemned by their ongoing allegiance to blood-borne tradition.[69]

As Jewish as is the setting of *Call It Sleep*, therefore, Fiedler holds that Roth's novel repeats a Christian "fable of redemption." He dwells on the book's return to Isaiah, what might be seen as evidence of determinate Jewishness:

> The *Haftorah* passage from the prophet of priestly caste, which so obsesses David, includes not just the image of the burning coal held to that prophet's unclean lips, but the verses, "For a child is born to us / A son is given to us And the government [also, "authority"] is on his shoulders." But this has, of course, been read by Christian interpreters as a prophecy of the coming of Christ, the Son of God, the Son of Man, the Suffering Servant (also a metaphor smuggled out of Isaiah by Christologists), the Redeemer of Fallen Humanity. That Roth thought of humanity as fallen no reader of *Call It Sleep* has ever doubted; and Roth himself has declared, "there is one theme I like above all others, and that is redemption."

It initially looks like Fiedler deploys a narrative from ethnic particularity to cosmopolitan universality: that is, "Jewishness" becomes the particular frame through which David (and metonymically through him Roth and synecdochically through Roth American Jewry) activates a universal possibility by transcending its limits. But Fiedler renormalizes this narrative in terms of an essentialized category of the Jew: though these writers "Christianized the Jewish tradition of which they came," Fiedler insists that they also "Judaized the Christian culture to which they assimilated." In this sense, I think the reifying title of the essay in which he introduces the term *Jewish Christolatry*, "The Christian-ness of the Jewish-American Writer," reveals Fiedler's reliance on generativity and kinship as the means to hold on to a categorical Jewishness and to situate these books in a securely Jewish American canon.[70]

For the record, Fiedler describes Nathanael West, another Jewish Christolator, as a "crypto-Jew" who "made no attempt to hide his own mythological identification and that of his characters with the self-proclaimed Jewish messiah rejected by his own people," and he calls *Miss Lonelyhearts* "an even more egregious example of Jewish Christolatry" than Roth's novel. Miss Lonelyhearts "aspires to the role of the Crucified Christ, whom he thinks of as 'The Miss Lonelyhearts of Miss Lonelyhearts.' . . . When we see him last he is reaching out in Christlike, all-forgiving love to his worst enemy. To be sure, the enemy is not converted by his love but shoots him dead, which serves, of course (despite the irony with which the scene is rendered) to reinforce rather than undercut his identification with the mythological Son of Man."[71] And I would claim that Mike Gold's *Jews without Money* inhabits this structure, too, with its use of the Joey Cohen character. Joey, the innocent of Mikey's gang of Jewish boy-hoodlums, the "dreamy boy in spectacles who was so sorry when he killed the butterfly," is killed one day by a horse car in the street. But if he is destroyed by the fallen Lower East Side, he is resurrected on the very next page: "Joey Cohen! you who were sacrificed under the wheels of a horse car, I see you again, Joey! . . . Morning is here, and, Joey, your father gave you a whole nickel. Together we set out to spend it."[72] A chapter-long narrative of their trip to a candy store follows, told in the present tense, that, though adding insult to injury by ending in Joey's molestation by a deranged bum and in yet more violence, can be seen to complement the redemptive Christian logic of the book: Joey's sacrifice to industrial modernity is redeemed as his resurrection here (however temporary) prefigures the novel's closing fusion of Messianic and socialist imagery: "O workers' Revolution, you brought hope to me, a lonely, suicidal boy. You are the true Messiah. You will destroy the East Side when you come, and build there a garden for the human spirit."[73] Though it can be argued that the Messiah was Jewish long before Christianity ran with the concept—and indeed, the book calls up a specifically *Jewish* Messiah for socialist service—the associations and implications of the innocent being martyred for the redemptive good of humanity are unmistakably Christian.

Fiedler obviously belongs in a genealogy of literary critical semitism. There is a lot to agree with in his treatment of identity as, primarily, an object of desire and recognition, and his discussion of Jewish Christolatry emphasizes—very usefully for literary history—the practices in which identity inheres: there are obvious compensations in situating one's writing in dominant, recognizable vocabularies, and just as obviously a dominant Christian milieu or discourse is going to make certain paths available, unavoidable, and/or unavailable to a writer. But as incisive and original a reader as Fiedler is, his reliance on an essentializing, racialized concept of identity reinscribes a dubious historicist paradigm; having discovered the spectrality of Jewish identity, he suppresses it in favor of ethnohistorical security. In fact, books such as Malamud's and Roth's and West's and Gold's all more or less turn away from a Jewishness secured by the generativity of heredity and ethnic cohesiveness. Semitism articulates an alternative account of literary Jewishness to the undertheorized racialist positivism we see in Fiedler, and repeated across the history of Jewish American literary study, informing field-defining beliefs (however unarticulated) that literature is Jewish when Jews write it or literary historical claims (however undemonstrated) that since the large-scale entrance of Jews into the mainstream of American literature during the twentieth century, it is now appropriate to claim that American literature bears a touch of the Torah brush. A critical practice oriented by what I have called semitism allows us to hold on to categoricality not by retaining a positivist determining ground—a genetic or historical origin—but precisely by traversing or displacing it in desire.

With the help of recent literary historians, we can tell a relatively easy story about the literary critical approach of Fiedler and others of his cohort who first started talking seriously about Jewish writers in the postwar period, when assimilation emerged as an important problem for the accounting of Jews and Jewishness. Fiedler writes of the problem facing these Jews "only minimally Jewish," a group in which he includes himself: "the very success of Jewish-American writers in thus becoming mouthpieces for all of America meant their disappearance as Jews, their assimilation into the anonymous mainstream of our culture. But was this not what we had been all the time wanting really, participants all of us, to one degree or another, in what has been called the 'silent Holocaust'?"[74] Alter uses less inflammatory language: "I would suggest that Jewish life since the entrance of the Jews into modern culture may be usefully viewed as a precarious, though stubborn, experiment in the possibilities of historical continuity, when most of the grounds for continuity have been cut away. The serious literature produced by Jews in this period draws its distinctive creative energies from the modern Jewish predicament and at the same time revealingly documents that predicament in all its pained self-contradictions and confusions."[75] Both writers are responding to the same problem of cultural integration: this earlier generation, via an identification with the writers and their literature, preserved the categorical Jewishness of Jewish literature by historicizing the Jew through race or at least through heredity-borne culture, which in the wake of assimilation preserved Jewish identity. Nowadays, in the age of literary multiculturalism, we seem to be historicizing the Jew through culture or other ethnic metonyms, but as we can see with the help of critics such as Kramer, Franco, Michaels, and Douglas, such culturalist interpretation relies on the same kind of racialist error, however suppressed this justification is. The racialism of Fiedler's generation was deployed for obvious social and political reasons that we can surely understand, even sympathetically defend; but we certainly do not need to reproduce that logic in our own times, as we take up the critical task of reading the literature of that generation. Now, and for the future of Jewish American literary studies, the pressing—and pressingly political—epistemological problem is how to pursue a thorough critique of categorical Jewishness, a displacement, which is neither an ignoring nor a claiming or reclaiming, of the legible generative categories in which Jewishness inheres.

How else can we talk about the Jewishness of "Jewish" literary texts? We need to seek possible ways to talk about Jewish literature outside of a likely essentialist, and certainly nationalist, predictive and predicative practice that looks for marks of Jewishness (or even just categoricalness) in a canon already safely recognized as Jewish, a practice whose procedures are supported by a prefab identitarian process; for such a historicist paradigm, identity is an authoritative framework that polices or administers the labor of literary scholarship. While it is probably impossible to evade recourse to an already-recognized Jewish canon—merely citing a text under the auspices of Jewish literature or identity certainly suggests we have already assumed (at some level) that the text is relevant to a discussion of Jewish identity in literature—it would be nice to imagine a critical Jewish literary history that would be something more than, maybe as a displacing theorization of, this relevance. Taking seriously the fact that our choice or desire to read a particular text as "Jewish" forms part of the matrix that produces the text's categorical Jewishness is a start. If, as Fiedler suggests, the Jewish Christ in Roth, Gold, West, and Malamud represents an escape from the prison of determinate, othered particularity—the ends of the Roth and Gold texts, certainly, quite explicitly signal to us a departure from the ethnicized ghetto in the direction of a universalized, cosmopolitan future, a theme common enough in so much canonized Jewish American literature—then I would like to ask how this escape already deconstructs itself, having become a way of talking about spectral Jewish differencing or identification that does not operate under a nationalized sign of representation. The Jewish Christ may attest to universal subjectivity, but in its pure excess, in its irreconcilability with any historical order, it also makes something that is not at all self-evident analytically available, if only as a displaced and displacing specter haunting the desire for a "universal" agency—itself an ideal whose impulse toward cultural nonspecificity, as Daniel Boyarin reminds us, can never not amount to the suppression of difference from a dominant norm.[76] Approaching the Jewish identity of Jewish American literature critically through what I have called the semitic procedures by which Jewishness is predicated or identified rather than mimetically or metonymically through the forms in which Jewishness is represented reveals how the literature is already, at least in part, about the problem of its own categoricalness. Seen in this way, the literature thus makes an irreducible claim *about* its canonicity rather than a simple assertion *of* its canonicity. Roth's closing, not-quite-sarcastic gesture is promising: David might as well call sleep the incessant, destabilizing movement between past and future, memory and present experience, person and collective, self and other, archive and individual that has taken erotic control of his imagination since his resurrection; there is certainly nothing else to call it. But that is where identity is.

2

Against the Dialectic of Nation

Abraham Cahan and Desire's Spectral Jew

This book began with a politically and professionally motivated desire to develop a way to talk about the Jewishness of Jewish literature that is not coordinated by an inevitably unsavory nationalistic project to recognize the history, culture, ancestry, descent, and society—that is, by a historicist project to secure the identity—of The Jew. As I hope I have made clear, by gesturing toward a genealogy of the term I do not mean that we should not be studying literature from the perspective of identity; that the constellation of territorializing forces we call "identity" currently underwrites our shared ability to think about the meaning of experience and history, for example, certainly recommends it as a powerful instrument, but it must be deployed critically, against the ethnicized and anthropologized self-evidence that its normalized use now reproduces. We must remain suspicious of literary historical approaches that expect the machine called representation, via the operator "identity," to peg literature to a conceptually coherent, nationalistically limned, and often racially secured entity—a specifically, legibly Jewish subject—existing recognizably, self-evidently, and autonomously outside of literature. It is one thing to say that modes of Jewish culture and self-presentation have changed or multiplied over the years since Abraham, but it is quite another not to take for granted that this nominally Jewish history is categorically and canonically unified under the aegis of a representationally identifiable Jewish subject that self-evidently determines it. What I try to do in this book is reconstitute the canon of Jewish American literature—not around the representation of an identified subject the recognition of which we do not really question but around the desire for an identity that we do not yet know how to recognize. Rather than claiming its authorization from a secure look backward on an essentially continuous history of the Jewish subject dialectically coordinated by the protocols of recognition, this reimagined canon would derive its sanction from a future it cannot take for granted as self-evident.

In this chapter, I begin the project of establishing and articulating a literary historical legitimation that can be a resource for a critical practice invested in the legibility and circulation of Jewish categoricalness—in the interest of a critical literary history that originates in an analysis of the ways in which the Jewish American literary canon will have already challenged the nationalist expectation, anchored in a presumably secure past, that Jewish American literature is about Jews—often specifically about the accommodation of Jews to America. The historical subject that the dominant nationalist paradigm of interpretation expects as Jewish literature's substratum can never be anything other than a reification of historicism's institutional-classificatory desire, of the processes and practices through which historicism always finds in literature what it is looking for. But armed with Foucault's idea of strategic reversibility, a responsible criticism can displace this chimerical subject from the site of its legibility. The point is not to stop talking about figures of Jewish identity in a literary canon that can be marked as Jewish; rather, we must use this very categoricalness and this very legibility as resources in the critical effort to contest the self-evidence or naturalness in whose name a nationalist canonical subject is legitimized. *The Impossible Jew* has been arguing that it can make sense to call this scholarly desire for self-evidence "Zionist": though I certainly recognize the polemical downside of using this term, I cannot think of a more efficient way of marking the pernicious historicist tendency—itself bearing a racialist heritage—to think about Jewishness in statist terms. Such statism, manifesting itself in the expectation of a coherently identifiable historical body that representationally anchors all things Jewish, reduces historical, doctrinal, and cultural difference as epiphenomenal to the gravitational subject that administers historicist literary work.[1] I should reiterate that when I speak of representation this way, I do not mean some particular representation of Jewish identity—though I obviously do engage particular representations of Jewish Americans here. Rather, I am suggesting that the academic field of "Jewish literature" has too consistently been administered by a historiographic logic according to which the literary archive's categorical function is imagined to represent—that is, in either the literature's represented content or, more frequently and more subtly and powerfully, its representational subject or authorial agency—an actually existing, specifically Jewish subject (that is, in the form of Jews, Jewish history, and/or Jewish culture) and that as a corollary to this field-organizing assumption the literary intellectual operating under the identity rubric and in articulation with this professionalized practice is expected to discuss that function.

To be sure, it is not easy to think about identity outside of the representational paradigm; indeed, it is tempting to look on the institutional histories of establishmentarian Jewish studies and academic multiculturalism as leveraging their inertial persuasion—as it takes form in professional incitements such as academic positions, funding streams, and publication venues—against the possibility of thinking critically about the concept of identity. *The Impossible Jew* sets itself against this structural inertia in the hope of critically reviving the study of Jewish identity; luckily, in this task it can look to some exemplars. A notable exception in Jewish studies to the professionally legitimated practice of taking for granted the representational-functional nature of culture is, as I have suggested earlier in the book, Jonathan Boyarin, in particular in his gestures toward what he has called "critical post-Judaism," a way of thinking about and naming "an already-existing but unidentified commonality, a way of being Jewish 'otherwise than being,'" outside the seductive structure of currently dominant multicultural positivisms. Destabilizing to statist modes of imagining identity in literary and cultural studies, the analysis of critical post-Judaism would be part of an "effort to begin to imagine a future for Jewish communities beyond the vision of a closed world of contiguous, monocultural nations." Boyarin's undertaking strikes me as a crucial element in the genealogy of the practice of critical interpretation carried out under the banner of identity. Boyarin calls on critics to challenge a tradition of Jewish historiography that shares two broad characteristics: a totalizing rhetoric of corporate national identity—that is, the assumption of the Jewish people—and a confident, historicist chronological periodization, which, among other things, secures Jewish identity by means of anchoring it in the past.[2]

As we theorize our way into this semitic criticism, however, we must remain vigilant against the seductions of alternative positivisms and should keep in mind that even as it is important to steer clear of an inevitably dubious literary critical Zionism, the solution is not instead to valorize Diaspora as the representational key to Jewish literature; as Caryn Aviv and David Shneer point out, Diaspora no less than Zionism calls on a corporate historiographic "center" that orients interpretive practice.[3] Jewish American literary history can disclose the possibility of a postnationalist interpretive practice by not presuming that its job is the historicist coordination of literature with an already recognized and legitimized image of an identifiably Jewish subject that has been sanctioned across a variety of powerful institutional, cultural, and political networks. This counterdiscourse of identity would hold literature to be, as Joseph Riddel once put it, primarily critical or analytical rather than representational,[4] a repetition with difference—a rewriting—of our fixation on identity rather than simply a transcription or record of identity. Contesting the statist temporality of identitarian literary history, such a criticism would see literature as primarily engaged in producing the terms by which identity can come to be realized rather than reflecting or referring to a self-identical or self-possessed historical subject that has been already professionally legitimated, undermining a literary critical paradigm that casts the relationship between literature and history as primarily positivist and indexical.

Therefore, a new literary historical *B'reshis*: in the beginning (at least close to it from a literary historical perspective), Abraham Cahan—surely a patriarch of the Jewish American literary canon—manifests a challenge to modernism's nationalist epistemology. Situating his 1898 novella "The Imported Bridegroom" in an interpretive context provided by *The Rise of David Levinsky* and some of his best-known journalism, I show here that a central problematic in Cahan's work is the absence of precisely the kind of historical, social, and theoretical coherence that underlies the positivist nationalism of our current representation-administered Jewish literary historicism. Cahan's text persuasively suggests that "the Jew" retrievable from literature is not the nationalistically legible Jew underwritten by a recognizable past, the represented Jew we insist we recognize because of its legitimizing circulation through a variety of statist itineraries, but an emergent, desired one, the spectral Jew that, as the proleptic inducement to an as-yet-impossible identification, compels as the unconfident trace of the past projected from an inscrutable future.

Jew-ish

I start twenty years after "The Imported Bridegroom," at what is often considered the modernist wellspring of the Jewish American novel. In the final chapter of *The Rise of David Levinsky*, Cahan's titular protagonist-narrator famously asks, "Am I happy?" The ladies'-cloak-and-suit magnate's answer, in spite of the economic ascent charted by the preceding narrative, in spite of the moments when he is "overwhelmed by a sense of [his] success and ease," is not so sanguine.[5] He admits that he is now "lonely" (526) despite his pride in helping to "build up one of the great industries of the United States" (529); and he acknowledges that "the gloomiest past is dearer than the brightest present" (526). If Levinsky's seemingly triumphalist American story seemingly confirms ambition's victory over class, it also suggests that this victory, like class, may not be so important. The book—which looks in so many other respects like a kind of American economic bildungsroman we Americanists get paid to already know how to recognize—leaves us in this last chapter trying to figure out what category does finally matter to this Jewish American novel.

An answer is indicated in the intersection of two concepts whose link the book highlights in these closing pages. The first is what Levinsky calls "race." Levinsky has had love affairs with three women over the course of the novel, each woman suggesting a different Jewish type: a wealthy assimilated Jew in Russia, the wife of an ambitious ghetto entrepreneur on the Lower East Side, and the avant-garde daughter of a Hebrew poet in Harlem. These affairs, however, fail to develop into sanctioned relationships for respectively typically appropriate reasons: class boundaries in the first case, domestic obligations in the second, and aesthetic and political commitments in the third. But Levinsky does admit to there being one other woman whom he "might have married if she had not been a Gentile." As he tells this woman, "It's a real pity that there is the chasm of race between us. Otherwise I don't see why we couldn't be happy together" (528). The unbridgeable "chasm of race" between Levinsky's Jewishness and this gentile woman's American Christianity seems more fundamental than their similar class position. His elaboration of this connubial obstacle is noteworthy: "I saw clearly that it would be a mistake [to propose to her]. It was not the faith of my fathers that was in the way. It was the medieval prejudice against our people which makes so many marriages between Jew and Gentile a failure. It frightened me" (527). By locating the differencing power of race in the "medieval prejudice" of gentiles against Jews rather than in "the faith of my fathers," Levinsky points toward an important aspect of how the machinery of identification functions in Cahan's work. After Levinsky's eye-opening immigration to America a sixth of the way through the book, he unsurprisingly—unsurprising especially to anyone familiar with Jewish American literature—becomes perfectly capable of contravening the orthodox expectations of his European "fathers" whose "faith" no longer seems relevant. But if Levinsky has lost the faith of his fathers, he fears that gentiles continue to carry the prejudices of theirs.

In the wake of the destabilizing variety of Jewish self-identification available in the book (including secular, religious, nascently bourgeois, liberally educated, domestically traditional, sexually adventurous, and capitalist), Levinsky cannot take his Jewishness for granted as an internally coherent identity formation under the administration of some controlling factor such as the authority of "my fathers"; instead, the boundaries of Jewishness seem policed at least as much from without as they are determined from within.[6] He implies that he is "frightened" by the prospect of being identified as a Jew in a process over which he exercises little control. What Levinsky withdraws before is the unrecognizability of American Jewishness, whose inscrutability itself remains unmarked even as it exercises persuasion. Levinsky's term "race" spans this ambivalence, figuring an erstwhile authority anchored in the past and reinscribed by an emergent authority that compels from an as-yet-indeterminate future.[7]

But this concept of race seems to be at odds with the second idea presented at the close of the book, only a couple of pages later: that of an "inner identity." Levinsky suggests that his "inner identity" has been betrayed by the trappings of his present American success but that he was true to it in his impoverished Russian youth in Antomir, the shtetl where he lived a pious life dependent on the local shul until he left for America at the age of twenty: "I can never forget the days of my misery. I cannot escape from my old self. My past and my present do not comport well. David, the poor lad swinging over a Talmud volume at the Preacher's Synagogue, seems to have more in common with my inner identity than David Levinsky, the well-known cloak manufacturer" (530). A paradox emerges here: though Levinsky suggests that his inner identity is unproblematically Jewish, in appealing to his race a few pages earlier he has implied that Jewishness is no longer inherently convincing. As Julian Levinson puts it, Levinsky here "embodies the American Jew as split subject," alienated from the only identity he has got.[8] However, there is more to this problematic crossing than a chestnut about Jewish American alienation. The tension between Levinsky's two terms, "race" and "inner identity," is resolved to a degree with the realization that they correspond to two different methods of understanding the compelling force exercised by claims of Jewish identification. If Levinsky used the term "race" to describe the "chasm" between himself and the wealthy gentile woman with whom he stops just short of a romance, it also quickly becomes apparent that a similar chasm, one that is likely far more significant for the novel than the first, opens as well between himself and his father's more self-evident Judaism. That is, Jewishness as "race" in fact circumscribes a coherent—and differential—set of beliefs and/or practices, such as might distinguish between a Jew like Levinsky and a Christian like the wealthy woman or between a Jew like Levinsky and a Jew like his "fathers." A phrase like "inner identity," however, implies a different account of compulsion: rather than relying on a set of practices to distinguish or differentiate itself, Jewishness as "inner identity" relies on an existential or naturalized criterion for its normative power, a criterion that readers today have little choice but to understand in racialized terms. In the crossing of these two terms, the novel powerfully enacts the incompatibility or irreducibility of these simultaneous paradigms of identification, between desire and heritage. Once Jews get to America, Cahan's novel suggests, Jewish identity fails to be self-evident precisely in the desire to rely on it.

In this passage about inner identity, Stephanie Foote reads a rhetoric of loss characteristic of what she calls immigrant fiction's dialectic of ethnic subjectivity, which repeats "the process of reification in a capital economy." Thus, if "ethnic or immigrant characters" experience a "dislocation of identity" that they mistake "as an *effect* of Americanization," they are "in fact being initiated into a chronic sense of dislocation underwriting American identity at large." As the ethnic subject mourns a real, but intensely private, true self, Foote sees ethnicity represented "as a factor in, rather than the final horizon of, the negotiations between private identity and public citizenship" on a national basis.[9] Foote's revised and updated melting pot transforms a residualized and mourned Jewishness into the medium through which American identity is articulated and experienced. Illuminating the high literary historical stakes of this Americanism, Isaac Rosenfeld, writing in *Commentary* in 1952, claims that in *The Rise of David Levinsky*, which he admits he had long "avoided" on what he concedes was the mistaken assumption that it was little more than "a badly written account of immigrants and sweatshops in a genre which—though this novel had practically established it—was intolerably stale by now," Cahan wrote a powerful novel that is both American and Jewish; and he moreover concedes that the characteristically Jewish theme (the persistence of Levinsky's differential Jewish inner identity) powerfully connects with and amplifies the book's characteristically American theme (that the millionaire finds life at the top empty). As Rosenfeld puts it, "He was writing an American novel par excellence in the very center of the Jewish genre."[10] What is important about the genre of immigrant fiction in this view is precisely its reliance on—and maintenance of—the legibility of identity categories. Even if the category of Jewish American, for example, resolves in difference from both traditionally Jewish and American identities, the institutional scholarly stability of that difference depends on the persistent legibility of both Jewish and American. Far from suggesting the subversion of categorical fixity, this dialectic of identity reinforces it.

This kind of categoricalism constitutes one of the chief mechanisms of the fundamental nationalism of dominant historicist patterns of Jewish studies thought that *The Impossible Jew* analyzes, and it is perhaps particularly conspicuous in the liberal scholarship characteristic of the emergence of Jewish cultural studies in the early '90s. Though Amos Funkenstein does not explicitly make this point (nor, for that matter, is he reading literature), for example, this kind of move strikes me as a conclusion that he might want to endorse given his polemic against Jewish studies' reliance on "false dichotomies" such as (most importantly) that between a "stable 'essence'" of Judaism and "assimilatory 'appearances'" absorbed from Jews' historical cultural environments. The

"contraposition of 'assimilation' against 'self-assertion, self-expression'"
is "misleading" insofar as "Jews expressed their uniqueness, and still do,
in an idiom always acquired from their environment." As he continues,

> The question: what is original and therefore autochthonous in Jewish
> culture, as against what is borrowed, assimilated, and therefore of alien
> provenance—that question is more often than not wrong and ahistori-
> cal. We rather ought to look for originality in the end product, not in
> the origins of its ingredients. The end product, no matter which sources
> fed into it, is original in some respects if it is unlike anything in its
> environment. . . . Even the self-assertion of Jewish cultures as distinct
> and different is articulated in the language of the surrounding culture;
> assimilation and self-assertion are truly *dialectical* processes.

Despite his useful destabilization of a conceptual structure opposing Jewish identity as a static and recognizable essence to assimilation, Funkenstein's goal here is unequivocally to preserve the "genuine
individuality" and categorical "uniqueness" of an identifiably and self-
evident Jewish subject. Funkenstein can devalue the difference between
essence and assimilation, it seems, because he never questions the existence of a historically, geographically, and socially continuous Jewish
identity; Jewish identity has "always" persisted thus.[11] Thus, as Rosenfeld
sees it, *David Levinsky*'s powerful significance arises in its suggestion—
its revelation—of a complementary relation between Jewish and American "character" (today we would probably say "identity"): "the old world
Yeshiva student is essentially an American in ethos." "Diaspora Man,"
who "drags the whole past after him,"[12] can simultaneously embody the
striving intelligence of American capitalism—and Cahan's theme can be
both Jewish and American—only because of the foundational Americanism subtending the gesture of the dialectic of ethnic identity: in recognizing Jewishness, America recognizes itself.

Cahan certainly seems to attest Rosenfeld's (and Foote's) comple-
mentarity in his 1898 essay on the "Russian Jew in America," in which
he pragmatically insists that Jewish immigrants—that is, in their very
immigrant Jewishness: in their Yiddish literacy, in their devoted industrial organization, in their religious community-mindedness—make for
ideal American citizens: "The Jewish immigrants look upon the United

States as their country. . . . The Russian Jew brings with him the quaint customs of a religion full of poetry and of the sources of good citizenship."[13] Precisely in their otherness Jews make good Americans. Starting from the assumption that Jewishness is a recognizable category and that Jews have a recognized history—and in an effort to prove that Jews have a justified and functional role to play in American society—Cahan seeks in the "Russian Jew" essay to describe Jews in terms acceptable to Americans who might potentially fear for the future of a self-evident American identity.

But a few years later, Cahan offers a quite-different perspective on this potential paradox—and on the fate of Jewish identity in America. In his arresting 1902 eulogy of Rabbi Jacob Joseph, the analysis is launched not from the standpoint of a past that secures identity but from the standpoint of a future that cannot take identity for granted. The essay, more than memorializing the man, in fact eulogizes the recognizability of the Judaism that so many immigrants brought with them to America. Rabbi Joseph was imported to New York from Vilna by a coalition of Orthodox congregations in the hope that as chief rabbi (an office without any real precedent in the US and whose title became largely worthless after his death), he could unify and fortify Jewish religious life in America. Rabbi Joseph's tenure, however, was marked most conspicuously by discord and, for Cahan, a "gap . . . yawning between the chief rabbi and his people, one which symbolized a most interesting chapter in the history of Israel, but which foreshadowed the tragedy of the newcomer's life in this country." As Cahan describes it, "Rabbi Joseph remained the man of the third century he had been brought up to be, while his fellow country people," that is, those who had also immigrated to America but who, almost universally, were only "lackluster" in their attention to him here, "whom he came here to lead, were in hourly contact with the culture of the nineteenth century. . . . He remained absorbed in the intricacies of his Talmud; remained absorbed in the third century, in which he had dwelt all his life." Cahan displays little confidence about what this "gap" represents for a definition of Jewishness in America: "Chief Rabbi Joseph was the epitome of a world which was and still is, but is doomed not to be. The Talmud, which he knew so well, is the soul of a people; but another soul, the Modern Spirit, is crowding it out of the bosom of life on to the dust-covered shelves of history. In the Ghettos of

America this process goes on much more rapidly than it does in Rabbi Joseph's birthplace. The celebrated Talmudist died here like a flower transplanted to uncongenial soil."[14] Rather than taking for granted an assimilated American identity as the fate of Jewish immigrants, an identity whose sanction and coherence derive from a past with which it is continuous, a mediation between American and Jewish identities, Cahan here resists a compulsion to yoke interpretation to the teleological legibility of identity—that is, as he can be seen to have submitted to in the "Russian Jew" essay, which is so frequently administered by the secure legitimacy of both the American and the Jewish. US civilization—which for Jewishness represents the destabilizing inscrutability of the future rather than the stabilizing influence of the past—cannot help but undermine the legible coherence of Jewish identity. History, rather than carrying the categorical coherence of identity forward, is revealed to be far more disruptive than conservative. Cahan's tenses here are insistent. While Rabbi Joseph claims only a "was" that "is doomed not to be," the Jewish Ghetto of the metropolitan US, which is subject to an elusive historical agency and which Rabbi Joseph could not represent, teems with a present that is "crowding . . . out" confidence—a confidence that could find its erstwhile sanction only in the past—in the nature of Jewish identity. Rather than depending on a metaphorics of the self-evident past, Cahan here reorients identity as a machine that compels from an indeterminate future.

In the case of *David Levinsky*, it might be too hasty, therefore, to say that David's inner identity as a Jew provides a kind of historically continuous racialized substrate for our interpretative desire to work with that the "faith of my fathers" can no longer provide. Jewishness may have been unquestionable back in Antomir, but America makes the continued expectation of such self-evidence look farcical. Certainly, "race" as it appears in the novel is far from being simply biological or otherwise deterministic; instead, the term displaces a fundamental indeterminacy about what Jewishness—specifically American Jewishness—actually amounts to. The problem disclosed at the end of the novel is that Levinsky lacks the terms with which to recognize his Jewish identity, that such terms may in fact no longer be available. But though Jewishness no longer looks like the Judaism to which his fathers were faithful, it remains a powerful axis of desire.

There are obvious attractions in inscribing this potential disruption of legibility in a dialectical historical narrative of nationalistic modernity and thereby containing it: to interpret it via a narrative of immigration or assimilation or Americanization, a process that presumably both occurred and finds expression in literary or cultural artifacts. But Cahan offers a warning about ignoring the potential threat to such a historicism posed by the displacement of a historically coherent Jewish identity. Though Americanization is so often the great theme of Cahan's writing, it is curious that this theme has also become, in a reduced form, the dominant paradigm through which literary criticism conforms this writing. Jules Chametzky, the author of the first major monograph on Cahan's work, demonstrates precisely: insofar as "Cahan played a crucial role in the acculturation of the Jewish immigrant masses" and "was a pioneer explorer in the duality of Jewishness and American[ism]," his work should be read for how it "mediat[es] between various sensibilities, languages, and cultures—Yiddish-Jewish, American-English, and Russian."[15] This becomes a key trope in Cahan's literary history: his work dialectically bridges languages, political systems, nations, and practices. As Chametzky puts it, Cahan embraced "contradictions," "mediating a difficult synthesis." Shown to render identity legible in the new grammar necessitated by modernity, Cahan, with one foot in an identifiably Jewish world and the other in an identifiably American one, representing Jews' "conver[sion]" from traditional Jewish learning to "the delights of Western thought," can become, in Chametzky's words, "the leading interpreter of Jews to the American world"—and, accordingly, to literary historians.[16]

This assimilation or Americanization narrative has by now become the preeminent literary critical typology, a machine that, by way of what, following Chametzky, we can call a "mediation" operator coordinating the cultural present and future in terms of the securely essential past, produces largely predictable results; it is structured to find what it is looking for, namely, Jewish identity. Cahan can "mediate" a "synthesis" of Jewish "contradictions" only because dialectical assumptions already unify all those contradictions under the sign of a coherent Jewish identity. Funkenstein is again instructive—and representative—here, insofar as even in challenging a too-easy critical reliance on an "assimilation" rubric, his argument fundamentally relies on the historically self-evident continuity of Jewish identity; to put it bluntly, we still discuss assimilated Jews as Jews; they may become self-haters, but they never simply become *goyim*, do they? Writing of *David Levinsky*, Philip Barrish, for example, argues that "the specific forms of Levinsky's self-division work as primary mechanism of the rise, in both its cultural and economic aspects"; in Levinsky's despair over the discrepancy between his American ascent and his more genuine traditional self, Barrish finds an ability to capitalize this genuine if irreconcilable ethnic remainder as the "raw material" of his economic and cultural success.[17] As it did for Foote, therefore, assimilation—which inscribes the present (and future) in terms of the past—rather than effacing ethnic difference, becomes the means by which Jewish identity is focused in Cahan's work. The Americanization machine's dialectical mediation—ultimately a modality of the expectation that identity is essential in, determinative of, and therefore retrievable from literature—casts a long shadow over Jewish American literary history.

Initially promising an alternative route is the work of Sara Blair, who wants to recover Cahan as a key figure in a heterodox modernist tradition that embraces mixed linguistic and cultural roots. The vital role of Lower East Side Yiddish culture in the "rapid transformation of the US into [the] avatar of modernity" is often lost for Blair in orthodox modernism's genteel marginalization of Yiddish as "a vestigial, atavistic culture, its exponents adrift within the very modernity their diasporic energies were catalyzing." Displacing the problem of Jewish identity with the historical fact of Yiddish culture, Blair hopes to avoid the assimilation rubric, which she claims to indict for suppressing "the effects of competing modernisms—Yiddish and English, high and low, idealist and naturalist, individualistic and collective—on the ground, at the very site where diasporic, dominant, and emergent cultures unpredictably collide." For Blair, Cahan "gestures toward a collage aesthetic—or perhaps more accurately, toward collage as a historically salient mode of culture making" proper to modernity. Yet she appeals to the familiar typology: Cahan "understood his work to be mediating literary and more broadly social responses to modernity for US writers and intellectuals." Rather than occupying what she calls an eddy of native realism, an "epigone" of Howells, his great patron, Blair's Cahan is newly positioned at the heart of American modernism, because of his work's articulation of "the felt realities of mediation": the "paths of cultural mediation," the "cross-fertilization of contiguous communities," and the "simultaneity of competing frames for reading cultural experience." Thus "Cahan understands his text's mediation between Yiddish- and English-language life-worlds to be assisting in the birth of new cultural forms suited to the mobility and dislocation of their subjects."[18] Yiddish becomes a figure for Jewish,[19] and this metonymic association is anchored in the past, by a history in which the relationship between Yiddish language and culture and Jewish people is secured as self-evident by the machine of Jewish identity. Even as Blair steers clear of the explicit assimilation typology, she reinscribes Chametzky's historicist mediation as the determinative link between past and present at the heart of her appeal for the literary historical importance of Cahan: in effect, she rewrites Cahan's "Russian Jew" essay, demonstrating Cahan's usefulness to literary historians of modernism in its conservation of a Jewish difference that she takes for granted.

Philip Joseph produces a more nuanced critique, critically deferring a solution to the problem of the function of identity in the canon (even if, like Blair, he maintains an overly positivistic interest in self-evident metonyms of Jewish identity). Joseph situates Cahan in the ferment of US Yiddish socialist journalism of the 1890s, particularly in its response to the question of Jewish identity. Though American Yiddish socialism in Joseph's account demanded rigid adherence to the goal of assimilation—that is, to the goal of making Jews indistinguishable from other workers, in the interest of ending the Jewish Question that many people found America, of all the nations, uniquely capable of effecting—by the end of the 1890s, Cahan had become suspicious of this goal and unsure about the fate of Jews and Jewish identity in America. And so Cahan turned to the English language and to realism, which afforded him the liberty of not having to have an answer. "Rather than compromising either his prominence as a Yiddish-speaking socialist or his wish to explore more fully the subject of Jewish identity in the US, Cahan chose to write for audiences who had never openly debated the Jewish question and who were uncertain about the racial placement of Jewish immigrants." For Joseph, this move into English-language fiction "cannot simply be explained as a literary 'fall' from Yiddish: a capitulation to the conventions of American local color in order to gain credibility. . . . The world of English fiction offered him . . . an intellectual hiatus from the obligations and narrow conventions of Yiddish journalism." The American English-language literary market offered Cahan "a greater scope in relation, very specifically, to the question of Jewish identity" insofar as he "could postpone taking a position" and "could remain undecided about the outcome of the Jewish exodus to America," a possibility unavailable to him in Yiddish.[20] Thus in so much of Cahan's writing—for example, in *Yekl*, "The Imported Bridegroom," and *David Levinsky*, canonical works all—we see, most palpably, uncertainty about the future of Jews in America. As Joseph puts it, Cahan in his English-language work wonders how Jews will "turn out in a context where tradition seemed untenable"; that the "the way of life associated with Eastern European Jewry was not viable in the US" was obvious to Cahan, but his work insists that this cannot become for literary history a mere platitude. Cahan's fictional characters "do not forfeit their identity, but neither do they possess it entirely. . . . Committed to understanding the Jewish resettlement in America, [Cahan] is at the same time reluctant to plot its end."[21] Though Joseph remains committed to the assimilation typology—he has deferred an answer to the question of how the past determines the present, but he has not given up on the historicist presumption of the determining relationship—his contribution is refreshing.

What ends up happening in so much of the criticism on Cahan is that several powerful modernist antinomies—such as those between public and private, autonomy and heteronomy, autotelism and heterotelism, and individual and collective, for example—are deployed to limn another antinomy, that between the work and the writer, an antinomy in turn underwritten by the racialized legibility of national identity. The literary significance of Cahan's oeuvre in this dominant account pivots on and is derived from a presumed historical self-evidence of the texts themselves: they are positioned as part of the cultural history of an identity, and literary history is articulated to extract that history by means of the expectation of that identity. There is little question that this is an institutionally powerful model of literary history, but there is no more question that its possibility is built on a foundation of taking for granted a historical and theoretical coherence—a legibility—of identity that Cahan's work can be justifiably seen as resisting. The problem I am addressing in this chapter is not a failure to recognize the definitional crisis presented for a categorical Jewish identification by immigration to America—in a word, a failure to attend to assimilation or Americanization. On the contrary, the problem is that literary history often takes the dialectical representation of assimilation for granted. Rather than attending to the categorical threat of emergence, an ascendant model of literary history has transformed the typology of assimilation into an undertheorized machine for the secure, and subversively nationalistic, recognition of Jews. Thus, as Jewish and American inscribe each other's possibility, the typology of Americanization operates as an agency of Americanism. The result will always be a historicist reinscription of the nationalist fetish of ethnic identity. But Cahan's great value is in disruptively figuring this fetishistic desire from the very heart of the canon that supposedly satisfies it. I propose, therefore, focusing not on those categories that Cahan's work is presumed to mediate from the perspective of their presumed mediation—on identity terms presumably anchored in historicism's history—but on how the desire machine of "Jewishness" operates in Cahan, at the outset of what we now categorically recognize as the canon of Jewish American literature.

Cahan offers us an opportunity to reinvigorate the criticism of Americanism—that is, of America as an organizational force—in the larger historical analysis of American Jewish identity by replacing a nationalist expectation to recognize the continuity and/or conceptual coherence of "Jewish identity"[22] with a more skeptical focus on the desire that makes texts available to criticism—a desire that works both in and on texts. Rather than assuming our field-organizing object of study (namely, a concept of Jewish identity that remains coherent—and compelling, both affectively and critically—across history, geography, and cultural technology), I suggest as a more legitimate critical enterprise a focus on the attractive forces that administer the texts we pursue and the methods we use in their study. Instead of looking for historical entities that we presume to understand in order to coordinate them in an articulation of Jewish identity—terms such as immigration, socialism, America, Yiddish, or tradition—we should concentrate on how texts make these terms recognizable and available to a desire for identity. The pressing critical question we should ask of Cahan's writing is not how it represents some sort of historical possibility or problem we

already know how to articulate—whether that be about Americanization or ethnicity or modernity, for example—but rather how it responds
to the instrumental Americanist questions we ask of it, which in this
case ultimately circulate around the legibility of Jewish identity. By staging the expectation of identity's self-evidence, Cahan's 1898 novella "The
Imported Bridegroom" makes available a nonnationalist Jewish American literary history oriented not by dialectics and recognition but by
emergence and desire.

Jews?

Twenty years before *The Rise of David Levinsky*, Cahan offers a pen-
etrating critical anatomy of the curiously problematic Jewish American
emergence. "The Imported Bridegroom" is the story of three characters groping toward an identity crossed at once by *Jewish* and *American*.
Asriel Stroon is a widower who came to America with nothing, made
a fortune in flour and baking, and now lives in comfortable luxury on
Mott Street since converting that fortune into real estate. Frightened into
rediscovered piety by a "newly landed preacher," however, this Bowery
rentier finds himself growing wistful for his hometown shtetl even as
his religion divides him from his American-born daughter, Flora.[23] He
returns to Pravly, his birthplace in Poland, in order to revisit his father's
grave but also in an effort to rediscover what he calls the "genuine Judaism" (99) he associates with his Old World youth—and that he fears
has been undermined by his American sojourn. While there, he outbids
a local *macher* in a marriage auction for the naïve Talmudic prodigy
Shaya Golub, whom he intends to wed to Flora in order to save her from
the apocalypse of Americanization—and in the bargain, he himself will
gain someone to say *kaddish* for him after he dies, on the anniversary
of his death.

Stroon, flush with confidence from his triumph in Pravly, returns to
America with Shaya, but Flora, though "amused and charmed," refuses
to consider the greenhorn. Indeed, her aversion is staged as predictable.
We come across Flora on the novella's first page reading Dickens's *Little
Dorrit* (whose theme of imprisonment will later become conspicuous)
instead of the mass-culture *Family Story Paper* and *Fireside Companion*
that her former classmates like to read; unlike her less refined (if more

typical) ghetto peers, she is "burning to be a doctor's wife. . . . Flora hated the notion of marrying as the other Mott or Bayard Street girls did. She was accustomed to use her surroundings for a background, throwing her own personality into high relief. But apart from this, she craved a more refined atmosphere than her own, and the vague ideal she had was an educated American gentleman, like those who lived uptown" (94). Meanwhile, Shaya is spurred on by the English tutor whom Stroon has employed for him, whose radical secularism (unnoticed by Asriel) positions him as a fifth column in the conservative Stroon household, and he becomes mesmerized by gentile learning and soon forsakes the synagogues and *tisches* where the braggart Stroon had hoped to show him off in favor of the Astor library, where he exalts in studying Western philosophy and natural history. When Flora catches wind of this transformation—indeed, in "less than six months," he has bested her in "Arithmetic and English Grammar," beaten her, as it were, "on her own ground" (135)—her desire is aroused, and she calculates that she may yet marry her doctor even while satisfying her father's wishes. And so a secret arrangement is engaged, with Shaya ingenuously promising to do anything so long as he can read gentile science and caress Flora (from whose lips, we learn, Yiddish sounds like "the language of the Gentiles" [123]) and Flora pledging herself in return for Shaya's transformation into a doctor who can eventually, we suspect, move uptown. In one scene that is particularly evocative of the desires underwriting this double conversion, Flora encourages Shaya, "encircling Shaya's neck with one arm, and producing with the other an English textbook on Natural Philosophy, which had lain open under the huge Hebrew volume" (142). When Stroon finally learns of Shaya's treasonous, monstrous reversal from prodigy to secularized apostate—he is told by an old, impoverished member of his synagogue who resents Stroon's boorish, nouveau-riche ostentation and inauthenticity—his dislocation is complete, and he feels himself no longer able to imaginatively situate himself in America: "The clamor of the street peddlers, and the whole maze of squalor and noise through which he was now scurrying, he appeared to hear and to view at a great distance, as if it were on the other side of a broad river, he hurrying on his lonely way along the deserted bank opposite" (149). Once Flora, still hoping to reconcile with her father, admits to him that she and Shaya have eloped, Stroon resolves to marry his earnestly observant housekeeper Tamara, herself the widow of a celebrated rabbi, and together they plan to abandon America, which, he says, "robbed me of my glory" (154) and is now "*treife* to me" (158) and poisonous to the very possibility of Jewishness, and decamp to "the Holy Land" (157). Parodically restaging how the dialectic of assimilation conserves the self-evidence of Jewish identity, Stroon the historicist hopes to restore the self-evidence and legibility of Judaism in Palestine, the origin that presumably coordinates history and identity.

But Flora, too, is destabilized by Shaya's importation. On their wedding night, with Flora "all of a flutter" and "impatien[t]" with "joy" (158), instead of returning to the Stroon residence to "pacify Asriel as best they could" as Flora would have preferred, Shaya takes her to the bohemian salon where he has been enthusiastically reading about Auguste Comte (on Clinton Street, incidentally, which is notably *not* uptown from Mott). Flora is "dazed" and "felt a lump growing in her heart" at the thought of Shaya "at this minute interested in anything outside of herself and their mutual happiness" (159). She feels "kidnapped" (161) as he "drew her up the two flights of stairs almost by force," and "before she had time to recover from the shock she was in the over-crowded attic" (159). The real surprise, however—for readers expecting a Jewish American referent as much as for Flora—is to be found with the immigrants crowded into this attic. Shaya insists that his fellow intellectuals are "such nice gentlemen, . . . genuine Americans—Christians" (159). Initially, this sounds like it is coordinated with the kind of language Flora used to describe her ideal mate at the book's opening, where she is "burning to be a doctor's wife" and where she "crave[s] a more refined atmosphere than her own," with her "vague ideal" of "an educated American gentleman, like those who lived uptown" (94). And it also sounds like it repeats the opposition between American and Jewish that Stroon takes with him to Palestine. If Flora herself does not explicitly articulate the "Christian" that Shaya uses, her father all but does, as when, in the beginning of the early paragraph in which Flora describes her matrimonial plans, Stroon dismisses a recent matchmaker: "old Stroon had cut him short, in his blunt way: his only child was to marry a God-fearing business man, and no fellow deep in Gentile lore and shaving his beard need apply" (94). His fear may be well founded: we are also told early on that Flora watches her father praying in Hebrew and thinks it a "novel" scene, looking on "with the sympathetic reverence of a Christian visiting a Jewish synagogue" (96). If Flora craves a more "refined" setting, Stroon reveals a link between her desired refinement and Christianity, a link he later expands by way of an elemental association with America; from Stroon's perspective, at least, it seems only natural that Americanized Flora desires to be less Jewish and more like the gentiles to whom America seems properly to belong. Flora and Stroon each illustrate the danger that this book locates in a desire for what is taken for granted; rather than securing a categorical territory, this kind of desire engages a destabilizing vector of epistemological escape.

But in Shaya, Cahan's story does not maintain the opposition between American and Jewish—far from it. Indeed, the book moves decisively away from the static categories with which Stroon and Flora are comfortable. Once up in the attic salon, Flora "gazed about her in perplexity" (160). She has imagined what married life would be like with her uptown doctor—she "pictured a clean-shaven, high-hatted, spectacled gentleman jumping out of a buggy, and the image became a fixture in her mind. 'I won't marry anybody except a doctor,' she would declare, with conscious avoidance of bad grammar, as it behooved a doctor's wife" (94)—but this "haunt of queer individuals . . . was anything but the world of intellectual and physical elegance into which she had dreamed to be introduced by marriage to a doctor. Any society of 'custom peddlers' was better dressed than these men, who appeared to her more like some of the grotesque and uncouth characters in Dickens's novels than an assemblage of educated people" (161). If this scene indicates that her exceptional reading of Dickens in the novel's opening has proven itself not completely without relevance east of the Bowery, at least in offering her metaphors by which to orient herself, the future resolving into incontrovertibility, which transfigures the arguably gentile "buggy" of her assimilationist imagination into the decidedly Jewish pushcart of the "peddler," promises something other than the American marriage she had expected:

> There were some ten or twelve men in the room, some seated—two on chairs, two on the host's trunk, and three on his bed—the others standing by the window or propping the sloping wall with their heads. They were clustered about a round table, littered with books, papers, and cigarette

stumps. A tin can was hissing on the flat top of a little parlor stove, and some of the company were sipping Russian tea from tumblers, each with a slice of lemon floating in it. The group was made up of a middle-aged man with a handsome and intensely intellectual Scotch face, who was a laborer by day and a philosopher by night; a Swedish tailor with the face of a Catholic priest; a Zurich Ph.D. in blue eyeglasses; a young Hindoo who eked out a wretched existence by selling first-rate articles to second-rate weeklies, and several Russian Jews, all of them insatiable debaters and most of them with university or gymnasium diplomas. (159–160)

It is little surprise that Flora is "perplexed," what with "Scotch," "Swedish," "Catholic," Swiss, "Hindoo," "Russian," and "Jew[ish]" crowding out any possibility of the simply and recognizably "American" she had so long taken for granted. Testifying to her confusion, the room itself, "full of smoke and broken English" (161), mocks her.

And yet if the smoky room suggests that Flora cannot see things clearly through her purblind expectations—she feels "jealousy" (162) in the face of everything in the room that does not comport with her desires, a suggestion, perhaps, of other desires working the room—this scene offers a picture of the interpretive rupture presented by Jewish immigration from Europe to America and indeed where trouble may lie for literary historicists' (not just Cahan's characters') confident presumption of securely recognizable referents. Where Flora sees only a foreign threat to her assimilated desire, Cahan here reverses her disappointment in an image—if still dubious—of Jewish American futurity. Though Shaya's intellectuals bear the markings of decidedly non-American beginnings, their shared, albeit "broken English" suggests that their diverse histories, as much as being "clean-shaven, high-hatted, [and] spectacled" (to say nothing of having a "buggy" to jump out of), despite Flora's vain wishes, may represent an American characteristic; broken English, rather than the good grammar Flora believes becomes a lady with "uptown" pretensions, looks to be the lingua franca of a future America. Indeed, despite what she may insist about a "doctor's wife," Flora's first spoken words in the novella—"Just comin' from the synagogue, papa? This settles your fast, don't it? You ain' goin' to say more *Thilim* tonight, are you, pa?" (95)—suggest something less than completely proper elocution. Even if to these "genuine Americans" "a

Jew is the same as a Gentile" (159), as Shaya, voicing the utopian promise of heterotelic amalgamation, insists, there does seem to be something Jewish about the identity emerging on the Lower East Side. If
they are potentially no more nationally errant than any clean-shaven
and bespectacled uptown gentile, by conspicuously gathering in a group
of "ten or twelve men," this motley group of immigrants looks a lot
like a *minyan* that, if paradoxically American, is potentially as Jewish
as Stroon's atavistic, European (and then Palestinian) orthodoxy.[24] Of
course, I am talking about our literary historical desire here; there is
no way we can really prove that the categorically Jewish referent of the
minyan, appearing elsewhere in the book, is repeated here in the image
of ten men gathered together in philosophical study. But given that the
book is explicitly about the desire for supposedly self-evident referents,
this is precisely the literary semitic point of reading Jewish American
literature for a Jewish American referent.

The possibility of Jewish American identity in "The Imported Bridegroom" at once appears and escapes in the intersection of a number
of compelling, apparently perspicuous oppositions that seem, initially,
to promise just such a coherent Jewish referent. The contrast between
America and Europe from which Stroon expects so much is built on
a foundation laid by the religious distinction between earthly life and
the afterlife: landlord Stroon is wracked with anxiety that his "earthly
title deeds" will not entitle him to a "share in the World-to-Come" (98),
but it took a sermon delivered by a "newly landed preacher," whose
recent immigration to America has presumably not yet corrupted his
Jewishness, to reverse Stroon's American profanity and revivify his
piety. Stroon's "genuine Judaism was somehow inseparably associated
with Pravly" (99) because in his worldview the contrast between gentile
secularism and religious devotion is clearly demarcated along national-
regional lines. For Stroon, at least after his religious reawakening,
American success leads to the forgetting of Judaism; one simply cannot
be both Jewish and American. Of course, it is worth nothing that, paradoxically, it is precisely this success that offers him the option of his geographical return to piousness. Buttressed by this cartography, moreover,
identity seems coordinated by linguistic difference, too. Stroon's preference for Jewish-marked languages is opposed to Flora's earnest attention
to English; Flora insists on answering her father's quotidian Yiddish in

what we imagine she hopes is "uptown" English, and Stroon insists on praying in Hebrew, which sounds like "Chinese" to Flora (125). Finally, the book also appears to propose a chronology of identity: Stroon's age is opposed to Flora's youth, and Stroon's interest in moving backward, to the European past ("I want to be there [Pravly] as I used to" [97]) and then the Palestinian origin, is opposed to Flora's interest in moving further into the American future, which she imagines is uptown, away from the immigrants "a few years in this country" (94) who dominate the Lower East Side. The ascendant assimilation-Americanization narrative takes for granted a cultural and geographical temporality: the past is Jewish, and the future is increasingly American.

But if these contrasts appear straightforward to Stroon and his daughter as they vie with each other over Jewish American identity, the text treats them with a notable irony: Stroon and Flora are both defeated by their vanity, by their shared presumption that they can successfully construe—and control—experience. Flora's experiment in directed Americanization goes wildly awry, and Stroon, who often admits his boorishness, is downright moronic in his remarkable capacity for misreading cultural cues. Even as he announces a self-evidently hierarchical distinction between Europe and America, Stroon is obviously a lot more American than he permits. Though he insists to Flora in announcing his plans at the start of the book to return there that he remembers Pravy "better than Mott Street; better than [his] nose"—"I was born there, my daughter" (97)—he proclaims on the same page a surprising defense, eliding "Jewish" and "American," against any possible interference by the Russian police, which Flora, remembering stories Stroon has told about his youth, worries about: "Show a *treife* gendarme a *kosher* coin, and he will be shivering with ague. Long live the American dollar" (97). And once he gets to Pravy, this American nationality powerfully reasserts itself. At shul, an auction is held for the privilege of reading the weekly Torah *parshah*, and though Stroon is certain he has submitted the highest bid, the honor of reading goes to a local community leader, a turn of events—and an elevation of moribund and byzantine Old World authority over vital and transparent New World assertion—that leaves Stroon "stupefied." Stroon "thunder[s]" a protest, "suddenly feeling himself an American citizen" (108), but is rebuked by the synagogue elders for comporting himself as if in "a market place. . . . If he can't behave in a holy place let him go back to his America!" (109). And indeed, when he *is* in America, the Hebrew that sounds like Chinese to Flora is no less "incomprehensible" (96) to Stroon. Far more than he acknowledges, Stroon elevates what he takes to be debased American virtues over the supposed traditional protocols of European Jewishness. Returning to New York with Shaya, even as he warns the prodigy, "stick to your Talmud, and don't give a *peper* for anything else" (119), he assumes (not altogether incorrectly) that the best thing he can do to improve "his importation's" (120) chances of appealing to the Americanized Flora is to dress him in modern clothes. Stroon thinks the "completely transformed" Shaya "easily the handsomest and best-dressed man on Broadway. . . . Barring the prodigy's sidelocks . . . he now thought him thoroughly Americanized" (120). Despite Shaya's abject American commodification, Stroon can still murmur to himself that "it is the Divine Presence shining upon" Shaya (120), rather than his stylish duds, that makes the imported bridegroom look so good. Cahan's wry comedy is at its most incisive in challenging the Stroons' attempts at management, as each tries to claim the keywords of Jewish American identity by locating Shaya in a network of oppositions that are not nearly as self-evident as they presume.

Seen in the light cast by Asriel's and Flora's arrogant and ludicrously failed attempts to overwrite conspicuousness with perspicuousness—a light that shines unsettlingly on historicist literary criticism's romance with mediation, as well—the book challenges the demand for self-evidence. But in undermining a certain kind of literary history that expects to find in Jewish American literature the secure representation of a Jewish American subject it wants to recognize, Cahan's text also illuminates a path toward an alternate literary history, a counter-discourse to the dialectical conservation of a Jewish identity anchored in the past. Refusing to take for granted the recognizability of Jewish identity, eschewing the urge to coordinate and articulate Jewishness via presumably self-evident metonyms secured by a confident history, this text, aware finally that the Jew it wants to represent does not (yet) exist, opens up the futurity of identity—a futurity that is coincident with unknowability but that makes available a present liberated from past legibility. Identity in this text is decoupled from the reactionary lure of critical rubrics such as assimilation or a dialectics of identity, representational structures ultimately underwritten—they cannot be otherwise—by a determinative essentialism, by the presumption of an identifiable subject, that this subject persists through history and that its past can, without too much trouble, be linked up to its present precisely in this past's ability to determine and administer the terms by which this present is located and understood. These rubrics work in tandem with an assumption that it is the responsibility of literary history to uncover these links in literature written by or about Jews. But this text disrupts this hegemonic responsibility. Asriel and Flora are both defeated in their expectation of recognition: Stroon in his attempt to protect an impossible representation of Jewishness from what he takes to be an American threat and Flora in her attempt to shed a Jewish identity she impossibly takes to be hostile to her Americanness. This is the logic of the golem: they are both dispossessed by powerful epistemological procedures they have put into motion. Jewish identity abides these attempted reifications in Cahan's story, persisting despite both Asriel's idealization and Flora's dismissal—despite, that is, its presumed legibility. As identity is displaced from a secure representational configuration, the possibility of representing identity is displaced onto a desire.[25]

The only one comfortable in modernity as it exists, rather than as it is expected or desired to be, is Shaya. Flora, become "background" herself as she sees her new husband turn from her to Comte's positivism and able to "neither speak nor stir from her seat" (162), is immobilized by an America that refuses her desire.[26] Asriel flees to Palestine from an America that refuses his desire, even as he suggests despite himself that America may yet be kosher. Only Shaya, who eschews the representational self-evidence of Jewish and non-Jewish/American that Asriel and Flora take for granted, remains open to Jewish American possibility, precisely in that possibility's inscrutability. When first presented by Stroon, back in Pravly, with a photograph of Flora ("representing her," we are told, "in all the splendor of Grand Street millinery" [112]), Shaya is able to hear in the word "America" a "fascinating ring, and the picture it conjured was a blend of Talmudic and modern glory" (113). But Shaya stares at the picture with "undisguised, open-mouthed curiosity" (112), as it destabilizes his expectations about Jewishness and his own identity: "His own formula of a bride was a hatless image. The notion, therefore, of this princess becoming his wife both awed him and staggered his sense of decorum. Then the smiling melancholy of the Semitic face upset his image of himself in his mind and set it afloat in a haze of fantasy" (112). Shaya retains the reader's sympathy as neither Asriel nor Flora can, but there is odd value to be found in his ingenuous attraction, as he certainly clarifies nothing for Cahan's readers about what sort of American Judaism is going to replace Stroon's outmoded and outmatched "genuine Judaism." We are presented not with a perspicuous opposition between authentic and phony Jews but rather with a question—that is, one that cannot be answered—about what Jews in America are going to look like, indeed about how they can be represented. Cahan's story in its closing scene reveals a disruptively irresolvable tension between Shaya's cosmopolitan *minyan* and the not-necessarily-Jewish "genuine Americans" it comprises. If a new American Jewish identity—a proper, maybe even genuine, identity, such as might presumably authorize and satisfy nationalist, which is to say Americanist and/or Zionist,[27] historical and literary critical inquiry—will have been emergent here, it paradoxically transgresses the statist purview of its erstwhile securely self-evident authorizations and representations: its classical and Rabbinic genetics, its European traditions, its strict linguistic boundaries, its generational hierarchy, even its blood-borne racial authorization. The Jew's future may well come at the price of its being unrecognizable, as "the Jew" comes—will come—into focus only as object of a Jew-ish desire.

The Negative Desire of Jewish Representation;
or, Why Were the New York Intellectuals Jewish?

Though the New York intellectuals are widely acclaimed as the preeminent American intellectual group, certainly of the twentieth century—Irving Howe wrote that "the New York intellectuals are perhaps the only group America ever had that could be described as an *intelligentsia*"[1]—their political, historical, and critical legibility remains contested; for a good forty years now we have had a fairly steady stream of work from across the political and academic spectrum that has fought over, in an attempt to secure, the relevance and significance of these highly visible critics. Yet too often scholarship devoted to them imagines itself as engaged primarily in the documentary historiography of an already-identified subject—often of the second-generation immigrant or Jew in America, sometimes also of an American political subject or Cold War citizen, more rarely as the Marxist in his or her confrontation with the eccentricities of the American political scene—and a result of this historicist-sociological predisposition is that this contestation remains a dead end, stuck in bookkeeping conflicts over who can be organized as representative of what category. Most visibly these days, we see this evacuation of criticism in action exerting ideological control over discussion of the New York critics insofar as they are now approached largely as the ancestors of the neoconservatives, a discussion coordinated by the supposedly determinative intersection of these intellectuals' Jewish biography and a later concern with the US-Israel relationship. We can work to free analysis of the New York intellectuals from this positivist impasse, however, by reimagining the project of understanding this analysis as a critical history not of a Jewish subject we already recognize but of the processes, figures, and institutional itineraries through which we are able to recognize and identify such a Jewish subject. Critical analysis of the New York intellectuals—at least critical analysis that is at some level concerned with the problematic of Jewish identity—should begin not with an assertion of the fact and consequence of Jewish identity but with a question about the legibility and affectivity of Jewish identity. Thus can the inevitably political problematic of literary criticism be liberated from the pernicious orbit of biologistic nationalism.

Jewish Afterlives

A few years after Lionel Trilling's death, Mark Krupnick wrote of a much-remarked moment in Trilling's overdetermined history among the New York intellectuals. The Columbia English Department's decision to hire (after first deciding not to hire) Trilling as an assistant professor in the late 1930s is widely accounted a significant moment in the institutional acceptance of Jews in America:[2] the first Jew hired to a tenure-track position in the theretofore anti-Semitic English department. There is, however, official disagreement among the chroniclers of New York's Jewish intellectuals about what actually went down. As Sidney Hook recalled it in 1979, department chairman Ernest Hunter Wright called then-instructor Trilling into his office in 1936 to tell him that there was no future for him at Columbia; though no word about ethnicity or faith was uttered, "Trilling was absolutely convinced that the only reason he was being cast adrift from the Columbia department was that he was Jewish." Hook by his own admission counseled an atypical course of action for Trilling, "fundamentally a very gentle person," to follow:

> My proposal required that he make a public scene—the first and perhaps the only one he would make in his entire life. . . . You must jump up from your chair and at the top of your voice, you must shout: "This is unfair—absolutely unfair! The only reason for telling me this [i.e., that Trilling lacks a future at the school] is that I am Jewish and that the Columbia English department doesn't want Jews as colleagues. It doesn't object to accepting Jews as students but it can't stomach Jews as teachers. Your genteel anti-Semitism differs only in degree from that of Hitler and the Nazis. They are driving Jews out of their university posts but you are making sure Jews never get in. You won't be able to keep the real reason for my dismissal from the press and the community of New York."

Hook claims to have "never expected Trilling to agree to act" on the suggestion, and "when he agreed," Hook "never expected him to carry it out." But as Hook tells it, "A few days later the phone rang, and over it came Lionel's jubilant voice: 'It worked, Sidney, it worked!'"[3]

In a dueling 1979 reminiscence, Diana Trilling also recalls Columbia's hiring of her husband. In her version, "The departmental spokesman said he [Trilling] would not be reappointed for a next year because 'as a Freudian, a Marxist, and a Jew' he was not happy there. Lionel said he *was* happy in the department. They said he would be 'more comfortable' elsewhere." After a few days, Trilling responded, and "the action he took was the single most decisive move of his life." Instead of making a "public scene," as Hook rendered it, Diana's Trilling confidently "confronted those members of the department whom he knew best: [Mark] Van Doren, [Raymond] Weaver, [Trilling's dissertation adviser, Emery] Neff. He didn't reason with them, he didn't argue with them. He told them that they were getting rid of a person who would one day bring great distinction to their department; they would not easily find another as good. It was his habit to speak quietly but now he spoke so loud that Neff was distressed, closed the transom. It wasn't a ploy, it wasn't planned—for the rest of his life Lionel would recur to this deeply uncharacteristic moment." What follows—Trilling presents Columbia president Nicholas Murray Butler with a copy of his just-published-by-Norton erstwhile dissertation on Matthew Arnold while Diana charms Butler at a formal president's tea—secures Trilling his job.[4] According to Krupnick, "Mrs. Trilling writes that her husband believed in later years that 'it was this that had accomplished its miracle: with such high opinion of himself, was it not possible that he deserved their high opinion?' In this account, it was not Trilling's threats but, more positively, his affirmation of his own worth which saved his job."[5]

Though Krupnick claims that "the differences between Sidney Hook's account and Diana Trilling's do not seem to be important,"[6] if we are interested in analyzing the New York intellectuals while being attentive to the literary critical problem of Jewish identity, then in fact it is precisely the difference—that there is an apparent difference—between the two reports that is important. Both Hook and Diana Trilling refer to Trilling's aberrantly outspoken behavior in claiming a tenure-line position, and both accounts take on characteristic shades of hagiography—Diana's mostly of Lionel and Sidney's mostly of Sidney—but they present opposed pictures of Trilling and of the importance of this event for a literary history of Jewish identity. In Hook's presentation, the department persists in genteel euphemism, and Trilling confronts it with the anti-Semitic truth of this euphemistic surface, the specter of an unwelcome Jewishness; while in Diana Trilling's version, the department plays the anti-Semitic Jewish card, and Trilling triumphs over it with a straightforward assertion of his indisputable and identity-blind intellectual merit. Both reports, that is, present Trilling speaking truth to anti-Semitic power, overpowering an anti-Semitic regulatory regime with one appealing to meritocratic values (a move that is itself a powerful historiographic metonym in narratives of Jewish American assimilation), but while Hook's Trilling calls out the department's anti-Semitism and confronts it with his Jewishness, Diana's Trilling dismisses as insignificant and corrupting the concern with Jewishness and indeed the whole issue of identity—though only after she has spent the bulk of her essay discussing Trilling's Jewish biography (and despite the subtitle of her essay, "A Jew at Columbia"). Recalling (in our deliberate scholarly manner) that Trilling was not teaching literature with any particularly (or certainly explicitly) Jewish content, we can argue that there is no better example of the Jewish Problem as it currently haunts the humanities. While Hook tells us that Trilling's Jewishness is an essential framework for the consideration of his career, Diana Trilling paradoxically reproduces the essentiality of Jewishness in Trilling's biography even as she insists that it has no place in the appreciation of his work and should withdraw before a standard of literary value. In both cases, Jewish generativity secures and circumscribes the field of professional literary historical analysis. The alternation between these two poles demonstrates how the writing of intellectuals such as Trilling remains vital to a Jewish American literary history attentive to the unresolvable problem of identity. Diana Trilling's and Sidney Hook's opposing yet linked appeals to Lionel Trilling's Jewish biography in considering his work and career—Hook barrels toward it, Diana Trilling ostentatiously demurs even as out of the corner of her eye she makes sure it is there—focus the persisting hold of a biologistic conception of identity in the study of Jewish American writing. When I say "biologistic," I do not exactly mean "hereditary" or "genetic" but something more like "racialist"; I use "biologistic" because it affiliates with the term "biopolitics," in the sense that it underwrites[7] or links to the production of instrumental-ized knowledge about, or to the adumbration of the life of and in the process the subjectification of, a population-as-historical-agent. The biography—insofar as it transcodes and conserves the heredity—of a writer functions as a transit point whereby an identified archive of liter-ary production connects to, often as the representation or representative of, an identifiable historical subject. Once Jewishness is taken to be the defining predicate of a recognized subject or historical agent, then it has already become the potential pivot of a set of police operations that establish a generative order, that classify and adjudicate a distribution of representations. Thus do an understanding of Jewish literary studies that imagines Jewish literature to be representative of a Jewish historical subject and a historiography that referees what is proper to and there-fore appropriate for such a historical subject rely on the same funda-mental organization of the Jewish archive. However, this archive and this organization, and therefore the relays through which representation links a categorically identified Jewish population and a canon of writing that we associate with it, via operators such as relevance or description, are anything but self-evident.

The point is not to beg the question by coordinating the lives and works of the New York intellectuals in terms of some historical narra-tive of assimilation, a Jewish bad conscience, or a return of the ethnic repressed; there have already been too many attempts to index Trilling's career to his deliberate (and painstakingly interpretable) early *Meno-rah Journal* stories, for example, and I hope not to reassert historicist bookkeeping as the final word on Jewish American literary history.[8] Conceptualizing a secure Jewish identity as the end of the practice of interpretation, this kind of documentary positivism will find in lit-erature only those identitarian narratives it sets out to find: for such a reading, Trilling simply provides yet another document in the self-evident archive of an assimilation narrative whose essential Jewish identity such critics have no intention of questioning or reimagining. Daniel O'Hara offers a refreshing critical corrective to such documen-tary interpretation; rather than standing as the end or goal of reading practices, O'Hara allows us to see how the Jewish identity of Trilling (or anyone else, for that matter) can become a beginning or opening for revisionary acts of interpretation. For O'Hara's Trilling, Jewishness is one in an assemblage of names for the "ethical disaster" of repression or narcissism, suspensions of the "liberating horizon of moral possibility" through which imagination subversively supplements and speculatively complicates one's own recognizable position. The specter of Jewish self-hatred haunts O'Hara's Trilling, especially in early stories such as "Impediments," "Notes of a Departure," and "A Light to Nations," in which the truth contained in anti-Semitism's charge of Jewish self-hatred becomes palpable.[9] But as O'Hara sees it, such spectral self-hatred becomes beneficial for Trilling, by providing an ironic shield against both self-victimization and the apocalypse of the American sublime, where identity and eccentricity are sacrificially capitalized in favor of the recognitive compensations of the market. Far from attesting to a simple desire to erase his heritage, Trilling's repeated assertions of independence from Jewishness attest to his fear that achieving representative status within one selective context might compromise his intellectual integrity: as O'Hara puts it, "Self-conscious detachment from any position he might passionately adopt defines Trilling's ironically heroic stance. Trilling thereby protects his imaginative freedom from suffering the uniquely American fate of willing self-defeat." Thus, in Trilling, the power of repression can be transfigured as the work of liberation when it is dramatized or played out in the revisionary creation of a self-critical text.[10]

Rather than be seduced by the positivist project, we should follow O'Hara's revisionary lead—not to reproduce his argument or readings but to look for traces of how the texts of Trilling and his fellow recognizably Jewish New York intellectuals parody (which is in part to say render conspicuous) the interpretive compulsion to recognize or identify them as Jewish; critics operating in such a mode would analyze how the New York writers, already caught up—in their own work as much as in scholarship about them—in a tensioned alternation between discontinuous forces organized by the possibility of identification, contest the interpretive will to read their work in terms of a literary historical criterion of represented Jewishness.[11] In this context, the alternation between Hook's and Diana Trilling's narratives is readable not as a stable choice between a biographical and a literary criterion but as an expression of the unstable problem that identity presents to literary history, precisely the problematization that is suppressed by identitarianism. It is one thing to assume that—by asking how—the history of the frequently Jewish New York intellectuals and the larger literary history of Jewish America are part of the record of, and/or represent, US Jewry as a historical subject. It is another thing entirely to register and analyze the important role played by our historical desire in operations that link the frequently Jewish New York intellectuals to the historical agency we already recognize in US Jewry in the literary history of Jewish America. In the first case, identity guarantees a stable inquiry, insofar as the text is imagined to representationally bear the legible Jewish identity of the subject that generated it—thus, in our example, Jewishness provides the framework for understanding Trilling's career, as the self-evident historical elephant in the room with Trilling and Wright (and in another room with Trilling's oeuvre and us) that had either to be acknowledged via explicit activism (pace Hook) or suppressed via liberal assimilation (pace Diana Trilling). In the second case, however, identity functions as a beginning of an insecure critical inquiry insofar as the manner in which a text represents the Jewish identity we read in it is no longer at all self-evident or definitive. It is in this problem of identification that the field of Jewish American literary study is constituted.

Thus humanities-based critics of Jewish identity should not be content to imagine Jewish American studies as essentially a matter of adjudicating the links between a recognized Jewish subject of history and a canon that represents it; rather, let us set ourselves the goal of imagining Jewish American studies as a matter of criticizing the vocabulary, practices, and institutional demands in which we mutually recognize this canon and the Jewish identity we read in it. Once identity is considered a positive, documentable characteristic of authors and texts, the categorical mark of a historical population or subject, critical practice interested in a criterion of identity has little option but to engage itself with representation in an essentially nationalist way: literary history and interpretation as much as the literature they engage are necessarily, before anything else, administered by a presumed Jewish subject in which cohere all identifiably Jewish historical phenomena. Whether the critic chooses to engage with Trilling's Jewishness in a consideration of Trilling's work is the only question, and it is a question that cannot contest, and is not interested in contesting, the nationalist logic underlying this kind of identitarianism. However, there is another way of looking at this disagreement over the Jewish significance of Trilling's hiring at Columbia. If we shift the locus of Jewishness from a Jewish population of which Trilling is a member to the interest in or desire for Jewishness of a discontinuous series of critical practices—including, to be sure, Trilling's own but extending as well to our interest in Trilling—the nationalist logic that always already expects to read the legible traces of a Jewish subject is displaced from the site of its operation and opens itself to revisionary critique. Critics would do well to resist dismissing this question about the Jewishness of the New York intellectuals as a niche or precritical inquiry primarily because a dominant context in which questions about the New York critics are now raised—by both scholars and laypeople—is an interest in the neoconservatives' gestation in the womb of the New York intellectuals, a narrative of emergence administered by a concept of Jewish identity.

* * *

Alan Wald begins his important book on the New York intellectuals by arguing that a "mystification" makes studying political culture and politically engaged critics in the US difficult. Wald points to a "neoconservative self-portrait being created by many of the New York intellectuals" that, among other things, has been instrumental in "perpetuating an amnesia" about these critics' "previous political history" as "Marxists." Though many of these writers and critics migrated during the Vietnam era far to the right to become the state philosophers for the Nixon, Reagan, and Bush regimes who justified such reactionary triumphs as the supply-side unraveling of the social safety net, permanent war in the Middle East and South Asia, and the sovereign ideology of ownership militated against New Deal practices of solidarity, Wald—writing in the mideighties, we should note, before much of the fruit of these triumphs was fully ripe—wants to illuminate the suppressed itineraries through which anti-Stalinist intellectuals committed to revolutionary Marxism increasingly "came into harmony with the dominant ideology of the liberal intelligentsia during the Cold War." This "amnesia" papers over important differences between the "anti-Communism (originally, opposition by revolutionary Marxists to Soviet Communism, after the rise of Stalin, as a deformation or perversion of socialism)" that these writers shared in the 1930s and '40s and the intransigent "anticommunism (in the United States, an ideological mask for discrediting movements for radical social change and supporting the status quo by amalgamating these movements with Soviet crimes, expansionism, and subversion)" that came to characterize a significant subset of them in the decades that followed. Wald's interest in rescuing the New York intellectuals as an important part of a vital American Marxist intellectual tradition that young radicals today can turn to for sustenance is not precisely mine, but his key point here—that the New York critics' "ultimate evolution was not the only one possible"—offers a powerful antidote to a dominant neoconservative narrative.[12]

As repeated efforts by scholars on the left to retrieve the relevance of the New York writers' Marxist (or maybe Marxist-allied) critique attest, it is hard now to see the New York intellectuals outside the framework that neoconservative history has constructed, a history that on the one hand dismisses as irrelevant, misguided, and sometimes even un-American the Marxism and Trotskyist idealism that characterized the group in the 1930s and '40s and that on the other hand—in the course of a process of a kind of ideological selection—justifies only those currents in their anti-Stalinist thought that can be retrospectively organized as constitutive of neoconservatism, legitimating the neocons as the non-leftist redemption of the New York intellectual tradition. Recent historians such as Wald, Terry Cooney, and Harvey Teres have done important work in retrieving the political legacy of the New York intellectuals from the ideological clutches of the neocons; here I want to continue that labor but by focusing on one of the crucial pivots of the neoconservative narrative, one that has so far been inadequately analyzed by left scholarship: the New York intellectuals' Jewishness. More or less clear links can obviously be narrated from (some of) the frequently Jewish intellectuals writing against totalitarian forces at home and abroad in periodicals such as *Partisan Review* and *politics* in the late '30s and '40s (and in some cases into the 1950s and '60s) to the right-wing Zionism and reactionary hack grandstanding that characterizes a journal such as *Commentary* today, but such recognitive associations are not the whole story. More fundamentally, an instrumental neoconservative narrative that redeems the New York intellectuals primarily to the extent that they can be seen to conform to the development of a programmatic "Reaganism,"

often encompassing a militantly racialist Zionism, has become dominant (admittedly despite pockets of left-liberal resistance). We can trace
at least three points at which this narrative has been leveraged: beginning in earnest with Irving Kristol's participation in founding *Encounter* magazine in 1953 (though I think in this regard it is not necessarily
significant that this was effected with funding and support from the
CIA-backed Congress for Cultural Freedom) and with Norman Podhoretz's ascent to the editorship of *Commentary* in 1960; cemented in
the decades to come by Kristol at the helm of Basic Books and the *Public
Interest* and by the celebrants of his rise into official political circles;
and advanced most audibly in the Academy these days by scholarly
fellow travelers such as Ruth Wisse and, to a lesser extent, Susanne
Klingenstein. This rightist narrative is dependent on the same nationalist organization of the Jewish archive that today orients the identitarian
mainstream of humanities-based Jewish studies.

My point here, echoing Wald, is that this neoconservative vector is
neither the only line that can be drawn from the immensely productive
ferment of the New York intellectuals to the present nor, importantly,
an inevitable one. Through analysis of the 1944 forum "Under Forty:
A Symposium on American Literature and the Younger Generation of
American Jews," which appeared in the *Contemporary Jewish Record*
(*Commentary*'s predecessor journal) and collected essays by eleven
young Jewish American literary intellectuals who were asked to reflect
on the importance of the "Jewish heritage" to their thinking and writing,
but also and as importantly through analysis of how that symposium
and its emphasis on Jewish identity has circulated in academic criticism
of the New York intellectuals, I aim here to uncover the possibility and
legibility of a critical alternative to the dominant rightist narrative that
structures—and limits—our understanding of the New York intellectuals. A countertext to this dominant account can begin with the realization that "Jewishness" has functioned as a reinscriptive lynchpin of this
structure's narrative authority. We need to consider in analyzing how
we approach the New York intellectuals the powerful role in our most
ready-at-hand interpretive practices of a hegemonic historicism, manifesting itself (in part) in the stock narrative of Jewish American political transformation: from early twentieth-century immigrant socialism
to midcentury deradicalization and liberalism to post-'67 Zionism.

Attending this storyline is a set of identitarian clichés that contribute to the legibility in academic scholarship of an ultimately racialistically and nationalistically limned Jewish subject presumed to organize Jewish history: equally perspicuous in the American landscape, for example, is the Jewishness of such recognizable figures as the Lower East Side socialist, the Mississippi Freedom Rider, and George W. Bush's neocon brain trust. Indeed, these clichés are so firmly rooted by now that we might want to say that Irving Kristol's quip that a neoconservative is a liberal who has been mugged by reality is simply a repetition of the familiar chestnut about being a liberal in your twenties and conservative in your forties—but for a Jew.

Essential in this recognitive structure, of course, is the ideological gravity of Israel and its association with Jewishness in the post-'67 statist realignment of Jewish identification. If Kristol, his wife Gertrude Himmelfarb and brother-in-law Milton Himmelfarb,[13] Norman Podhoretz, and Sidney Hook were relatively unsuccessful recruiting their coreligionist peers to vote for Nixon in 1972, by the 1980s many more Jews were comfortable voting for Reagan. In both cases the key point was Israel: in 1972 little constituency existed for the argument that Nixon was more concerned for Israel than any other US president, but by 1980 enough people felt that the claim was much easier to make of Reagan.[14] A more recent variant of this mechanism can be seen in Susanne Klingenstein's defense of the neocons against the attacks of paleoconservatives. In pursuit of her mostly unsubstantiated claim that criticism of neoconservatism amounts to anti-Semitism, she argues that the neocons have been branded as Jewish in the popular American imagination. Klingenstein's polemic takes shape largely as a reaction to John Mearsheimer and Stephen Walt's (in)famous 2006 "Israel Lobby" paper,[15] which Klingenstein argues "used themes and rhetorical strategies long familiar from the rhetoric of leftwing anti-Zionism," a fact that merges in Klingenstein's account with evidence of anti-Semitism. This particular case of the "Israel Lobby" paper becomes representative of another phenomenon, that paleocon resentment against the political ascent of the neocons, first during the Reagan administration and then in the Bush 43 administration, increasingly took shape according to anti-Semitic patterns. But her argument proceeds almost entirely by way of circumstantial evidence: a typical gesture is her claim first that

a paleocon such as Russell Kirk writes that neocons "insinuated" themselves into the Reagan and Bush White Houses and then that because
"insinuation" was a common anti-Semitic charge, that Jews insinuated themselves into positions of power and influence in gentile society, Kirk must have been anti-Semitic. One of her key conclusions is
that the foundation of the public anti-Semitic association of neocons
with Jews was "the decades-old linking in the public mind of Jews
with Israel," which is an interesting claim, given that it is precisely by
means of this linkage that the neoconservative narrative has inscribed
itself—and given that it is likely precisely on the warrant of this linkage that Klingenstein, suggesting Podhoretz on Nixon before her, takes
criticism of Israel and/or Zionism as a metonym for, and symptomatic
of, anti-Semitism.[16] We need to note in both these instances the pecu-
liarly powerful political valence of "Jewishness": neoconservatism has
justified itself by legitimating not only a narrative of its own rise out of
socialism's self-immolating excesses but at the same time a narrative of
the putatively self-evident relationship between Israel and Jewishness
and of the inevitability of American Jews' feelings in regard to this association. That is, the neoconservative account of the New York intellectuals can be seen as taking form as a particular history of the Jewish
subject. Challenging a paradigm of Jewish literary study that imagines
itself positively organized by the representation of a Jewish subject, I
will show how the "Under Forty" symposium belongs to the archive of
an alternate literary history of Jewish spectrality.

* * *

In 1944, the American Jewish Committee's journal *Contemporary Jewish
Record* (*CJR*)—the journal that the following year, under editor Elliot
Cohen, was succeeded by *Commentary*—published a symposium titled
"Under Forty: A Symposium on American Literature and the Younger
Generation of American Jews."[17] The symposium collected brief essays
by eleven young Jewish writers, including not only Trilling but also
Muriel Rukeyser, Alfred Kazin, Delmore Schwartz, Ben Field, Louis
Kronenberger, Albert Halper, Howard Fast, David Daiches, Clement
Greenberg, and Isaac Rosenfeld, who were asked to reflect on "the par-
ticipation of writers of Jewish descent in the development of Ameri-
can letters" (3), as the first sentence of the editors' introduction puts

it. The editors begin from the assumption that with this rising generation, American Jews "are taking their place in the front ranks of American literature. They function in every sphere of literary creation—as
poets, novelists, playwrights and critics. Their work is part and parcel
of the national literary product, and this is clear evidence of the fact
that American Jews have reached the stage of integration with the native
environment. They are spectators no longer but full participants in the
cultural life of the country" (3). Specifically, the editors suggest to the
"representative group of American authors" whom they have "invited"
to "record their views and experiences" (4) that "the Jewish heritage is
historically of so remarkable a character, and its effects are so significant
on every level of existence, that the American writer of Jewish descent
can hardly dismiss it as irrelevant to his problems" (3); this is to say
that the editors asked the symposium participants to gauge the relationship and relevance of the "Jewish heritage" to the "problems" of[18] "the
American writer of Jewish descent" (3).

As suggested by the use of the word "representative," the editors
take Jewish literary production as the record of an agent in history, or
subject. To be representative, of course, is to be representative *of*, and
what this group of eleven writers is representative of is The Jew, specifically as this Jew becomes American. Already in the first sentence of the
one-page introduction, the editors seem to be staking out a geography
of Jewish American literary study that must look fairly familiar to us
now: they take as axiomatic that Jewish literature is Jewish because it is
marked or informed or explained by the "Jewish heritage," a categorical
archive that differentiates Jewish cultural production. The explicit claim
is that Jewish American literature is part of the American "national literary product," but the categorically Jewish identity in which the symposium editors are invested draws for its coherence and legibility on a
national logic, too. The introduction evinces a dedication to the evi-
dentiary legibility of certain categories or sets, including Jews, America,
and literature—specifically as they define the field of a Jewish American
literary production, along with the conditions of possibility of its canon,
its literary history, and its criticism, constituted as the object of analysis.
Attesting to a categorical historical subject, the editors' archival "heritage" thus already functions as a nationalist prescription, tasked with
policing the boundaries of the representation of Jewish identity.

In fact, the symposium participants' essays take on this nationalistically administered heritage and critically destabilize this generative prescription that takes form in the introduction as the self-evidentiary foundation of the editors' interpretive confidence—precisely by exposing it as a *desire*. Functioning in the editors' introduction as the statist archive of a historically secure Jewish subject, "heritage" is better understood in the symposium as the disruptive archive of a spectral history that displaces Jewish identity from the coherent cultural narrative that the introductory statement expects to evince. The symposium will contest the positive organization of a heritage with a strong spectral negativity, a tension between authoritative modes of Jewishness as currently legitimized and Jewishness as a framework for resolving possibilities that could be, that destabilizes the summons to document the archive of a self-evident Jewish subject that underlies any identitarian literary history looking for the representation—that which either offers an image of or gives voice to—a given, recognized population. Muriel Rukeyser, for example, rejects the possibility that she is representative of a normative Jewish subject,[19] instead claiming that this tension "guarantees" against aligning with some particular authorized version of Jewish life: a vigilance against rather than an assertion of. Others, such as Howard Fast and Albert Halper, develop this sense of vigilance as an activist social consciousness, arguing that the Jewish heritage produces not a comforting particularist self-image but a universal platform to fight injustice. Delmore Schwartz argues that his sense of Jewish identity is beneficial but only insofar as it allows him to gauge his alienation from an American normalization, and Lionel Trilling, similarly, sees his Jewishness not as a positive identity but as a kind of spectral ethics, marking his unwillingness to be "provincial and parochial" (17). Isaac Rosenfeld argues that Jews in America are "overconscious" (34) of their own particularity, of how they are recognized at the present time, and so feel that they may at any time be called to account for this overdetermined identity. "Under Forty" is important not primarily for the reasons laid forth by the editors—because it marks the historical moment in which Jewish intellectuals could imagine themselves as American intellectuals, because it more generally stands as some other document of assimilation, or even more generally because it provides representational access to Jewish America—but because it critically figures an interpretive desire invested in a concept of Jewish identity. The symposium makes it possible to pursue a criticism of the specter haunting the literary historical desire for literature to be "about" the subjects we recognize in it.

In the symposium, the desire to explore how a "representative" group of Jewish American writers represents Jewish America—what forms the "Jewish heritage" takes in Jewish American writing, how it is discernible there, and how its cultural efficacy can be described—interrupts the possibility of policing this interpretive order as Jewishness becomes less a positive archive and more the negative specter of an inheritance, a mode of critique that challenges—albeit sometimes implicitly—the representational statism underlying a generative or documentary understanding of the Jewish heritage. In the name of "representation," a biologistic concept of identity so administers how we now think about literary and cultural production that it is now difficult to loosen the links and explore the space between literature and the subject we consider it to represent, to survey and investigate the relays—between genealogy and vocation, between group and action, between text and archive—that this symposium reveals. Interrupting the establishment of this field by displacing the possibility of policing a secure positivization of Jewish identity, however, the "Under Forty" symposium compels us to conceptualize identity not under the positivist aegis of recognition but as a form of criticism.

New York "Jewish" Intellectuals

The juxtaposition between *American* and *Jewish* in the editorial introduction of "Under Forty" can be read as a liberal wager that Jewish intellectuals can thread a subtle line between simple assimilation and crude cultural nationalism. Jewish American writers can now be considered part of the national literary product, the argument goes, but in achieving this categorical identity, they are also identifiably Jewish, marked by the Jewish heritage: becoming identifiably American can be identified as a Jewish achievement. Interested in an alternative at once to ethnic erasure and to a fascist politics of identity, the *CJR* editors assume that anti-Semitism will be overcome in a political concept of American identity operating in a separate register from a cultural concept of Jewish identity and therefore not contradicting it: a liberal nationalism in which "Jewish" neither opposes, reduces to, nor alternates with "American." Nathan Glazer has argued that even as the New York intellectuals grew out of a contingent confluence of remarkably "time-bound" historical accidents—including developments in the publishing industry, in US immigration patterns, in the institutionality of US universities, in American Judaism, in the demography of New York, in the intellectual geography of the US, and so on—and even as there was therefore nothing particularly necessary or inevitable about this emergence, the New York critics were, significantly, identifiably Jewish. This definitive categorical identifiability differentiates them for Glazer from later Jewish intellectuals. "What is interesting today is that despite the vast increase in the number of Jewish academics and cultural figures in all fields, we have no sense that they make up a distinctive political and cultural environment, a circle, a world."[20] As influential and as widely distributed across American society as individual Jewish figures may now be, that influence is not now recognized collectively, as that of "a linked group that one can name": they are influential as individual academics, journalists, college presidents, foundation executives, and so on but not specifically as *Jewish* academics or journalists and so on.[21] The unitary logic of a concept like "circle" or "world," evoking the linked promises or specters of coherence and historical agency, is obviously a key interest for any history of the New York intellectuals (literary or not), even more so for one specifically attentive to or based in a concern with Jewish identity. For Glazer, one needs to keep in mind when considering the New York intellectuals that one thinks of them as a categorically Jewish historical body or "circle." And this collective coherence is missing now in the intellectual sphere, except in one offshoot of the New York intellectuals: "The idea that we can find a 'corporate identity' as intellectuals and as Jews linking a group of Jewish intellectuals today is found only in the case of the neoconservatives."[22]

Glazer's historiography is notable given his claim a couple of years earlier, while speaking of the writers and critics associated with the journals *Commentary* and *Partisan Review*, that "[the] editorial group at *Commentary* reflected a divorce between Jewish writers and intellectuals and Jewish life—Jewish issues—that would be unimaginable today."[23] "We could see no connection between the Judaism and the Jewish life we knew—none of us came from educated Jewish homes—and the culture, politics, and civilization to which we aspired."[24] *Partisan Review* may have been the more egregious offender—Glazer wondered why, "despite its many Jewish editors and writers, [it] had published nothing on Jewish issues during the years of its greatest influence"—but *CJR*'s "Under Forty" becomes the case study for this disconnection; referring specifically to the 1944 symposium, he writes, "It was a remarkable demonstration of the almost total distancing of young Jewish writers from anything that could be called Jewish. For example, Alfred Kazin wrote [in his contribution]: 'I learned long ago to accept the fact that I was Jewish without being part of any meaningful Jewish life or culture.' Clement Greenberg, shortly to become managing editor of the *CJR* and to continue for many years thereafter as a senior editor of *Commentary*, wrote: 'This writer has no more of a conscious position toward his Jewish heritage than the average American Jew—which is to say, hardly any. Perhaps he has even less than that.' "[25] For Glazer, "Under Forty" is located at the crossing of two conspicuous identitarian vectors—the desire on the part of many Jewish intellectuals to dissociate themselves from ostentatiously Jewish "life" and "issues" and the desire of those Jewish intellectuals who went on to become the neoconservatives to avow a Jewish identity. Under such epistemic conditions, a documentary literary or cultural history that imagines itself as part of a positivist representation of a subject is inevitable.

There are obviously a number of reasons why, or contexts in which, we now think of the New York intellectuals: as a chapter in Jewish American history or American intellectual history, as part of a story about the professionalization of US universities and US criticism, as an important site in twentieth-century US political realignment, as an occasion to chart the contours of US Cold War thought, as an episode in the urbanization of American society and culture, and so on. The list goes on, and there is obviously no definitive category through which one must recognize the significance of the New York intellectuals. This polyvalence arises in part out of the general problem of what critics and historians tend to desire of or expect from the intellectual. Rebecca Walkowitz has written that to ask questions about intellectuals is to attempt "to locate the place from which intellectuals speak,"[26] a formulation that rides an unstable line between on the one hand authorizing a question about for whom or in what interests intellectuals speak and on the other standing as a summons to open up the whole critical problem of representation—between asking about the *who* or *what* of representation and inquiring into the *how* of representation. If intellectuals *speak for*, they do so, as a special kind of agent, precisely by questioning the terms in which it is possible to *speak* (let alone *for*) in the first place.[27] Intellectuals are representatives but only by contesting the possibility of representation—a theme to which Edward Said returns repeatedly in his 1993 Reith Lectures.[28] Intellectuals always highlight processes that indicate an identifiable historical subject: we cannot criticize the intellectual's representation of a position without also criticizing the terms in which we recognize the subject of that position. In exposing a fundamental question about the legibility and legitimacy of possible vectors of action, intellectuals are always also second-power, or double-order, agents, always engaged in, and engaging, what are essentially political questions about representation. Understandably, this focus on the political significance of representation characterizes much of the historiography of the New York intellectuals. Thus for Alexander Bloom, the New York intellectuals are primarily important for their recapitalization of social history as intellectual history: "They exchanged the peripheral world of the immigrants for the marginal world of radical intellectuals."[29] For Terry Cooney, the New York intellectuals forged out of an intellectual cosmopolitanism that was decreasingly cohesive by the 1920s and '30s a coherent tradition of intellectual liberalism as the proper expression of American identity, a liberal identity grounded in an image of the intellectual as an individual rather than as an affiliated member of a party or nation or race; the New York intellectuals gave "institutional form" to a developing body of liberal thought that emphasized the cosmopolitan individual as a discrete intellectual position.[30] Following the direction of Cooney's analysis, Harvey Teres explains the significance of the New York writers in terms of subjective experience— that they figured out, in contrast to many leftists before and since, who had and have sacrificed an interest in subjectivity before the altar of ideological conformity, how to articulate the importance of the "direct experience of individuals"—and argues that as a result they deserve critical rejuvenation as part of an indigenous American left political tradition interested in the individual.[31]

For these critics and many more, the New York intellectuals are significant because they produce political possibility—specifically, they offer the possibility of giving voice to constituency. Whether the focus is on immigrant ethnicity, intellectual activity, or leftist agency, the key term in scholarship on the New York writers is the relay structure between Walkowitz's "place from which intellectuals speak" and the subject for whom they speak. In this scholarship, the New York writers' concern with the Jewish heritage (at least the concern of the Jewish ones), including their burgeoning critical interest in questions about Jewish identity, starting in the '40s (whether in "Under Forty" or elsewhere) is understood insofar as it enabled these intellectuals to further theorize the intellectual's status—as outsider, exile, paradigm, and/or spokesperson. Cooney, for example, emphasizes how critics such as Kazin and Greenberg laid great stress on the fact that Jews, like other Americanized and Americanizing groups, have to a great extent had to create their own sense of culture as a practical matter. Jewish identity is legible not so much on its own terms but as a framework in which liberal individuality is reinscribed. This dominant trope of constituency partly explains why Glazer seems so unnerved by what looks to be the rejection of origins on the part of some of the New York writers and why, also, the neoconservatives emerge as the heroes (albeit the qualified ones in places) of his specifically Jewish history: they recover the genetically significant Jewish origins that so many of the other New York intellectuals too often neglected. I want to argue that "Under Forty" provides, rather than evidence for an account of how Jewishness is represented, an adumbration of the absence of—reinscribed by and for literary criticism as a desire for—a self-evident vocabulary for describing the Jewishness of Jewish writing. The Jewishness of the New York intellectuals is best seen not as anchoring a biologistic regime of representation but as unsettling precisely the mutual articulation of representation and historical subject that such biologistic identitarianism activates. Rather than serving as the historical bedrock for a set of symbols that literary criticism and intellectual history index and interpret, Jewishness in fact functions as a contested site that mediates between history and representation.

While Glazer is bothered by what looks to be the refutation of origins on the part of some of the New York writers, Irving Howe, another native informant, will in fact theorize this line of flight as precisely the field of a Jewish predication. In his well-known synoptic essay—written in 1968, once the major fault lines that would lead many of the anti-Stalinists of the '30s and '40s to far more conservative politics in the '70s and '80s had already appeared, and intended therefore as a kind of retrospective postmortem (he asserts, rather unequivocally, that "whatever the duration or extent of the influence enjoyed by the New York intellectuals, it is now reaching an end")[32]—Howe initially seems to have little difficulty identifying the New York intellectuals, that is, as a "circle" or "world" in Glazer's terms, as Jewish. This easy identification is complicated, however, when he ends up offering three accounts, each successive one supplanting the one previous. His first explanation seems quite straightforward: "The social roots of the New York writers are not hard to trace." With a few "delightful exceptions," he points out, "they stem from the world of the immigrant Jews, either workers or petty bourgeois." Thus, though he notes that some of the writers "who have been associated with this milieu" or group that we now identify easily enough as the New York intellectuals were not Jewish, he says, "I am working on the premise that in background and style there was something decidedly Jewish about the intellectuals who began to cohere as a group around *Partisan Review* in the late '30s—and one of the things that was 'decidedly Jewish' was that most were of Jewish birth!"; thus, he admits, when he uses the phrase "New York intellectuals," he does so as "a shorthand" for the more "awkward" phrase " 'the intellectuals of New York who began to appear in the 30's, most of whom were Jewish.' "[33]

But Howe complicates this simple sociological explanation by pointing out that the identifiably "Jewish" New York group emerged "at a moment in the development of immigrant Jewish culture when there is a strong drive not only to break out of the ghetto but also to leave behind the bonds of Jewishness entirely."[34] "Most" of the New York intellectuals may well have been Jewish, but if what is Jewish is a vector of escape from the cultural patterns in which Jewishness has historically inhered, then Howe wants to introduce, at least, a problem of definition. He admits that this tendency to "leave behind the bonds of Jewishness" is not necessarily anything new, that earlier generations "had known such feelings," and that in fiction written by Jews "as early as the 1890's this pattern had already come into view." But if this literary paradigm diminished further into the twentieth century, with its last "significant expression" coming in Philip Roth's stories, in which "the sense of Jewish tradition" becomes "feeble" in comparison to an "urge to escape its suburban ruins" that is "extremely strong,"[35] Howe suggests the reason may be that the parallel sociological paradigm to which it is representationally indexed had essentially completed itself—in the wake of a largely successful American assimilation, all we can really point to with any degree of accuracy as legitimately "Jewish" is Jewish genealogy. The New York intellectuals, that is, most of whom were born in the US to immigrant parents (exceptional was the case of someone like Philip Rahv, already a generation older than many of the other New York writers who came to prominence and who was himself an immigrant), "were the first generation of Jewish writers to come out of the immigrant milieu who did not define themselves through a relationship, nostalgic or hostile, to memories of Jewishness," for whom, in other words, "the recall of an immigrant childhood does not seem to have been completely overwhelming." Indeed, not only was the decisively Jewish immigrant past not "overwhelming[ly]" determinative of the New York critics' intellectual maturation, but their very categorical visibility as a group did not derive in any substantive way from the Jewish practices in which manifests the identity that Howe otherwise takes for granted in recognizing them: "precisely at the point in the 30's when the New York intellectuals began to form themselves into a loose cultural-political tendency, Jewishness as idea and sentiment played no significant role in their expectations—apart, to be sure, from a bitter awareness that no matter what their political or cultural desires, the sheer fact of their recent emergence had still to be regarded, and not least of all by themselves, as an event within Jewish American life."[36] While Howe seems perfectly comfortable identifying the New York intellectuals—a group both in whose formation and chronicling he was a decisive member—as Jewish by right of genealogy, according to the logic of descent, he at the same time suggests that the "idea and sentiment" of this Jewish identity persists almost entirely in being outworn.

And so Howe's second account arises in a kind of dialectical negation of the first: the emergence of the New York intellectuals is for Howe a Jewish event precisely because it stages a line of flight from a positive Jewish predication; precisely in attempting to escape from a particular historical pattern of Jewish visibility is the Jewishness of the New York intellectual vector reaffirmed. Thus does Howe reinscribe the potency of the logic of descent: the emergence of the New York intellectuals is a Jewish event not insofar as the content or focus of their writings bear decisively Jewish marks—after all, Howe suggests these writings often did not bear such explicit marks, just as Glazer points out that the writers often deliberately avoided such overt themes—but insofar as this event can be narratively charted along a Jewish trajectory whose categorical coherence and consistency are vouchsafed and administered by a logic of descent.[37] If Glazer does not quite know what to do about this flight from Jewishness, Howe goes a step further and provides a way of theorizing this absence of explicitly Jewish content as Jewish. Though as a purely "literary group and no more than a literary group" the New York writers "will seem less important than, say, the New Critics, who did set in motion a whole school of poetry," the "main literary contribution of the New York milieu has been to legitimate a subject and tone we must uneasily call American Jewish writing."[38] He has already noted that themes such as escape and the dwindling persuasiveness of religion had been apparent in literature written by Jews since the end of the nineteenth century; here he is arguing something different. It is not simply that the "fiction of urban malaise, second-generation complaint, Talmudic dazzle, woeful alienation, and dialectical irony" appeared in the pages of journals such as *Partisan Review* and *Commentary*; it is that this fiction, "in which the Jewish world is not merely regained in memory as a point of beginnings" but "is also treated as a portentous metaphor of man's homelessness and wandering," is staged as the field of an analytic, of a method of literary criticism.[39]

Thus finally the third version of Howe's Jewish accounting of the New York intellectuals effects a synthetic reconciliation of the initial two accounts. The New York intellectuals "legitimate[d]" the "subject and tone we must uneasily call American Jewish writing" not simply by being Jews who wrote about Jews, and not simply by escaping a determinately Jewish milieu by which they had been determined, but by legitimating a critical vocabulary and thereby constituting a field of literary analysis; the New York writers produced a set of themes—including the aforementioned "urban malaise," "second-generation complaint," "Talmudic dazzle," "woeful alienation," and "dialectical irony"—as a characteristic index of Jewish history. And yet it is a complex analytic, functioning at once centripetally and centrifugally: at the same time that this canonization of themes was consolidating a field as the "expression" of Jews, it was also being constructed as an "emblem" of something universal, precisely insofar as these themes "form a notable addition—a new tone, a new sensibility—to American writing."[40] Here Howe echoes the terms in which the *CJR* editors introduce "Under Forty." On one hand, they assume that Jewish writing is now part of the American national product—that Jewish writers are now identifiably American. On the other hand, even as they are American, their "heritage" segregates them, identifies them as belonging, at the same time, to a separate category—by the same nationalist logic that purportedly renders them American. Though it looks like the editors, like Howe a generation later, mean this ideological maneuver to preserve the possibility of a generative understanding of particularist cultural identity—that is, against the threat of a disruptive universalism—in the interest of a liberal cultural nationalism, I would like to argue for a different kind of Jewish predication: only in traversing Jewish particularity does this Jewish sensibility rightfully claim the mantle of specifically Jewish categoricality.

The reason that Howe can ground his Jewish predication at precisely the site that bothers Glazer—namely, the frequent lack of decisively Jewish content in the writings of the New York intellectuals—is that Howe refocuses the analysis of the New York intellectuals. Despite "our earlier claims to have shaken off all ethnic distinctiveness," despite the fact that "our Jewishness might have no clear religious or national content" and that "it might be helpless before the criticism of believers," Howe claims of his cohort that, at least in the wake of the Holocaust, "Jews we were, like it or not, and liked or not": "but for an accident of geography we might also now be bars of soap."[41] An ingenious maneuver: Howe finds in the crossing of two threats to Jewish predication—Americanizing assimilation and Hitlerian genocide—a new mechanism to ensure it, calling attention in our interest in the New York intellectuals to their need to theorize their Jewishness without primary reference to a self-evidently Jewish content. Thus as Howe lays it out, at precisely the moment when the New York intellectuals are establishing the field of Jewish American literary study, they are facing the peculiar problem of feeling themselves Jews while lacking a vocabulary to express that identification. "We could no longer escape the conviction that, blessing or curse, Jewishness was an integral part of our life, even if—and perhaps just because—there was nothing we could do or say about it."[42] If Howe is able to relocate the categorical Jewishness of Jewish writing to a critical desire to approach it as such only because that desire is legitimated by a biologistic confidence in a generative account of culture, he nonetheless offers a powerful resource to identity-based literary studies.

For Glazer, writing categorized as *Jewish* needs to satisfy two criteria: not only must it pass a genealogical test, but the writing must also be about Jews in some way or work for Jews in some way—it must serve some kind of legibly and legitimate Jewish function. Howe, by contrast, depositivizes the second criterion, abandoning Glazer's strictly and pragmatically recognizable "Jewish life" and "Jewish issues," even if only by way of rendering this second criterion dependent on the first: writing by Jews that is not self-evidently "Jewish" is in fact Jewish precisely because that line of flight constitutes its Jewish predication, reinscribing the absence of Jewish content as Jewish. But this really just serves to emphasize the interpretive stakes of a biologistic nationalism and its racialist account of culture; indeed, we can take Howe's spectralization one step further. We need to evade the temptation to read the negation of a generative inscription of an identitarian concept of "heritage" in the New York critics as itself categorically Jewish and instead develop critical procedures and an analytical vocabulary for reading this contestation for a desire for Jewish representation, for the representational access to Jewishness it focuses. The genealogical criterion becomes an occasion in which these writers reinscribe the effort to find Jewish traces represented in a text precisely as a desire, rather than as generative identitarian origin.

Identifying "Under Forty"

Instead of a false choice between, in Glazer's terms, an "almost total distancing of young Jewish writers from anything that could be called Jewish" and demanding a representational link "between Jewish writers and intellectuals and Jewish life—Jewish issues," the "Under Forty" symposium offers an opportunity to imagine a different kind of identification. Many of the essays take the introduction's imputation of "Jewish heritage" and evacuate the concept of its generative normativity: the Jewish heritage that interests them is less a categorical archive—of practices, beliefs, dogmas, genealogies, and so on—that is reproduced or transferred from one generation to the next and more a machine that focuses or marks the individual's deviation from a hegemonic center. Or rather, the categorical or national coherence carried by the inscription "Jewish" is not positive but spectral: "Jewish" does not represent a securely recognizable subject position—a "culture" or "ethnicity" or "religion," for example—so much as it figures the countertextual displacement of one. That which might police the administrative categoricality of an identifiable subject marks instead precisely that subject's failed categorical self-evidence.

Muriel Rukeyser begins the symposium by mounting a challenge to the logic of representativity on which the editors' introduction premises its argument. Born with "not a trace of Jewish culture that [she] could feel" (5) and "no mark of Judaism in [her] childhood home except for a silver ceremonial goblet, handed down from a great-grandfather who had been a cantor, and a legend that [her] mother's family was directly descended from Akiba" (5), Rukeyser begins at the crossing of the recognition of a generative Jewish heritage and a Jewish identity that does not know how to recognize itself. As Rukeyser notes, this crossing destabilizes the expectations of representation with which the *CJR* editors begin. She explains that she knew only a "reformed Judaism" growing up, one whose practitioners "wanted a religion of reassurance; they listened to the muted organ, and refused to be involved in suffering that demanded resistance, and refused to acknowledge evil. If they had a mission as a responsible and inspired people, they did not want it. It was enough to be Jewish" (6). Visible here is a theme that will be common to several of the essays in the symposium: a corrupting and repellant bourgeois complacency characteristic of ascendant Jewish American self-regard. Rukeyser sought out militant "struggle" and "connections" and found them not in authoritative religious customs but in the richly dynamic Bible, which she read at *shul* "during the drone of the watered-down sermon and watered-down liturgical music" (7). In this tension between Judaism as she found it practiced and Judaism as a mode of possibility—but also between the "Jews who could put up with fascism as long as it left them alone, the Jews who objected to a poster against discrimination because it mentioned Jews and Negroes together" (8), on the one hand, and "the men and women in the Warsaw ghetto, standing as the Loyalists stood in Spain, weaponless against what must have seemed like the thunder and steel of the whole world," or those "planting Palestine and taking a fierce oath never to put down their arms" (8), on the other—Rukeyser admits, "I do not know how far I am representative of any group in Jewish life" (7). So she refigures the tension as a kind of call-out against shame, settling on what she hopes is a nonreified response to the editors' prompt, not so much a confidence in a sustaining Jewish heritage that informs and structures her work but a sustained demand, decoupled from any determinate content or affiliation, that oversees her work: "To me, the value of my Jewish heritage, in life and in writing, is its value as a guarantee. Once one's responsibility as Jew is really assumed, one is guaranteed, not only against fascism, but against many kinds of temptation to close the spirit. It is a strong force in oneself against many kinds of hardness"; what she calls "organized religion has not been able to take a strong stand against these things," but this assent to what she calls "responsibility," perhaps, can (9). It is an assent to critical negativity, to a vigilance against "clos[ing] the spirit," rather than an assertion of a recognizably Jewish subject whose "heritage" is a Jew's self-evident birthright. Once it is made, "the conflict enlarges and grows, with one's own life and writing swept up in it. And the imagination moves, the spirit opens, one knows again what it is to be Jewish; and what it will always be at its best in one's life and one's writing: memory and fire and poetry and the wandering spirit that never changes in its love of man" (9).

Alfred Kazin begins from a similar stance of uncertainty or ambivalence: he does not discount the possibility of the Jewish heritage being a beneficial inheritance, but he is incapable of taking this inheritance for granted in his own case, precisely insofar as he rejects an understanding of the Jewish heritage as the coherent archive of a nationalistically self-evident Jewish subject. He speaks admiringly of "Jews for whom the word [i.e., *Jew*] meant and means something" (9), and he insists, "What I admire in the Jewish tradition, and in certain Jews whom I know, is the texture of a genuine and received Hebrew culture; an indestructible belief in the spiritual foundations of a human life; the feeling for the book; the kind of universal curiosity which spring out of so profound a sense of nationality (not nationalism) that it lives on the illumination its sources provide" (9–10), and yet he does not see that in Jewish America: "I have never seen much of what I admire in American Jewish culture, or among Jewish writers in America generally" (10). For Kazin, there is a Jewish heritage, but neither its reception by Jews nor its categorical security in the American context is a foregone conclusion—a rupture that troubles the generative coherence that the *CJR* editors appealed to when they spoke in the first place of a heritage. Rather than functioning as an enfranchising, received tradition, Jewishness in America seems for Kazin to have been the victim of a kind of embourgeoisement,[43] transformed into an alienating spectral object of intention. Lamenting that "the American Jew can get into such an unhappy limbo—neither completely lost from what he thinks his ancestors had, nor found in what he wants; with an occasional ritual gesture that is like the rigor mortis of an Elks convention" (10), Kazin reads American Judaism as the space of a disruptive absence rather than the site of a secure categorical inscription. The American Jew, "especially in these terrible years," does not necessarily believe in anything "that separates him at all from our national habits of acquisitiveness, showiness, and ignorant brag" (10); what a "pity," therefore, "that he should feel so 'different,' when he believes so little; what a stupendous moral pity, historically, that the fascist cutthroats should have their eye on him, too, when he asks for so little—only to be safe, in all the Babbitt-warrens. When even his suffering may be so sterile, as his fears can be so selfish" (10). Far from a rich culture at once identifiably Jewish and securely American or even a frustrated or forestalled recognition subtended by a more fundamental, and secure, biologistic identity, the Jewish heritage fertilizes only an ersatz affect of cultural distinction: "When I read a novel by an American Jew that is at least as grounded in the life it rejects as [James T.] Farrell's *Studs Lonigan* or [Theodore] Dreiser's *Sister Carrie*, I shall believe in the empirical fact of our participation" (10). This is the apocalyptic threat of the American sublime that O'Hara finds Trilling reacting to. Kazin admits, "I know how easy it is for the American Jew, at least in my circumstances and of my generation, to confuse his timidity with devotion, his parochialism," he continues, "with a conscious faith" (11).

While Kazin's parents, though "not particularly devout," are "Jews for whom the symbols have had a direct and tender meaning, and for whom the code had a plain integrity," Kazin himself has "had no such luck" (11). He has "learned that Jews were 'different,'" but he lacks an adequate understanding of why or an adequate vocabulary to express that cultural differentiation (he believed, he claims with a bit of the deadpan, the reason they were different was "only because the ones [he] knew were always poor and usually scared"); similarly to Rukeyser, for Kazin, sincere assent to the doctrines and protocols of Judaism as he finds them is impossible: he was confirmed because it was "proper" do so, but he "never learned what the texts meant: only to repeat them" (11). Like many of his peers, he attended "Jewish religious clubs" and "Zionist clubs," but in them he "encountered only a dreary middle-class chauvinism" (11), merely an ersatz nationalist parody of the received heritage to which the editors appeal. And because he has "never found chauvinism any more attractive in Jews than in anyone else" (11), Kazin admits that he cannot take for granted a significant continuity between his generation and "the Jewish heritage": "I learned long ago to accept the fact that I was Jewish without being a part of any meaningful Jewish life or culture" (11). As a writer specifically, Kazin came to think that "to follow what [he] really believed in" was "more important" than "what would merely move [him] through associations or naïve community feelings" (11). And just as Rukeyser contested assent with critical negativity, the key for Kazin is active "belief," rather than sentimental "feeling": while the locus of "feeling" is "community," leaving the individual passive in the circuit of significant culture, the locus of belief is the "I," the individual. The writers who had the greatest impact on Kazin—"Blake, Melville, Emerson, the seventeenth-century English religious poets, and the Russian novelists"—lack any association for him with "Jewish culture" but call rather to "the fact that, like many another American," he says, "I have had to make my own culture" (11)—not a rejection of Judaism but a displacement of reception by spectral critique; Kazin cannot take for granted the significance of "the Jewish heritage" to his role as an American writer because Jewishness is not a fact or quality but a frame or mode of questioning. The identitarian imagination that might be able to take for granted the transmission of a coherent "Jewish heritage" to a securely Jewish American, in other words, breaks down on the absence of the transhistorical Jewish subject that might function as the biologistic channel or route of that transmission; as Kazin ends his essay, "When

Blake says, 'Truth cannot be so uttered as to be understood without being believed,' I know the deep sources of that faith in the Hebrew prophets. But the directness of that insight interests me now, not a fact in history which my mind knows as it knows that Szigeti is Jewish, and Einstein, and the woman who stepped on my foot in the bus and hates Negroes" (11–12). The possibility of Jewish identification for Kazin exists quite apart from an identitarian assertion of inclusion in a historically self-evident body of Jews (that may indeed include musicians, scientists, and taxpaying citizen-racists); he may know the value of the Jewish heritage, but he cannot take for granted that, and in any case he cannot yet, in Blake's vocabulary, "believe" that, it is properly his. For Kazin, Jewish identity exists only spectrally, in a desire elsewhere than his identification with it.

Delmore Schwartz speaks of the "naive and innocent pride, untouched by any sense of fear," that his "Jewishness" fostered in him as a child, but this naivete was the result of his being largely protected from any kind of significant anti-Semitism such as might make the fact of being Jewish more perilous, fraught, or maybe just insistent. Learning more about anti-Semitism—especially in the context of its great flowering in Europe that coincided with his maturation—allowed Schwartz to learn more about himself, he claims, insofar as it allowed him to understand aspects of his experience that distinguished him from others but that he had not been able to notice before. Thus, "I understood my own personal squint at experience; and the fact of being a Jew became available to me as a central symbol of alienation, bias, point of view, and certain other characteristics which are the peculiar marks of modern life, and as I think now, the essential ones" (14). He calls "the fact of Jewishness" an "ever-growing good" to him (and he says this with "diffidence" in the face of what was going on in Europe at the time of his writing). Thus, though he admits that it is "clear" to him that his Jewishness can be "nothing but a fruitful and inexhaustible inheritance," it seems that this inheritance, and specifically its fruit, is as a spectral negativity, externally sourced and producing the vocabulary in which he can articulate his "alienation," his "bias," his "point of view," and his other "peculiar[ities]" (14)—that is, his deviation from a norm, however indeterminate or undefined that norm might be. Now, it could very well be that such deviation from the norm is just another term for identity, but this semitic formulation displaces the easy biologistic self-evidence of nationalist identitarianism.

If Schwartz speaks of his Jewishness as a "good" that allows him to leverage his alienation as perverse self-knowledge, Trilling reveals a sublime self-criticism in this perversity: he speaks of his being Jewish as "a point of honor," but it seems a peculiar honor in the face of the fact that he opens his essay by stating that one's Jewish origin is something that a Jew of his generation cannot "escape." As he reiterates later on, "For me the point of honor consists in feeling that I would not, even if I could, deny or escape being Jewish" (15)—an honor, maybe, but one embraced completely in resignation, a claim of ownership only of what cannot be disowned. This ambivalence becomes more apparent in the "deep" and "visceral" effect that the word "Jew" produces for Trilling, a "reverberation" that is at the same time seemingly without content:[44] there is "no reason" the word should have such an effect on him, as he was never the object of prejudice or persecution, his family was well off, his childhood was spent in "a comfortable New York suburb," and while his parents were "orthodox," they "had a strong impulse to partake of the general life and to want it" for him (15). Here returns the Jewish counter-normative we saw in Schwartz: Jewishness is a kind of friction or tension in the normative, in the normalized experience of what is normal, the itch that assimilation cannot quite scratch. There is another valence of Jewishness's contentlessness (which other participants touch on, as well): "It is clear to me that my existence as a Jew is one of the shaping conditions of my temperament, and therefore I suppose it must have its effect on my intellect. Yet I cannot discover anything in my professional intellectual life which I can specifically trace back to my Jewish birth and rearing. I do not think of myself as a 'Jewish writer.' I do not have it in mind to serve by my writing any Jewish purpose. I should resent it if a critic of my work were to discover in it either faults of virtues which he called Jewish" (15). Thus for Trilling, Jewishness exerts a powerful, but seemingly empty, gravity: he understands it as a force but at the same time refuses to recognize any specific, positive lines of influence—to say nothing of products of that influence. He would find it distasteful if a critic were to find Jewishness to be determinative or generative of his work, find any qualities in his work that can be traced back to a Jewish origin. Trilling goes on to articulate this problem of negativity in terms of authority: "Modern Jewish religion at its best may indeed be intelligent and soaked in university knowledge, but out of it there has not come a single voice with a note of authority—of philosophical, or poetic, or even rhetorical, let alone of religious, authority" (16).

Trilling seems to understand the problem of Jewish cultural generativity—that is, the means by which cultural production can be identified as "Jewish"—in terms of authority but in the negative: in the "cultural" fields that matter to him (i.e., philosophy, poetry, rhetoric, and religion), no categorically Jewish administrative vectors exist such that might persuasively authorize recognizable generative structures. What is recognizably or self-evidently Jewish is what Trilling calls "provincial and parochial" in its "willingness to accept exclusion and even to intensify it," and it is therefore not persuasive; thus, the "Jewish social group on its middle and wealthy levels—that is, where there is enough leisure to allow a conscious consideration of social and spiritual problems—is now one of the most self-indulgent and self-admiring groups it is possible to imagine" (17).[45] To maintain a categorically Jewish identity, Trilling suggests, any kind of cultural formation needs to maintain such a stultifying level of exclusionary self-regard as to become "provincial and parochial," another way of describing which condition would be to say that it lacks any persuasiveness or "note of authority." The effort to police structures of categorically Jewish cultural generativity therefore fails the test for Trilling: "As the Jewish community now exists, it can give no sustenance to the American artist or intellectual who is born a Jew. . . . I know of no writer in English who has added a micromillimetre to his stature by 'realizing his Jewishness' " (17).[46]

Indeed, for most of the symposium participants, as for Rukeyser and Kazin, Schwartz and Trilling, Jewish identity functions less as a persuasive fact, a gravitational heritage of self-evidently Jewish practices, beliefs, or identifications, and more as the negative trace of such a positive archive, exerting compelling force precisely in the instability of the kind of identitarianism that would take for granted legible traces of a self-evident Jewish subject in the interpretation of Jewish writing. This is why I have suggested that it is not particularly helpful, and in fact dangerously misleading, to read the symposium through the tired biologistic nationalism of the assimilation frame; there is a more complicated and deliberate practice evident here. Ben Field fondly "remember[s]" his family's warm atmosphere of Jewish literacy (17), and, he says, it is "small wonder that at an early age I, too, leaped on the pen and galloped over reams of paper" (18). But if the subjects of his early "sketches" were those "which the family circle understood and approved of—the grandeur of Passover, the ghetto Jew, the pious mother forsaken by her Americanized children," these themes stood largely as easy clichés, and he was unequivocally "an American boy, educated in New York, playing ball in its streets" (18). And yet, as he turned to more politically moti-vated literary work during the Depression, he claims, "in my devotion to the underdog, in the wrath against the despoilers of the people, in the mysticism and religious fervor which color the tale of a schoolboy who goes to a country fair, I was expressing, even if in an unconscious fashion, my heritage as a son of the people of the book, of the people of the prophets" (19). It was specifically the rise of the Nazis that made him conscious of the compelling intimate relationship between his populist Americanism and his Jewishness: "Then I saw that I had made some growth toward understanding the little people, the little Jews who are always among the first victims of fascism. Then I recognized that my education as an American had helped to reeducate me as a Jew" (19). So an "American" event (the value-laden experience of class) reinscribed by an international event (the rise of Hitler) becomes an identifying event (Field's education as a Jew). His two roles—as writer and as Jew—cross rather than converge. He concludes with a heroic image (one that could stand to take itself a little less seriously) of the "American writer of Jew-ish birth": "suckled by two great breasts," Walt Whitman and Sholem Aleichem (19), quick to call "his brother" any immigrants such as "his parents," and "armed with a double-edged sword, the American Jew-ish writer stands out as a champion of the oppressed everywhere" (20). Though he is quicker to embrace a "Jewish heritage" than is either Rukeyser or Kazin, Field claims one that seems mostly metaphoric, or at best metonymic, operating through active inscription and reinscription rather than self-evident inheritance.

Louis Kronenberger admits, "The invitation to take part in this sym-posium made me realize that I had previously never connected my race with my profession—that I had never thought of myself as a Jew-ish writer" (20). Challenging the editors' assumption of generativity, Kronenberger says, "Doubtless much that I have written is colored by the fact that I am a Jew, but nothing—in the conscious sense—stems from it; creatively my Jewishness has been rather a fact than a force" (20); like Kazin, he lacks a vocabulary or narrative capable of articulating the generative self-evidence of his Jewishness. Accordingly, he has "never thought of a body of writing in America that could primarily be termed Jewish writing" (20). He does not deny that "the *problem* of the Jew stalks contemporary literature, in many realistic and symbolic forms—the Jew as rebel, as alien, as victim, as sycophant, as Puritan" (21), but these are essentially "traditionally roles," what we might call in less charitable moments clichés, "as freely drawn upon by Gentile as by Jewish writers" (21). Increasingly now, anti-Semitism is seen by Jewish writers "as but one facet of intolerance, and discrimination as but one facet of injustice," and this is making them "the less Jewish in their approach" (21), a process he terms "moral assimilation, in contrast to the old embittered isolationism of the ghetto" (22)—and it is a process that Kronenberger does not lament. He does see a "social conscience" sensitive to all of state capitalism's victims as a "distinguishing mark of American Jewish writers" today, one that "no one can doubt" arises from the historical fact that "they are Jews" (22), but this seems, of course, a paradoxical Jewish identification, operating as it does precisely by minimizing the Jewish inheritance with one hand that it might be seen to uphold with the other. Ultimately, "any search for labels in a group that includes, let us say, Ben Hecht, Jerome Weidman, Lillian Hellman, Waldo Frank, Lionel Trilling, Howard Fast, Muriel Rukeyser, Marcia Davenport, Alfred Kazin and Nathanael West, is predicated of a wish to find them rather than an indication that they are there" (22). He ends by averring that the best Jewish American writers transcend any kind of substantive effort to differentially identify them as Jewish, writing "increasingly in the native [i.e., generally *American*] manner" (23). Jewish writers in America seem to be most Jewish, that is, when they are most American.

Albert Halper also spectrally metonymizes the "Jewish heritage." Though "fifteen years ago" he might have responded to the question posed by the editors of *Contemporary Jewish Record* with an intemperate "Hell, I want to become a good American writer, what has being a Jew got to do with it?" (23), he now insists that he in fact is different from his "Christian colleagues": "Hitler has made me different,

Chamberlainism has made me different, the war has made me different, and the coming post-war decades will make me still more different" (23). Here the agency of differentiation is not a self-evident inherited Jewish essence, though some kind of identifiably Jewish kernel is certainly involved, but rather forces that produce a Jewish legibility. But it is a legibility in service to a metonymic universality. Though he "never witnessed a pogrom," Halper insists, "here in America I, and other writers, are witnessing every day a different kind of pogrom—the pogrom against human decency" (24). But this pogrom "is not limited to Jews. It is also directed against Negroes, against labor and against little people who earn under five thousand dollars a year. Unaccompanied by the rattle of machine guns, it is played, instead, against the muted legal obbligatos of 'free enterprise.'" Halper claims, "Being a Jew has helped me to see the terrifying deadliness of the whole business. We Jews are like undertakers: we have been to so many funerals, including our own, that we can smell a corpse quicker than any gentile can" (24). So the "heritage" of the Jewish writer is that he "do[es] not think the same as [his] Christian colleagues" (24) to the extent that he is more sensitive to capitalism's pogrom against the disenfranchised, and it is a heritage that the Jewish writer must claim for his own. But again, it is a heritage of metaphor, of metonymical affiliation, that operates by way of the specter rather than by positive self-evidence. In the gentile state, it is the Christian who maintains the particularist perspective; to bear a Jewish predication is necessarily to gesture toward particularity's self-overcoming in universality.

Howard Fast seems to agree largely with Halper that the Jewish heritage of the Jewish American writer consists largely, and at best, in a kind of metonymical responsibility to fight against injustice rather than in an identitarian claim to a differentially generative body of doctrine or practice that is, in his words, "cultural in value and historical in content" (25). He begins by admitting his "own uncertainty as to just what a Jewish heritage consists of," especially in his case, since he has "been occupied—and to an extent, preoccupied—by the American heritage" (25). He clarifies, "if a Jewish heritage consists of Jewish learning, Jewish tradition, Jewish religious influences, a Jewish historical memory, and a sense of my importance and insularity in this world as a Jew," then "I think I can say honestly and assuredly that my work bears no relationship to it" insofar, simply, as "I have been more or less untouched by these influences" (25). However, he insists, if the Jewish heritage is understood differently, as an "intimate" knowledge of "all the forces of hate and persecution," including "chauvinism" and "race hatred" (26), then it bears "a close relationship to all [his] work" and indeed to the Jewish American writer more generally (25). In Fast, the metonymization of Jewish heritage present in other symposium essays intensifies, insofar as the Jew's intimate knowledge of "the forces of hate and persecution" is explicitly of universal significance: "An extraordinary knowledge of all the forces, which through the centuries, have attempted to destroy the spirit and the hopes and the aspirations of mankind seems to me a part of the Jewish heritage—a part understood by some Jews at least—and to that heritage I owe much" (26). Thus, insofar as "knowledge" of the Jewish heritage in fact takes form as a familiarity with a general condition of "mankind"—what is specifically Jewish is in fact universal—a Jew's "heritage" seems to carry a potential to break down the walls that maintain the categorical integrity of "Jewish." Too infrequently, however, do Jews realize this inheritance, retreating instead within a narrow identitarian perspective in an attempt to maintain a self-evident categorical differentiation that can no longer be justified as coherent: "It seems to me that too many Jews fall into a sort of soul sickness, whereby they become the center of a universe—a dark universe where forces are pro-Jewish or anti-Jewish, where Jews are hated or persecuted or tolerated or loved—and so on, ad infinitum," the "logical end" of which is a dark "neuro[sis]" (26). Failing to refuse this soul sickness is coincident with the identitarian fiction that maintains in turn not simply categorical distinctions but also nationalism and chauvinism—and indeed anti-Semitism: "When a Jewish artist stops nursing his hurt soul and discovers that he has a brain and two hands to fight with, and that he does not have to fight alone, he is a step on the way to destroying anti-Semitism" (27). Displacing the question of a categorical difference between Jews and non-Jews with a focus on literary production (which is, after all, the focus of the symposium), Fast sees "no valid difference between the work of Jews and non-Jews," "certainly no one from which any conclusion can be drawn": "Does the Jew choose certain themes? I think Jews, as non-Jews, write of what they know or believe" (26). Given the Jewish heritage, Fast finds that no identitarian criterion can be imposed on their work: "A Jew isn't special, nor do I consider a Jewish writer to be such. I write of people, and sometimes they are Jewish and sometimes they are not. In either case, they have the faults, the ambitions, greeds, hungers and hopes of human beings" (27).

Isaac Rosenfeld, whose essay brings the symposium to a close, highlights the spectral critique of identitarianism's biologistic nationalism that we see so often in "Under Forty." He begins by pointing out that, as "everywhere" a "minority group," Jews face a "particular misfortune" to be a minority group these days in the US: "a conscious member of such a group is necessarily overconscious: he is distracted by race and religion, distressed by differences which in a healthy society would be considered healthful" (34). Whereas the "simple state of being a Jew" should "occupy no more of a man's attention than any ordinary fact of his history," it now "create[s] traumas, fears of violence, defenses against aggression" (34). Much as Hitler and "Chamberlainism" made Halper a Jew, Rosenfeld emphasizes that, rather than being self-evidently generative, Jewish categoricalness is produced in history. Specifically, this is the worst kind of environment in which an artist can operate. "An artist should first of all have the security of a dignified neutrality" (34); he should be able to consider himself "an equal, a man among men, a representative even if extraordinary individual. But a Jewish writer unconsciously feels that he may at any time be called to account not for his art, nor even for his life, but for his Jewishness" (35). Rosenfeld's term "representative" diverges or doubles: though on one level the term glosses the general "man among men," a suggestion that the artist ideally should generically represent universal humanness, be a representative, which is to say universal, man, Rosenfeld laments that the Jewish writer is inevitably taken to be representative in a very different way, which is to say of the identifiably Jewish category of humanity. As the other symposium participants attest, this process of being "called to account" has multiple itineraries, at once Jewish and gentile, alternately empowering and disenfranchising, serving no unified or coherent agenda. Rosenfeld's Jew, called to account, is overconscious because he or she is overdetermined, refused the comfort of self-evidence. Though many of the symposium participants hope to read this overdetermination sanguinely, as a beneficial inheritance, providing a kind of universal insight,

Rosenfeld emphasizes its disruption, the forceful challenge it mounts to any attempt—Jewish or not—at taking Jewishness for granted.

It is certainly possible to reduce the complex critique of identity in "Under Forty" to an already-legible drama about a self-evidently Jewish historical subject, to some stock story about assimilation, with its ambivalences and national narratives. But succumbing to such historicist seduction, by requiring thought to conform to precognized narratives of recognizable historical subjects, would be to ignore the deliberate contestation of the recognizable that irrupts in these essays. The spectral Jewish archive—the vast, incoherent, nonunified aggregation of discourses on, of, by, for, and about Jews—functions as the necessary supplement of any act of Jewish predication, whether a claim of Jewish self-consciousness or not. Any act of Jewish inscription is always already an act of reinscription, as in the Jew's desire he or she is always displaced from the site of the Jew's predication. One will have few greater opportunities to gauge what is at stake in the "Under Forty" essays' critique of identitarianism, to gauge the difference between reading them as the document of a nationalist narrative of assimilation and reading them as the difficult contestation of an identification that can never be taken for granted, than that presented by the Zionist concept of constituency through which neoconservative critics—in what follows I will focus on Ruth Wisse and Norman Podhoretz—have attempted to normalize a particular relationship between the New York intellectuals and the emergence of neoconservative statism.

You Can't Take the "Jew" Out of the "Intellectual," Right?

As professional literary critics go, few have worked more dutifully to oversee a professionally rigorous identity-based Jewish literary and cultural history with a normalized concept of national identity than has Ruth Wisse. For Wisse, the New York intellectuals as a group hold an equivocal value—though along largely unequivocal lines of demarcation. She finds dubious those forces operating in their work that she traces to their leftism, which she conflates with a pernicious, unyielding, and at once anti-American and anti-Semitic sounding "Marxism"; on the other hand, those forces that for her lead to the emergence of neoconservatism and to a self-evident equation between what she frequently and sententiously calls the "cause of the Jews" and a militantly racialist Zionism—an equation administered by her tendentious term "a Jewish polity"—are for Wisse historically justified and honorable. Like Glazer, she demands that Jewish cultural work serve an identifiably Jewish end; far more explicitly and aggressively than in Glazer's case, Israel operates as the fulcrum of her program to adjudicate Jewishness. If Marxism blinded the New York Jews to "the Jewish fate," as she polemicizes in her 2005 appreciation titled "The Jewishness of *Commentary*," she insists that Zionism and what later became the neoconservatism of some of them were two sides of the same identitarian coin. As Wisse sees it, the two marquee publications associated with the New York intellectuals function as a shorthand for her political anatomy of their output: while *Partisan Review* often, suspiciously, refused to commit to neoconservatism even as it doggedly eschewed Jewish content and themes, so *Commentary*, "by taking intellectual responsibility for the Jewish people and the Jewish polity," in fact "reinvented the intellectual calling,"[47] blazing the neocons' path by reaffirming political responsibility to their true constituency, the Jewish subject.

Wisse traces *Commentary*'s success to its founding by the American Jewish Committee in 1945 and the "unlikely merger" that editor Elliot Cohen effected "between two constituencies" in the Jewish cultural world, "an intelligentsia intent on maintaining its 'independence' and an institutional sponsor charged with protecting Jewish interests";[48] thus it bridged the divide between the prominent venues open to Jewish intellectuals before its emergence in 1945—on the one hand journals such as the *Menorah Journal* or *Jewish Frontier*, "which dealt almost exclusively with Jewish issues," and on the other magazines such as *Partisan Review* and the *New Republic*, "in which Jewish contributors wrote about general issues."[49] As this division in early twentieth-century Jewish intellectual life replicated (as the inheritor of) the "nineteenth-century Jewish Enlightenment's conceptual distinction between the Jew 'in his home' and the Jew 'in the street,'" itself productive of a split consciousness among Jews, acting one way within the community and another when interacting with the surrounding gentile world, it expressed also the long history of modern Jew hatred and the anti-Semitic mythos of the Jew perpetually alienated from and at odds with his or her nation of residence.[50] This history and mythos demand for Wisse one of two responses that continue to present an alternative that every Jew must face: genocide or Israel. If the Jews of *Partisan Review* effectively accepted this fundamentally anti-Semitic separation of spheres and thereby perpetuated dangerous patterns of self-hatred, *Commentary* replaced "this image of cultural bifurcation," as editor Cohen described it in the first issue's opening editorial statement, "An Act of Affirmation," with a model of integration that "will harmonize heritage and coun-try into a true sense of at-home-ness in the modern world"[51]—a reit-eration of precisely the liberal identitarianism that underlay the "Under Forty" introduction's figuration of Jewish American identity. But Wisse explicitly supplements this hopeful liberal description with the militant prescription that was always latent in its biologistic nationalism: the integrated Jew, newly recognized in the pages of *Commentary*, is newly capable of defending its "polity." That Wisse's racialist Zionism shares its foundational logic with the European genocide of the Jews to which she understands Israel as offering an appropriate (and necessary) response is precisely the point.

Though *Commentary*'s editorial policy was at the beginning reso-lutely "non-Zionist," for Wisse, the fact that the journal began publishing in the years between the end of the war and the founding of the Israeli state helped define the field in which it would operate and the "polity" and "cause" that it would come to represent. And in any case, Wisse finds after Israeli independence a new Jewish intellectual aggressiveness in *Commentary*; she notes in this context the 1949 essay "What Can We Do about Fagin?" by Leslie Fiedler—no natural ally of Wisse's—with its conspicuous use of "the first person plural pronoun," as marking a new willingness among Jewish intellectuals to "confront" and "counteract" the "negative myth[s]" existing about Jews in literature and culture.[52] Fiedler, Wisse notes, "does not mention in his article that he is writing a year after the British withdrawal from Palestine. I have not found in either the magazine or the memoirist literature any acknowledgment of the link between the two phenomena, yet it seems clear that the new Jewish cultural self-assertiveness accompanied the establishment and successful defense of Israel."[53] That her tendentious argument proceeds by circumstantial presumption (however "clear" "it seems") highlights the fact that she ignores the intense questioning of the meaning of Jew-ish culture—and of the possibilities, manifestations, and significance of what she too easily calls "Jewish cultural self-assertiveness"—in "Under Forty," not three pages after referring dismissively to the symposium, a dismissal that is notable for being grounded in an implicit but powerful equation of "Jewish cultural self-assertiveness" and Jewish nationalist statism. In a similar vein, Wisse celebrates the decision of Norman Podhoretz, who had taken over as editor of *Commentary* in 1960 after Cohen's death in 1959, to publish, shortly after Hannah Arendt's discussion of the Eichmann trial started appearing in the *New Yorker*, Jacob Robinson's attack on Arendt's "banality of evil" thesis and a little later his own condemnation of Arendt's "exculpatory portrayal of anti-Semitism and her denunciation of the Jewish leadership";[54] as she writes of Arendt in defending Podhoretz's "offen[se]" at the philosopher's "moral imbalance," "This intellectual razzle-dazzle seemed especially odious when the reputation of the Jews was at stake."[55] With her polemically blunt phrase "reputation of the Jews" muscling aside justification of any nuanced criticism of the Israeli state, Wisse correlates Jewish intellectual activity with a militant Zionism through the agency of what she calls later in the essay "the interests of their group"[56]—and at the same time delegitimizes Jewish intellectual work that fails this Zionist criterion.

Wisse's neoconservatism links the cultural fates of America and Israel.[57] The political "persuasion"[58] that Wisse celebrates in her elevation of neoconservatism emerged earlier than the more visible, general rightist reaction to the rise in the late '60s of the countercultural deformation of what Trilling famously called the "adversarial culture" and what Wisse aggressively calls "the New Politics that attacked not America's flaws but America itself."[59] And this earlier emergence was in "the Jewish component of *Commentary*," in "earlier articles on Israel, Judaism, and the Jews," which "promoted neoconservatism before the term came into use and before the rest of the magazine was prepared to conclude that the opposite of the Left would have to call itself the Right."[60] As Wisse insists, "it emerged earlier in that sphere because the threat to the Jewish polity and the Jewish future was more dire than the threat to America. This emergent Jewish conservatism did not hearken back to any sounder, better, or happier past, but warned that Judaism and the Jews had adjusted so completely to modernity that unless they now consolidated their practice they would evaporate altogether."[61]

The Jews of *Commentary*, sensitive to the threats faced by Israel at once in the Middle East and on the Upper West Side, cleared the intellectual ground for neoconservatism: "As the Arab war against Israel escalated in violence and hardened ideologically, it left the Jews exposed not only to Arab hatred but also to the ire of liberals who wanted to believe in conflict resolution. Neoconservatism was the logical consequence of defending Israel and the Jews from Arab belligerence and from the hypocrisy of liberal reproach."[62] Wisse emblematizes neoconservatism's emergence from a productive articulation between, on the one hand, an identitarianism—which we can probably justifiably gloss with terms such as *essentialism* and *nationalism* and, especially for Wisse, even *patriotism*—that functions centripetally, according to the logic of a consolidated, coherent, and recognizable national Jewish subject, and, on the other hand, an ethical and epistemological Manicheanism that legibly divides the world into primarily Good and Evil but also, ancillary to and bound up with this, us and them, friend and foe, and so on. Authorized by this coordination and faced by liberalism's Cold War prevarications, Wisse equates Jewish identification with a Zionism in which unconditional loyalty to a militantly Jewish Israeli state stands as the normalized expression of Jewish identity and figure of the Jewish subject. Thus can Wisse conclude that "its Jewish mandate drove the neoconservatism of *Commentary*": the defense of a perilous polity—legitimated only as Zionism—provided the theoretical apparatus that would ultimately result in neoconservatism's fetishism of ethical clarity and its uncompromising and absolutist political logic.[63]

So if the New York intellectuals who remained mindful of the "Jewish fate" and the "Jewish polity" more often than not wrote for *Commentary* and, when push came to shove, became the neoconservatives, what of those who did not persist in such mindfulness and who did not primarily write for *Commentary*? Wisse makes great hay of a key phrase in the "Editorial Statement" that opened the inaugural issue of the revived, anti–Communist Party *Partisan Review* in December 1937. In the statement's challenge to totalitarianism in its cultural, political, and social polyvalence, the editors insist that ideological conformity of any variety is necessarily anathema to any project that hopes, through the medium of "democratic controversy," to commit itself to the analysis and evaluation of the "literature of our time." Though the new *Partisan Review* "aspires to a place in the vanguard of literature today" and conceives of itself as being "revolutionary in tendency," neither of these qualities demand that the journal align itself with the Communist Party; indeed, in stark contrast to the "Editorial Statement" that opened the inaugural issue of the first, Communist Party–affiliated, *Partisan Review* in 1934, which declared that a literary magazine devoted to the revolutionary cause must set "the defense of the Soviet Union" as "one of [its] principal tasks," in 1937, the editors declared that they stand "convinced that any such magazine will be unequivocally independent."[64]

It is this phrase "unequivocally independent" (which Wisse cites as "unequivocal independence") that she finds particularly worrisome. She concedes that the forces from which the *Partisan Review* editorial statement explicitly declares independence are certainly the "Communist party, to which the magazine had originally been attached, and also . . . Stalinist dogmas that exerted an authority beyond the political organization Stalin had set in place,"[65] but through the lens of her biologistic statism, she can maintain that this resistance to Stalin's "worldwide apparatus" was actually not so impressive: "note," she insists, that "it was not to any *political* reality (such as a state) that the group mounted its active opposition, but rather to an ideology that had limited their freedom of expression and creativity. In real terms, *their* polity, the state in which *they* lived, allowed them to put out any magazine they liked, and even placed no restriction on the development of modernism (except in the area of obscenity)."[66] Though she admits that "it undoubtedly required courage to make a public disavowal of Stalinism in the intellectual climate of the time," the editors' putative claim of "independence" is illegitimate to the extent that "the liberty the *Partisan Review* writers championed was a liberty they already enjoyed"; because they were "declaring their independence not only from a system to which they were not subject, but also and at the same time their disaffection from its political alternative, the system that granted them freedom,"[67] their position is in Wisse's statist eyes of limited merit. Another boorish iteration of the jingoistic love-it-or-leave-it chestnut, but intensified by her powerful biologism, Wisse's formulation restricts the legitimate operating theater of the adjective "political" to discussions of legitimized states. But the full nationalistic power of Wisse's term "polity," which adds a racialist valence to her fetishism of the state form, is revealed in her insistence that it was not just ultimately Stalinism from which the *Partisan Review* editors sought liberation.

"Although *Partisan Review*'s declaration of independence did not mention Jews, for those of the New York intellectuals who were themselves Jewish (and they were the majority by far) it justified the same kind of disengagement from the idea (and, later, the reality) of a Jewish polity." As she continues, "even less than opposition to Stalinism required (as it seemed to them) enlistment in the cause of democracy did opposition to anti-Semitism appear to require enlistment in the cause of the Jews. And as in the former case, so too in the latter, Marxism provided the most obvious grounds for keeping one's distance."[68] To the extent that *Partisan Review* eschews alignment with a state, its resistance to totalitarianism threatens the statist Zionism that for Wisse—perversely, as threatened by the prospect of stateless Jewry as any fin de siècle Viennese burgher ever was—offers the only legitimate resistance to anti-Semitism. For a strident dedicatee to the state form such as Wisse, opposing the ideologies, practices, and habits of mind in which totalitarianism manifests itself cannot be considered "engagement" in "the cause of democracy" if such engagement is not administered by an actually existing, nationalistically or biologistically limned, and self-evidently identifiable state entity; the alternative is simply too dangerous. Just as the New York intellectuals' enjoyment of American political and civil rights should compel them to resist Marxism in the name of Americanism, so too should their Jewish heritage compel them to embrace the cause, and then the reality, of the Jewish state. The Jewish New York intellectuals were wrong to adopt Marxism because it is an ideology that is not proper to her racially defined Jews.

For Wisse, the *Partisan Review* Jews were duped, essentially, by Marxism, which aimed to dissolve national and class boundaries and "expected the Jews to lead the process of national self-dissolution because they lacked a country of their own"; the "end product" of this process of national "divestiture," at least for the Jews, would be a "perfectly deracinated, perfectly cosmopolitan creature," a "non-Jewish Jew."[69] Wisse concludes that, for the *Partisan Review* Jews, at least, their leftism disempowered their Jewishness as an anchor for nationalist-statist identification: "Admissible then, as an item of ethnic identification, Jewishness was forbidden any further claims. Orthodox Marxism denied the existence of a separate Jewish question; but resistance to orthodox Marxism did not imply political or communal allegiances of another order." If these misguided intellectuals professed to defy Stalinism, they were in fact also necessarily declaring their independence from "all forms of commitment, even to democratic and fraternal obligations that had been conceived as guarantors of freedom." Using Marxism to guarantee their independence as intellectuals, therefore, resulted in their independence, too, from "political accountability," which is to say necessarily also to the "Jewish polity," which can have but one legitimate form.[70] "Independence" from rightist Zionism is for Jews at once a metonymy for the failure of political commitment in general and a specific genealogical affront to those "fraternal obligations" that in fact guarantee freedom. Instead, "so great was the distance these Jews felt between themselves and their community that they voiced no sense of special responsibility toward the fate of their fellow Jews in Hitler's Europe." Though a recognition that "the century's history . . . was being written on Jewish flesh" should lead logically to "an attachment to the Jewish fate," which is continuous with, and indeed should be identical to, Zionism, Wisse sees the *Partisan Review* writers hamstrung by the simple fact that Zionism, like "other forms of Jewish political mobilization," was necessarily opposed by the "American Left": the New York writers on the left "expressed their sorrow at the massacre going on, and nothing more."[71]

Wisse claims that it "might seem peculiar" that so many of the New York writers were "disengage[d]" from the "Jewish polity" not only because most of them "had been the targets of active discrimination, limiting their access to the best American universities and their prospects of employment," but also because, "as Jews, too, they inherited the history of persecution that had brought their parents to America."[72] If the "dramatic rise of anti-Semitism between the world wars should have sharpened their sense of injury and danger," Wisse is puzzled that they dedicated themselves to a stateless Marxist critique of totalitarianism rather than to the identitarian statism that should have been "inherited" along with their parents' "history" and that for her provides the only legitimate means of defending—and is the only proper expression of—a nationalistically defined group. Wisse reveals herself a Wilsonian to the extent that she argues that the New York intellectuals' Jewish heritage should compel them to dedicate themselves to the "idea and, later, the reality of a Jewish polity" (34) because a racially pure state is the proper nationalist birthright of every—biologistically defined—group; she reveals herself something much more horrifying than a Wilsonian to the extent that she implies that refusing to dedicate oneself to a racially pure state amounts to genocidal self-hatred.

In Wisse's polemical logic, the Marxism of the New York intellectuals—at least the Marxism of those who did not renounce it in ultimately becoming neoconservatives, whom her 1987 article concludes by praising as the true heroes of American intellectual history—is inseparable from their abandonment of "the cause of the Jews," which is to say a biologistic Zionism. Thus, "one of the greatest moral and intellectual failures of the New York intellectuals was their disregard of the Jewish fate, both before and during World War II and in the decades that followed."[73] This is the dangerous inheritance of Wisse's powerful term "Jewish polity," her persistent linking of genealogical and political metaphors in the discussion of Jewish identity. She sets up a disturbing chain of associations that associates the Jewish fate with the Jewish state, specifically by linking concern for the former with militant identification with the latter, primarily by implicit reduction of any attention to the problem of Jewish identity, identification, or community to a Manichean identitarianism, resulting in the conclusion that the intellectual who defies Zionist orthodoxies—including, most notably, its racialist protocols, which in Wisse's example suggests that nationalist politics go hand in hand with the "Jewish heritage" that Jews, on the logic of the *CJR* editors of "Under Forty," presumably inherit from their parents—becomes treasonous or, what amounts to the same thing, a race traitor.

Wisse refers to the "Under Forty" symposium mostly in order to heap juxtapositional scorn on it by way of comparing it with the kind of work that would distinguish *CJR*'s successor journal. In the *Commentary* essay, Wisse writes of the new journal that "no less consequential than" its "confidence in the integral American Jew" was its "new expectation of the Jewish intellectual."[74] "At the very least," she avers, "the association of a Jew with *Commentary* implied some relation to the American Jewish polity. Over the course of time, *Commentary* went much further than this: In trying to be honest and truthful, it found itself confronting the actual situation of the Jews, which brought about a shift of direction. . . .

This shift of political and cultural direction, which included a new definition of the intellectual calling, occurred in conditions of maximal freedom, without any direct Jewish institutional pressure, and without the kind of anti-Semitic coercion that had affected Jewish intellectuals in other times and places."[75] In the mysterious, polemical phrase "the actual situation of the Jews" reappears a ghost of Wisse's powerful and axiomatic term "Jewish polity," laboring to derogate criticism, and the intellectuals who engage in it, of the kinds of Jewish cultural and political institutions of which Wisse approves as necessarily anti-Semitic, precisely like that which informed the "coercion that had affected Jewish intellectuals in other times and places"—the referents of which "other times and places," given the historical moment we are talking about here (i.e., 1944–1948) and all the time Wisse devotes in her essay to "leftism"/"Stalinism," "Nazism," and "the question of Palestine,"[76] we can assume Wisse expects to be perfectly perspicuous.

To make the point about "*Commentary*'s new expectation of the Jewish intellectual," Wisse cites the example of "Under Forty," which she takes to be representative of the self-serving and self-hating dead end into which Jewish intellectuals had been leading the "Jewish polity" before Elliot Cohen launched *Commentary*: "A year before its founding, when *Commentary*'s forerunner, the *Contemporary Jewish Record*, featured a symposium of leading members of the young Jewish intelligentsia, most of these intellectuals recorded their alienation from the Jewish community and their contempt for its middle-class parochialism. With their own sights set on entry into the universities and into American high culture, they dismissed as 'dreary middle-class chauvinists' those who championed a Jewish state in Palestine. Rather than credit their Jewish heritage for their collective intellectual energy, they claimed it had deteriorated into 'less than nothingness.'"[77] The two quotations she cites likely come from Norman Podhoretz's introduction to a later symposium, titled "Jewishness and the Younger Intellectuals," which appeared in *Commentary* in 1961, the year after Podhoretz took over from Cohen.[78] Podhoretz caricatures the essays in the 1944 *CJR* symposium as all more or less arguing that though "we know that integration into the surrounding culture is not the answer to anti-Semitism," the nineteenth century's answer, "national sovereignty," is now repellant "thanks partly to the Nazis" and that "the Zionists we have met are generally 'dreary middle-class chauvinists'—the phrase is Alfred Kazin's—and we have no wish to associate ourselves with them or what they stand for."[79] The symposium participants, at least in Podhoretz's rendering, worry that "whatever it may have been in the past, today in America" the "Jewish heritage" "has deteriorated into nothingness, or worse than nothingness. It has been integrated into a culture which is itself inferior and vicious, and it has taken on all the worst qualities of that culture while retaining nothing valuable of its own."[80]

Thus, of the two phrases Wisse quotes, one indeed can be found in the symposium—in Kazin's contribution—but the other is an inaccurate citation of Podhoretz's own characterization (itself of dubious accuracy) of what "Under Forty" undertook—one that functions to further misrepresent the 1944 symposium in the interest of Wisse's own right-wing Zionism. Kazin, a key prooftext of Wisse's umbrage, displayed in his "Under Forty" essay, like many of his fellow symposiasts, what is now a fairly recognizable modernist anxiety about faltering cultural transmission—in his case, of Jewish heritage from parent to child: though Kazin's parents, for whom the Jewish "code had a plain integrity," felt more or less untroubled in a Jewish identity that seemed to them largely self-evident, Kazin's own generation "had no such luck" and "never learned what the [religious] texts meant: only to repeat them," having "learned long ago to accept the fact" of Jewish identity "without being a part of any meaningful Jewish life or culture" (11). Such a sentiment is repeated in Kronenberger's admission, for example, that Judaism has been "rather a fact than a force" in his life, and it finds expression elsewhere, too, in reiterated anxieties about the diminished persuasiveness of Jewish institutional authority. But Kazin's worry about failed identitarian compulsion, that American Jews now identify with each other on the basis only of "sterile" and "selfish" "sentimental chauvinism," becomes in Podhoretz's scornful reading a simple racially self-negating failure to embrace Zionism. As the newly installed editor of *Commentary* saw it, most of the writers participating in the "Under Forty" symposium "were assimilationists," and "their assimilationism was grounded in the belief that the 'Jewish problem'—as it used to be called—was on its way to being solved in the modern world." But just as the "Dreyfus Case had persuaded Theodor Herzl that assimilationism would never work," so "the Nazis ought to have taught American

Jews the same lesson."[81] Podhoretz powerfully articulates three terms—assimilation, Herzl, and Nazis—so as to establish an equally powerful, and implicitly absolute, opposition between the twinned concepts of Zionism and Jewish identification and the twinned threats of anti-Semitism and genocide. A further turn of the rightist screw is effected when Podhoretz attributes the "assimilationist" disregard of the symposium participants for Jewish tradition and practices to the leftist vogue then enjoyed by the concept of "alienation," insofar as what they are alienated by and from, even as it triggers their critique, is, in the words of Kazin that so provoke Podhoretz and Wisse, the "dreary middle-class chauvinis[m]" and the bourgeois desire above all "to be safe, in all the Babbitt warrens," that exemplify twentieth-century American Jewry.[82] Thus, though he admits that "not all the contributors were socialists" and insists that "it has not in our time been necessary to embrace socialism in order to repudiate the life and culture of the middle class throughout the Western world," by arguing that "it was the middle-classness of the Jewish community which more than anything else accounted for the harsh words the young writers of 1944 had for their fellow Jews in America," Podhoretz links a leftist critique of bourgeois insularity and stultification, a critical vocabulary of alienation, and what he calls—with the help of the same biologistic framework that will inform Wisse's keyword "the Jewish polity"—"assimilationism" with an anti-Semitism whose inevitable outcome is genocide.[83] Indeed, twenty-six years later, Wisse, in her 1987 review essay, peddles this same constellation, hearing "the echo of Karl Marx himself" in so many of the "Under Forty" essays' "identification of the Jew with the smug bourgeois," through which they irresponsibly declined "an attachment to the Jewish fate"[84]—an echo, apparently, that accounts for Jewish self-hatred.[85]

If Wisse all but accuses the "Under Forty" intellectuals of complicity in the Holocaust, Podhoretz generously notes that many of these same writers, in the years to follow—and as the critical fortunes of the concept of "alienation" ebbed—ended up revising their "unfair and one-sided" views in favor of a more sanguine embrace of the "Jewish heritage" they found themselves unable to accept in 1944; indeed, as Podhoretz points out, "One has only to skim through the back files of *Commentary* to see how far many of the contributors to the *CJR* symposium (and others like them) went in revising their estimate of the 'Jewish heritage,'" and he gestures to those Jewish writers—Saul Bellow, Bernard Malamud, and Martin Buber are three he mentions—who appeared on the scene after Kazin's immature 1944 claim that Jewish American literature's failure so far to produce the equivalent of a James T. Farrell or a Theodore Dreiser has convinced him that he cannot yet "believe in the empirical fact of our participation"—here in this pronoun we again note the compulsory force subtending the neoconservative erotics of Jewish identification— in what the *CJR* editors called the "cultural life of the country."[86] For Podhoretz, the "severe and merciless indictments" that characterize so many of the "Under Forty" essays can be attributed to juvenility, a kind of childish irresponsibility that can be—and often was—grown out of. On the one hand, the more friendly relation to Jewishness and Judaism "expressed by the literary intelligentsia of the 50's developed merely as a consequence of the passage of years: what a man flees in youth he often learns to love in middle age"; but on the other hand, Podhoretz identifies a "new and more positive relation to America" that, recognizing at once "the menace of Soviet totalitarianism" and the changing "character of the American middle class," was itself a manifestation of a maturing intelligence.[87] Wisse cribs this judgment, as well, calling the inability to take "intellectual responsibility for the Jewish people and the Jewish polity" an "adolescent" posture[88] and labeling *Partisan Review*'s declaration of its "unequivocal independence" "an ideal of unencumbered boyhood,"[89] stunting mature embrace of "national sovereignty" as the only legitimate manifestation of Jewish inheritance away from which a misguided leftist response to fascism steered the 1944 writers. Echoing Podhoretz, Wisse insists, "And though most of the Marxists among them had lost their ideological fervor, they retained Marxism's hostility or indifference to the national aspirations of the Jewish people. As youths, they had traded in their Judaism for leftism. When they later cast off Marxist authority, they prided themselves on standing free of both alike."[90]

Whether the "Under Forty" symposium's non-Zionist leftism is dismissed as the dangerous product of albeit-reversible youthful irresponsibility or assailed as continuous with the cultural apparatus enabling some of history's worst genocidal excesses, its legitimacy is suppressed through a conspicuous deployment of an interpretive paradigm that conceptualizes identity primarily as a police function administering the re-presentation of a historical subject. My point here is not to claim that it is unfair to approach neoconservatism as part of the inheritance of the New York critics; it unquestionably is, at the very least insofar as neoconservatism's intellectual parents and many of its major ideologues were key figures in the New York intellectual milieu. On the contrary, my point is that the biologism articulating the concept of Jewish identity that ideologues such as Wisse (with the help of Podhoretz) use to delegitimize Jewish thinkers who threaten the conceptual or ideological foundations of her Zionism—in "Under Forty" and beyond—on her way to celebrating neoconservatism is inseparable from an undertheorized concept of representation for their mutual nationalist coordination of identity and politics.

Conclusion: The Zionist's Red Shoes

My goal in looking so closely at how "Under Forty" and the (Jewish) New York intellectuals *have been* characterized is obviously not first and foremost to argue for a particular way in which they *should be* characterized. Instead, it has been to expose the biologistic-identitarian trap into which identity-based scholarly work can fall. Humanities scholarship organized around the historiography of a legible subject—how this subject speaks, what traces this subject leaves, the vocabularies in which this subject is marked—necessarily grounds itself in a nationalist history that bears a potent and durable political affiliation that is anything but neutral and that moreover can end up relying on biologistic-racialist logic. My goal has also been to show, through a revisionary reading of a key text in the representation of Jewish intellectuals, how this critique opens up space for a nonnationalist literary and cultural history. Far from serving the reactionary critic's surveillance of the representation of Jewish identity, "Under Forty" can be seen as part of a counterarchive of Jewishness. Wisse and Podhoretz's biologistic identity-as-police paradigm is the monstrous offspring of a generative concept of Jewish heritage coupled with a statist understanding of literature as primarily representational. But this paradigm derives its legitimacy from the willful suppression of the critique of representation and the Jewish subject discoverable in "Under Forty," a critique that points toward a reconceptualization of Jewish American writing as a critical commentary on identity.

Nine years after "Under Forty," in the hilariously devastating essay "The Duchess' Red Shoes" (1953), Delmore Schwartz staged a second meeting with Trilling, this time in *Partisan Review*. Responding to a piece by John Aldridge on manners and the novel in *Partisan Review* the previous year that had admiringly cited Trilling's famous 1947 essay, reprinted in *The Liberal Imagination* (1950), "Manners, Morals, and the Novel," Schwartz skewered Trilling at once for instrumentalizing literary criticism in the interest of social criticism and for using a supposed critique of snobbery and manners in the social novel as cover for a more or less self-interested defense of the educated class.[91] Trilling's argument for moral realism, we recall, is really an argument against moral idealism, to which he finds liberalism too often degrades itself and which is all too often a proxy for the social idealism underlying the twentieth century's worst totalitarian excesses. Literature may not be able to confront fascism or Stalinism directly, but moral and social idealism, at their less genocidal levels, often take the form of class parochialism or "snobbery," and Trilling saw the novel as a fantastically perceptive analytical lens through which to "record the illusion that snobbery generates and to try to penetrate to the truth which, as the novel assumes, lies hidden behind all false appearances. . . . The novel, then, is a perpetual quest for reality, the field of its research being always the social world, the material of its analysis being always manners as an indication of man's soul."[92]

So far so good; the Trilling of 1947 seems to agree with the Trilling of 1944's argument for the importance of the universal as the critique of particularism. But Schwartz's Trilling promotes universality because literary criticism is the proxy or medium for his social criticism. He claims difficulty in defining manners—saying initially that manners are impossible to define, that they are neither "rules of personal intercourse" nor "mores, customs"—but Trilling soon after famously describes them as "a culture's hum and buzz of implication, . . . the things that for good or bad draw the people of a culture together."[93] Defined thus broadly, manners appear as a kind of social glue, the principle of coherence that traverses mere class and therefore defines the identity of a culture or society. That is, manners seem to be what allow one to say that a particular piece of literature refers or is relevant to or concerns a culture or society or group: manners are part of the identity machine that allows the critic to confidently believe that literature is categorically representative, that it is, in the final instance, *about*. And it is this operation that underlies the critic's moral realism: providing access to real manners—the hum and buzz—rather than to mere class-differentiated habits—for example, the hateful politesse that compels Proust's Duke and Duchess de Guermantes to count such proprieties as proper footwear and being on time to dinner more pressing than is their friend Swann, who has just informed them of his terminal condition—the novel allows the reader to critically pierce the restricted moral universe of an idealist, if only a snobbish classed, perspective.

Schwartz's problem with all this is not the overt critique of snobbery, obviously, but what he sees as a covert, instrumental attraction to high society: as he interprets Trilling (who, it should be recalled in this context, always challenged the value and vogue of proletarian fiction), "unless one is concerned with class and snobbery one is not really concerned with 'society.' One has turned one's mind away from 'society' unless one is at least in part concerned with 'high society' where, it is commonly believed, most snobbery begins or resides. And thus, since class, snobbery, and high society must be involved, the manners in question may after all be the good manners of so-called 'polite society.'"[94] In essence, Schwartz understands Trilling to be making a fetish out of bourgeois society: Trilling's interest in manners as the hum and buzz thus masks an interest in good manners, not the manners that hold a society together but the manners that admit one to high society.[95] Now, to be fair—and Schwartz himself certainly concedes this point—this criticism is less appropriate to Trilling's argument against idealism than it is to Aldridge's piece (which really does verge on the idiotic in its reduction of manners to good manners), but Schwartz is mostly right in pointing out Trilling's authorizing role here, that "nothing that Mr. Trilling had to say prevented Mr. Aldridge from arriving at his views."[96] As Schwartz sees it, Trilling privileges novelists who write about manners and snobbery because they are the ones who allow him to make his point,[97] which is ultimately an assertion not about literature but about the educated liberal intellectual, whose profession is literature, and about the dangers to which he is prone, as a lens on which it is litera-ture's primary value to serve: "Mr. Trilling is interested in the ideas and attitudes and interests of the educated class, such as it is and such as it may become: it is of this class that he is, at heart, the guardian and the critic."[98] As Norman Finkelstein points out, a "late version of the 'ordeal of civility' "[99]—that is, the bad conscience born at the overdetermined site of assimilation—is the epiphenomenal form taken by Trilling's attempt to yoke a docile historicist degradation of "literature" in ser-vice to his true interest, social criticism of the educated, "liberal," class. What is really at work here is a dominant, field-centering presumption that literature is representationally bound to historical subjects, to the agents, actors, and populations of whom historicist criticism imagines itself to be the historiography; Schwartz lets us see that an interpretive schema emerging from such a paradigm is always politically interested in the subject it takes for granted as represented.

One might say, following Finkelstein, that Trilling as Schwartz reads him wants the universal but is ashamed of the particular he actually invests with significance: it is not so much Jewishness that Trilling can-not escape, it is an acknowledgment of his desire that his criticism, in being "about" his world, is relevant to his times. This historicist desire for "aboutness" is precisely the ghost that haunts not only the historical reception of the 1944 "Under Forty" symposium but also more gener-ally Jewish American literary critical practice. The problem illustrated in this feud is germane to Jewish literary study not because the educated liberal intellectuals who so dominated Trilling's critical consciousness were overwhelmingly identifiable as "Jewish" intellectuals (however effectively one may be able to justify such a claim). The key claim to be made about the *CJR* "Under Forty" symposium, a document that remains a touchstone of discussions of the Jewishness of the New York intellectuals, is that it disruptively contests the possibility and legibil-ity of the Jewish heritage, suspending it between a positivist sense, as a generative force, a way of accounting for, measuring, and/or narrating continuity between past, present, and future, elaborating a species of reproduction of a categorical archive that enables a potential recogni-tion, and a negative critical sense, as a kind of ghost, whose real impor-tance is not positively where it makes its appearance but in the form of a revisionary archival desire for generativity. Schwartz and Trilling back in 1944, like their fellow symposium participants, critically displace Jew-ishness from the site of positive inheritance, but their continuing feud offers critics interested in the possibility of a usefully Jewish American literary practice so much more. Schwartz, in his needling of Trilling, makes it possible to pursue a criticism of the specter haunting the lit-erary historical desire for literature to be "about" the subjects we rec-ognize in it. Literature cannot be "Jewish" in itself or in the stuff of its representations but only elsewhere than where we recognize it to be so.

4

Why Jews Aren't Normal

The Unrepresentable Future of Philip Roth's The Counterlife

In the fifth and final chapter of *The Counterlife*, titled "Christendom," Philip Roth's narrator, the writer Nathan Zuckerman, attends a Christmas choral service in London with his pregnant, British, gentile wife, Maria, and her daughter (by her previous husband), mother, and two sisters. He has just that day returned from Israel, one of the novel's many sites of identity production and disputation, where he went to visit and, he had possibly hoped, rescue his brother, Henry, who has rather suddenly abjured his profane secular family life in New Jersey in favor of making *aliyah* under the psychically protective and ideologically coherent wing of the Kahane-ist settler Mordecai Lippman. Having hoped to convince Henry—who now answers to the Hebraicized name Hanoch—that his Zionist about-face is artificial in its reactionary fundamentalism, Zuckerman found himself instead attacked by Henry, Lippman, and the others at Agor, the West Bank settlement overlooking Hebron that Henry-Hanoch now calls home, as himself inauthentically Jewish and for hastening a second, quiet, American Holocaust of apostasy and miscegenation. A concern for "authenticity" more than the concept of authenticity itself circulates close to the heart of the book's contestation of Jewish identity, as the book alternately embraces and resists the concept in its displacement of Jewish normativity.[1]

It is not insignificant that it is Nathan Zuckerman who leads us into this tangle and critique. Readers know Zuckerman as a vital and recurrent character in Roth's oeuvre. *The Counterlife* (1986) had been immediately preceded by *The Ghost Writer* (1979), *Zuckerman Unbound* (1981), and *The Anatomy Lesson* (1983), which collectively told the story of Nathan's rise to literary prominence and celebrity and were republished together, along with the epilogue in the form of a novella *The Prague Orgy*, as *Zuckerman Bound* (1985). Nathan reappeared a dozen years later as the narrator of a second trilogy—*American Pastoral* (1997), *I Married a Communist* (1998), and *The Human Stain* (2000)—and then again for a reportedly final book, another handful of years later, *Exit Ghost* (2007). The initial Zuckerman trilogy stands as a magisterial comment on Roth's first twenty years as a public Jew, and the second offers a kind of guided tour of the second half of the Jewish American twentieth century. But scholarly commonplaces about Zuckerman being Roth's novelistic alter ego or his representational avatar—stoked, perhaps, by the playful (a true Roth scholar would say "mischievous") back-and-forth between Roth and Zuckerman in the "novelist's autobiography" *The Facts* (1988)—suppress critical reflection on Zuckerman's function, and on Roth's oeuvre more generally, in favor of positivist celebration of biographical and historicist legibility.[2] It is true that Zuckerman shares a lot with Roth. He writes a story about a family dispute over money, "Higher Education," which many of Roth's readers analogize to "Goodbye, Columbus," that gets a lot of respectable establishment Jews worried about stoking anti-Semitic fires, memorably represented by *The Ghost Writer*'s Judge Leopold Wapter, who asks Nathan a series of pointed questions aimed at "awakening [his] conscience," including, "If you had been living in Nazi Germany in the thirties, would you have written such a story?"; "What in your character makes you associate so much of life's ugliness with Jewish people?"; and "Can you honestly say that there is anything in your short story that would not warm the hearts of a Julius Streicher or a Joseph Goebbels?"[3] Then he is presented in *Zuckerman Unbound* having just published the sensational best-seller *Carnovsky*, which essentially all of Roth's readers analogize to *Portnoy's Complaint*, that pisses off the rest of the establishment Jews who had not already abandoned him, including, possibly, his own father, whose dying word, according to Nathan's brother, is "bastard" and is directed at Nathan,[4] and, magnificently, *The Anatomy Lesson*'s Milton Appel, the literary critic who initially defended "Higher Education" but then turned on Zuckerman after determining that *Carnovsky* went way too far, a character who, we are repeatedly told in the criticism, is analogous to Irving Howe, who, famously, initially defended Roth against the respectable establishment Jews who worried that "Goodbye, Columbus" would stoke anti-Semitic fires but then came around to accuse *Portnoy's*

Complaint in the pages of *Commentary* of replacing the powerful realism of "Goodbye, Columbus" with the easy and vile stereotype.[5]

The point, however, should not be to interpretively index Roth's literary output to the supposed manifest incontrovertibility of his life and career; this is a narrow vision of literary scholarship that assumes the transparency of language and the self-evidence of representation and that essentially reduces the work of literary criticism to an algorithm.[6] Moreover, it is a paradigm that Roth unequivocally challenges, often blisteringly so—at least since *My Life as a Man* (1974) and quite explicitly since the emergence of Zuckerman in his current form in *The Ghost Writer*.[7] If Nathan's chiropodist father cautions the young writer in *The Ghost Writer* that "people don't read art—they read about *people*," it is important to realize that *The Ghost Writer* (like everything Roth has written since) does not embrace this statement as a normative claim; rather, it is precisely Doctor Zuckerman's will to normalization—such as is embodied in his respectable worry about "what Gentiles think when they read something like this" and in Judge Wapter's respectable self-righteous indignation—that the Zuckerman books labor to displace.[8] Few contemporary writers have been as deliberate and explicit as Roth has been that reading is wrong to begin from the normative assumption that literature should be understood as part of the documentary record of an already-sociologically-legible group or part of the biographical record of an already-historically-identifiable individual and that therefore literature's value is primarily referential or representational. This dominant institutional formation, which has the effect of reducing literary study as a subdiscipline of history, usually takes the form of some variant of the question "what does this book tell us about the already-identified subject we recognize in it?" However much such a query may aid certain kinds of historical inquiry, it does not strike me as a literary critical question—certainly not a very interesting literary critical question. Instead of assuming Doctor Zuckerman's and Judge Wapter's Jew—and instead, more gravely, of underwriting an identitarian literary history continuous with and subtended by that Jew's nationalistic anxieties—Roth's oeuvre is more intelligently read as focusing on how literature produces identity as a critical category. The Zuckerman books become something other—and more—than biography, historiography, or ethnography in the hands of a Jewish literary criticism that actively detaches itself from the thought of its proper relation to an individual who can be biographically identified or an ethnic group that can be sociologically identified. *The Counterlife* helps articulate a critical Jewish American literary study that sublimely contests the terms in which we inevitably take for granted the self-evident categorical legibility of identity.

An important current of recent work in Jewish American literary studies—and indeed specifically in Roth studies—links the development of Jewish American literature in particular and ethnic literature in general to questions about the role of Jews in the elaboration of cultural pluralism as a sociopolitical program starting in the early twentieth century and, later, in debates about multiculturalism. The best work in this vein, such as Dean Franco's recent *Race, Rights, and Recognition*, subtly and critically troubles the priority of literary-studies-based and sociology- or political-science-based concepts of identity.[9] But more often this sort of scholarship, by emphasizing questions of political constituency and/or policy, works implicitly to naturalize an assumption that any literary-studies-based discussion of identity is necessarily oriented around or grounded in an empirical, sociologically or anthropologically limned, referential subject—precisely in such a way that reduces humanities-based discussion of ethnic literature by justifying it as an instrument of a sociological or ethnographic inquiry whose value is assumedly self-evident. Indeed, it is often quite difficult to imagine a concept of identity outside such empirical or positivistic coordinates. That said, an important archive of work supporting a more critical concept of identity can be articulated, and Roth's mischievous Zuckerman books, including *The Counterlife*, help chart how such a concept can contribute to a more theoretically justified—and a more literary critically interesting—Jewish literary study.

Chantal Mouffe has written that while reference to political community is crucial in questions about identity, such community "should be conceived as a discursive surface and not as an empirical referent." We commit a reactionary error when we assume that "politics" takes place primarily inside an already-existing and recognizable political community and between already-identified and coherent agents; rather, "politics is about the constitution of the political community," and this needs to be understood not in sociological or empirical terms but as "a surface of inscription of a multiplicity of demands where a 'we' is constituted." The vital political element in identification is not specious reference to historical self-evidence, therefore, but rather the establishment of an equivalence—which does not mean the elimination or reduction of difference—in which identity claims turn away from the security of self-evidence in relating to each other in conflict and diversity.[10] Jacques Rancière, participating in the same 1991 symposium in which Mouffe made her contribution, elaborates this notion of equality or equivalence as a challenge to an identitarianism that takes for granted the recognizability and coherence of sociologically or historically legible groups. Rancière is interested in the challenge to historically stable self-recognition that occurs in processes of relation. Like Mouffe, he discourages critics from thinking about identity in terms of sociological reference or the values or characteristics proper to an identifiable group. The equality in which a subject achieves identification is not a coherent universal value to which an identified self appeals and therefore a procedure of identity; universality is not in concepts such as Man or Citizen or Human Being that might authorize such identitarian claims but is rather in the "discursive and practical enactment" of such concepts, in the "mediation" or "relation of a self to an other" in "what follows" from appeals to such concepts. Rancière directs us to look at the processes in which subjects make claims for recognition as ones of "disidentification or de-classification"; it is always "in-between" referential identities and categories and classifications that the universality that underwrites equality is enacted. The "desperate debate between universality and identity," the false positivist distinction between the universal and the particular, therefore traps us into thinking about identity only in terms of sociological reference, of groups that can be historiographically identified. Rancière's interest in the demonstration of equality displaces precisely this identitarian logic of identification, allowing us to attend to the political processes—here Rancière and Mouffe are very close—whereby the place of the universal is constructed locally in identity claims that already disrupt their own coherent self-relation.[11] The point is not to suppress or ignore particularity but rather to realize that no assertion or recognition of particularity is self-sufficient and that we cannot take for granted the normalized coherence of the particular. As

Judith Butler points out in this same symposium, identification is necessarily doubled by a contestation of the normative recognizability of
identity terms inevitably underwritten and made available by exclusionary and positivistic procedures.[12]

Since the advent of Zuckerman, Roth's oeuvre displaces a positivist
concept of identity underwritten by the supposed self-evidence of sociological reference with a critical concept of identity as a form of desire.
I have argued elsewhere that a primary drama in Roth's fiction—at least
in the context of Jewish literary study's concern with Jewish identity—is
the failure of readily available terms and paradigms to express Jewish
identification: Roth's central characters do not know how to describe
themselves as Jews.[13] Thus, as much as Roth's books can be seen as texts
of Jewish identity or identification, they are just as forcefully countertexts of Jewish identity or identification—countertexts that displace categorical Jewishness from the presumably secure site where we expect to
recognize it. To read the initial Zuckerman trilogy from the perspective
of a Jewish American literary criticism underscores the crisis Zuckerman confronts throughout: that the securely Jewish context from which
he imagines himself to have emerged and that guaranteed the Jewish
identity he could take for granted—the Jewish place, community, people, practices, and linguistic patterns of his childhood—is not represented or indexed in his literary output and career in any way that he
can take for granted. If he undoubtedly feels more or less sure that he
is a Jew, his travails with institutional forms of Jewishness—embodied
most memorably in his family, in Judge Wapter, in Alvin Pepler, and in
Milton Appel—show that he cannot prove it unequivocally, least of all
to himself. *Operation Shylock*, doubling down on the vexed relationship
between Zuckerman and Roth, elaborates how identity can be conceptualized as an overdetermined desire. The book relentlessly explores the
conflict between identity as interior compulsion and identity as exterior
categorization, between identity as something you do or are or feel and
identity as something that happens to you or that others see in you; in
it, Roth's embodied reputation challenges him to an existential duel in
which Roth often finds himself outwitted precisely in his attempt to,
or his expectation that he should be able to, master his identity. Identity is hardly ever under the Jew's control here. "Being mistaken for" in
Roth's 1993 "confession" makes performative *acting as* irresistible, and

"writing" emerges as the paradigm in which this overdetermined Jewish desire, which can never be anything so simple as a choice and can never be evaded, is alternatively queried and practiced, as Roth suggests in describing (and performing) his identity-as-problem:

> The topic I could not really remember having chosen to shadow me like this, from birth to death; the topic whose obsessive examination I had always thought I could someday leave behind; the topic whose persistent intrusion into matters high and low it was not always easy to know what to make of; the pervasive, engulfing, wearying topic that encapsulated the largest problem and most amazing experience of my life and that, despite every honorable attempt to resist its spell, appeared by now to be the irrational power that had run away with my life—and from the sound of things, not mine alone . . . that topic called *the Jews*.[14]

"Writing" is the countertextual space where this "topic" is interminably, unstably, and obsessively reinscribed by desire.

Writing is also, of course, the grand theme of the second set of Zuckerman books. In these later novels, Zuckerman is repeatedly positioned as a kind of displaced but very interested witness to the twentieth-century confrontation of American and Jewish rather than the secure historian or autobiographer of it we might expect. He hears about and invents histories, even of people he knew and events he experienced, rather than unequivocally or confidently recording or transmitting them, and he finds himself always reimagining—rewriting—the American experience of the Jewish problem, an experience lacking a historically self-evident ur-text. Indeed, the first Zuckerman trilogy's brilliant critique of how an author is overdetermined by the imperial trope of identity is only amplified by the second trilogy's intensive investigation of narration, most magisterially enacted in *American Pastoral*, in which the attentive reader cannot ignore the fact that Nathan Zuckerman largely imagines everything we read. And yet the jealous, anxious destruction of the category of literature championed by Doctor Zuckerman and Judge Wapter continues to be pursued by a dominant strain of scholarship that persists in imposing a kind of positivist or documentary straightjacket on consideration of Roth's work, especially in the context of this second trilogy, reductively conceptualizing it as a representation of or reflection on especially Jewish experience in twentieth-century America—during the Weathermen sixties in *American Pastoral*, the McCarthyite fifties in *I Married a Communist*, and the Clinton-Lewinsky nineties in *The Human Stain*—emblematized in the label that this series of books has earned in such disparate contexts as the Philip Roth Society and the Library of America: "The American Trilogy."

The Counterlife stands as an ideal occasion for criticism, in its urgency that scholarship needs to—and can—reemphasize the force with which Roth's work, especially in the Zuckerman books, redirects the critique of identity away from a reductive orientation around representation and historical reference and toward the powers of normalization. Before finally returning to the novel, however, I would like to jump forward to the next Zuckerman book to make a final point about how Roth contests dominant patterns of Jewish studies and Jewish American literary study. Putatively about Seymour "the Swede" Levov's headlong crash into the fantasy of American normalization, *American Pastoral* is more subtly, and importantly, concerned with the possibilities and mechanisms by which such representationality is effected and imagined. The book begins with Nathan recalling how important the Swede was to the Weequahic Jewish community—precisely as a figure who, as the embodiment of their identification fantasies, was not necessarily bound by the protocols and legibility of their shared Jewish identification; as Nathan admits on the novel's first page, ostensibly regarding the Swede's athletic prowess, "through the Swede, the neighborhood entered into a fantasy about itself and the world, the fantasy of sports fans everywhere: almost like Gentiles (as they imagined Gentiles), our families could forget the way things actually work and make an athletic performance the repository of all their hopes."[15] The book that follows primarily records Nathan's attempt to imagine the Swede. The problem, of course, as the novel insists, is that the interiority of a figure—and I appeal to this term "figure" in at least two senses, as the individual but at the same time as the trope managing the interpretation or understanding of that individual—whose exterior enacts nothing so intensively as an imperial overdetermination is inevitably irretrievable in any kind of historically referential certitude. What we get in *American Pastoral*'s portrait of Swede Levov is a picture administered and legitimized not by historical accuracy—such a possibility's unavailability is the ultimate and important focus of Roth's "American Trilogy"—but by Nathan's Jewish desire. If the youthful Swede was revered by Newark's Jews because he represented better than any of the rest of them could their shared Jewish determination to be normally American, then this prized normativity is always foreclosed on. The Jewish American's inability to ever just be American, this interminable contestation of Jewish categoricality, is doubled in Nathan's imagination of Swede's stumbling before American normativity. Nathan describes it:

> The Jewishness that he wore so lightly as one of the tall, blond athletic winners must have spoken to us too—in our idolizing the Swede and his unconscious oneness with America, I suppose there was a tinge of shame and self-rejection. Conflicting Jewish desires awakened by the sight of him were simultaneously becalmed by him; the contradiction in Jews who want to fit in and want to stand out, who insist they are different and insist they are no different, resolved itself in the triumphant spectacle of this Swede who was actually only another of our neighborhood Seymours whose forebears had been Solomons and Sauls and who would themselves beget Stephens who would in turn beget Shawns. Where was the Jew in him? You couldn't find it and yet you knew it was there. Where was the irrationality in him? Where was the crybaby in him? Where were the wayward temptations? No guile. No artifice. No mischief. All that he had eliminated to achieve his perfection. No striving, no ambivalence, no doubleness—just the style the natural physical refinement of a star.[16]

Even in its apparent absence, categorical Jewish inscription continues to dominate the perception of Swede Levov. Illegible, indeterminate, the Swede's Jewishness remains his most important characteristic.[17] If Jewish American literary study categorically asks of its field a version of Nathan's question—"Where was the Jew in him?"—then Roth's work suggests that the desire authorizing this question displaces the very categorical historical referent it seeks.

One reason the Zuckerman books are so vitally important for Jewish American literary study is that they insist on a model of identification that cannot be reduced to the representational historicism authorizing the humanities' obsession with sociological reference in matters of identity. By critically figuring the literary historical procedures by which identifiable Jewish American writers and texts are understood as histo-riographic tools to resolve a set of experiences of an already-recognized Jewish American subject, they help Jewish American literary study work toward a nonidentitarian concept of identity that comprehends how the desire for historiographic reference overdetermines any poten-tial referential self-evidence. Zuckerman compels the reader of Jewish American literature to expand the ways in which Jewish studies in gen-eral can and should be conceptualized—not so much as a methodology for decoding the representation of a Jewish subject but as a critical anal-ysis of Jewish representation. Part of the process of clearing a path for such a paradigm of Jewish studies would therefore involve interrogating the ways in which—as *American Pastoral* is assertively aware—identity and normalization have come to operate in a dominant reactionary model of literary study as two sides of the same coin. Even as Jewish studies has come to embrace a set of truisms about the historical diver-sity of Jewish experience, it has continued to operate within the norma-tive regime of a more fundamental reactionary interpretive historicism that assumes the legibility of the Jewish subject, despite gestures to an epiphenomenal diversity. What makes *The Counterlife* so vital to the effort to replace this restrictive identitarian paradigm with a critical Jewish studies that contests the availability and legibility of identity is Nathan's narrative replacement of normative confidence with desire: he represents himself as a Jew by *desiring* a Jewish identification that seeks legitimacy in the future rather than by *indicating* actual evidence of a Jewish identity that finds legitimacy in the past. *The Counterlife* helps to displace the self-evidence through which normalization and identity buttress each other.

The Lives of the Jewish American

The formal experiment of *The Counterlife* is to cycle through multiply-ing alternate narratives and accounts of selves. The first chapter, called "Basel," details successful dentist Henry's flirtation with lines of flight from his happy family life in South Orange, New Jersey. Successive versions of escape take the form of "Maria," in this opening chapter a married Swiss woman with whom Henry maintains a torrid affair until she returns to Basel with her husband (and with whom at one point he consummates a second, illicit marriage through "anal love" [27]);[18] "Basel" itself, for which Henry for a time obsessively imagines himself trading his family in the dark period after Maria leaves; "Wendy," his sexually dynamic dental assistant, with whom he opens an affair years after Maria's departure by impersonating himself (as Henry describes it to Nathan, "she pretended she was called 'Wendy,' and I pretended I was called 'Dr. Zuckerman,' and we pretended we were in my dental office. And then we pretended to fuck—and we fucked" [34]); and then death, which we learn in the second chapter is only apparently his final line of flight, the result of a risky elective heart procedure that he insists on undergoing despite his doctor's advice because the beta blockers he takes for a new heart condition, for which he holds his heartbreak at Maria's departure responsible, render him impotent and therefore unable to participate in his daily sessions with Wendy in his office, dubbed by Nathan Henry's "atelier" because in it, with Wendy, he is able to craft creative variations on—counterlives of—his normative married existence (35). Nathan himself, professional writer of stories, is presented in this first chapter as another experimenter in counterlives, especially as he tries after his estranged brother's death to piece together a coherent narrative of Henry's imagination. In the second chapter, Henry has survived his open-heart surgery but, in the wake of a debilitating depression that sets in afterward, takes a different line of flight, this time in the form of the militant religious Zionism of the settler movement. In this second chapter, titled "Judea," we recall that "Basel," before, and more than, locating Henry's fantasy of returning to Maria, was also the site of Herzl's first Zionist Congress in 1897. As Nathan will later point out in a letter he writes to Henry but never sends, Zionism was a globally productive line of flight, the "construction of a counterlife that is one's own antimyth" allowing Jews all over the world to refashion themselves (147). Insofar as Henry—like Nathan and like Henry's wife, Carol—has up to this point been contentedly secular, giving his putative Jewish identity very little deliberate attention, his newly adopted stance of right-wing Jewish fundamentalism is another in this expanding series of counterlives. And likewise, Nathan is put in the position of defending his own brand of secular, citational Jewishness, claiming it as deliberate and his own. The third chapter, "Aloft," puts Nathan on a plane returning to London to *his* "Maria"—here his pregnant wife—after failing to convince Henry.

On the plane with him is Jimmy "Ben Joseph" Lustig, whom Nathan had met two nights before at the Western Wall (in chapter 2), an antic American Jew hailing from suburban New Jersey who idolizes Nathan, recognizes himself in Zuckerman's writing (as readers may recognize a parodic version of Roth in him), studies at the "Diaspora Yeshiva" on the top of Mount Zion (92), and wants to play center field for the "Jerusalem Giants" (94). When Jimmy tries to hijack the plane and force it to land in Germany in order to publicize his "Forget Remembering!" manifesto, which calls on Israel to close Yad Vashem in order to topple anti-Semitism by destroying its foundation in the Jewish manufacture of gentile guilt, the Israeli counterterrorism agents on the plane hold Nathan partly responsible because the ideas in Jimmy's manifesto are, they say, "your ideas" (175). And in the fourth chapter, it is Nathan who has had heart trouble and has died during the unnecessary procedure, and estranged brother Henry, who would never sleep with his assistant, steals into Nathan's apartment after the funeral and discovers the manuscript of what looks like the book we have been reading; Nathan, author of the productivist lines of flight that seduce him, makes the book's agency an object of our attention. The novel's concept of the "counterlife," at least partly authorized by Zionism's "will to remake reality" and the fact of its "laboratory in Jewish self-experiment that calls itself 'Israel'" (147), is never as simple as a purely fantasized fiction safely insulated from the demands and protocols of normative existence; rather, it is itself produced out of those demands and protocols, a form of friction against the normative activated in the desires in which the normalizing forces of social life take root.

At Agor, Henry-Hanoch parrots a normalized discourse of Zionist Judaism's historical self-evidence to justify his transformation. He claims that Hebron is Abraham's city and that the Jews' claim on the land and the land's claim on the Jews amount to the same thing: "*This is Judaism, this is Zionism, right here where we are eating our lunch!*" (109). For Henry, the Jewish settlers have chosen to face the undeniable, self-evident reality of "history"—albeit it a "history" that refuses to acknowledge the histories of two thousand years of postexilic, pre-1967 geography—while self-hating Diasporic Nathan self-indulgently frolics in the decadent make-believe of "psychoanalysis" (137, 140). Nathan, however, abjures the ground of Henry's Zionist normativity, challenging the exclusivity of the settlers' claim to the normal; he asks, "What's any of it got to do with you?" To Henry's claim that "we are Jews, this is Judea, and the heart of Judea is Abraham's city, Hebron," Nathan responds, "That still leaves unexplained the riddle of Henry Zuckerman's identification with Abraham's city" (109). For Henry, Zionism expresses Jewish normality: if Judea is Judaism, then it is normal for Jews to live there, and Jews are normal only when they are there, where normal is being Jewish in a self-evidently Jewish place sharing a self-evident Jewish history with other people who share this identification (but not with the people who also live there but who lack this normative identification with the land). For the Agor Zionists, normality means being able to describe oneself and narrate one's existence in a vocabulary of exclusive and self-evident Jewish genesis. Judea is and only is Jewish, so that is where Jews should be in order to be Jewish. Conversely, it is not normal for Jews to live, as Henry puts it, "camouflaging behind goyish respectability every last Jewish marking. All of it from them, for them" (111). Nathan protests that in suburban Newark, Henry was normal insofar as he "lived like everybody [he] knew": "You accepted the social arrangement that existed," explaining, "Carol for a wife, dentistry for a livelihood, South Orange for a home, well-behaved kids in good private schools—even the girlfriend on the side. If that's not normalcy, what is?" (110). To this, Henry insists, "Only the arrangement that existed was completely abnormal" (110)—normal for gentiles, abnormal for Jews. Normality is a powerful term in this book: if Nathan bristles at Henry's adoption of a stock Zionism that to him "seemed mostly platitudes gleaned from a turn-of-the-century handbook of Zionist ideology," his chief justification for his opposition to it—certainly in Henry's case—is its "having nothing whatsoever to do with him" (111). That is, Nathan's problem with Henry's Zionism is that it is abnormal for Henry specifically, inappropriate, just as Henry's problem with Nathan's Diasporic secularism is that it is abnormal or inappropriate for Jews generally. If there is something normal for the Zuckerman brothers, Nathan suggests, it is Newark, which certainly was Jewish in some of the contexts in which it existed for Jews like the Zuckermans but which certainly was not self-evidently or exclusively or essentially Jewish, was not *properly* Jewish; as Nathan imagines telling off Lippman back at Agor (but notably does not say, perhaps signaling an ambivalence about Lippman's persuasiveness in the book or about the persuasiveness of Lippman's normative vocabulary of Jewish propriety or at least about Lippman's charisma as it functions as a proxy for this persuasiveness), "in our family the collective memory doesn't go back to the golden calf and the burning bush, but to 'Duffy's Tavern' and 'Can You Top This?' Maybe the Jews begin with Judea, but Henry doesn't and he never will. He begins with WJZ and WOR, with double features at the Roosevelt on Saturday afternoons and Sunday doubleheaders at Ruppert Stadium watching the Newark Bears. Not nearly as epical, but there you are. Why don't you let my brother go?" (133). Henry sarcastically asks Nathan, "Is it at all possible, at least outside of those books, for you to have a frame of reference slightly larger than the kitchen table in Newark?" and just as defiantly Nathan responds, "The kitchen table in Newark happens to be the source of your Jewish memories, Henry—this is the stuff we were raised on" (138). Nathan defies Henry-Hanoch's desires for neither Jewish identification nor a narrative of Jewish history, but he does defy the Zionist administration of those desires. Henry and Nathan both appeal to a discourse of the normal for their justification, but it is Nathan who is left looking the schlemiel as Henry storms off, "furious, and before he could be talked into going home" (140), bungling even his claim of fraternity with his reestranged brother. That said, it is hard not to believe that the book here invests a good deal of significance in Nathan, who, as schlemiel, destabilizes the hegemony of Agor's normative fundamentalism by introducing the possibility of counternarratives of Jewish normality.

The book draws attention to itself in its occupation of the contested, productive boundary between fantasy and self, between proper and improper, between authentic and inauthentic, between normal and abnormal, and in how Jewish identity, which is never simply an affair of genealogy, is crossed by all these demarcations in the representation of its persuasiveness. Very close to the end of Nathan's doomed visit, he revises his earlier appeal to authenticity, which had initially seemed to underlie his argument against Henry's existential about-face, by taking a cue from the first chapter's Henry: "Look, I'm all for authenticity, but it can't begin to hold a candle to the human gift for playacting. That may be the only authentic thing that we ever do" (138). Even as Nathan tries to challenge the ethical foundation of Henry's newfound "Jewish confidence," he perhaps unwittingly furnishes him the perfect justification for his new life—because it is the same justification that Nathan imagines for Henry's sexual escapades in "Basel" and that he himself appeals to for his own new British excursion. "Authenticity," then, initially appearing to code historically self-evident essence, in fact ends up, after a confrontation with normativity, reading as an ironic displacement of itself, as a new productivist paradigm of identification emerges in the book, in which Nathan feels compelled to write himself into an uncertain yet intractable historical narrative of Jewishness that is legible largely to the extent that it has been fantasized by others.

Back in the church, it looks like London, no less than Israel, is another site of identity's productivity. Though Nathan has returned from Judea to his new wife in Christendom, his "mind" is still "suffused" by the conflicts he engaged in Israel, "all those implacable, dissident, warring voices and the anxieties stirring up their fear and resolve," and this church in London at Christmastime now offers itself up as the very opposite of "that unharmonious country" (255).

> The men with briefcases, the shoppers with their parcels and bundles and bags, those who at the worst of the rush hour had come all the way into the West End with overexcited little children or with their elderly relatives—no longer were they unattached and on their own, but merely by opening their mouths and singing out, this crowd of disparate Londoners has turned into a battalion of Christmas-savoring Christians, relishing every syllable of Christian praise with enormous sincerity and gusto. It sounded to me as though they'd been hungering for weeks for the pleasure of affirming that enduring, subterranean association. (258)

Desire for this "subterranean association," this sense of connection, of playing a part in, being a constituent of, is what Nathan has diagnosed in Henry, but Nathan's insight here is that this comfortable appropriateness properly operates only in, and as, the absence of a desire for it: that is, these churchgoing Britons precisely do not feel the self-conscious yearning for the sense of connection they enjoy by simple performative right of "opening their mouths and singing out" and that Henry believes he has found at Agor. The normality that so attracts Zionist Henry does not survive this desire. "It may be a little hickish to find the consolations of Christianity a surprise, but I was struck nonetheless to hear from their voices just how delightful it was—in Zionist argot, how very *normal* they felt—to be the tiniest component of something immense whose indispensable presence had been beyond Western society's serious challenge for a hundred generations" (258). In the church among the Christians, Nathan understands that normativity offers a way to code the transformative compensations of hegemonic thinking.

Meanwhile, if Nathan's Jewish alienation seems equally insistent in Israel and in England, it serves to further clarify the experience of normative identification that has emerged—refracted through the trope or mask of Jewishness—as *The Counterlife*'s chief critical focus. Once the Christmas music starts, the "mild current of antipathy" Nathan knew to expect rises up in him. "It never fails. I am never more of a Jew than I am in a church when the organ begins. I may be estranged at the Wailing Wall but without being a stranger—I stand outside but not shut out, and even the most ludicrous or hopeless encounter serves to gauge, rather than to sever, my affiliation with people I couldn't be less like. But between me and church devotion there is an unbridgeable world of feeling, a natural and thoroughgoing incompatibility." As he continues, "I'm not repelled by Christians at prayer, I just find the religion foreign in the most far-reaching ways—inexplicable, misguided, profoundly inappropriate" (256). What Nathan, fresh from the front lines of the Zionist discourse of normalization, now calls normality or feeling "normal" therefore marks the hegemonic ability to mark "affiliation," an affect whose frustration is coded by the word "foreign." Nathan has come a long way from the historical self-evidence that Henry, coached by Lippman, expects from Jewish identification—or, for that matter, from that historical self-evidence that he himself located in Newark. The novel seems to be more invested in exploring the mechanisms of identification through a more nuanced and complex discourse of normalization than through the novel's array of relatively simple discourses of authenticity, but only as glossed by Nathan's term "playacting" and Henry's earlier term "pretending."

While at the Kotel the night before he went out to see Henry at Agor, Nathan indeed had encounters both "ludicrous" and "hopeless"— the former with Jimmy Ben-Joseph Lustig and the latter with a Chasid who, appealing to their shared Jewishness, implores him to *daven* with him. But however ludicrous or hopeless, these encounters mark Nathan's Jewish bona fides. Jimmy, "high as a kite on Jewish commitment," is the "high-flying Jew" to Nathan's "grounded Jew" (93), while to the Chasid's puzzlement as to why Nathan would marry four "shiksas" (initially the Chasid's word, but Nathan adopts it) even when, as the Chasid rightly suspects, Nathan was "a Jew who was bar Mitzvah" (89), Nathan responds, "That's the sort of Jew I am, Mac" (90); in both cases, Nathan can still take for granted that the affiliating identifier "Jew" is shared when little else is. The normative Jewish "affiliation" "gauge[d]" in both of these experiences, therefore, is not mimetic, not the signpost of a similarity: affiliation is not an index of how some essence is represented. Rather than with representation, identification looks to be most intimately associated with the procedures of normalizing desire that anchor it.

Certainly part of the reason Nathan feels like a foreigner in the belly of Christian normativity is that he actively seeks to set himself apart, authorized in part by his own kind of Jewish confidence. Another part of the reason is that, similar to what happened at Agor, he is denormalized by some people who enjoy the privileges of normativity, as we see in his encounter with Maria's troublemaking older sister Sarah, who tries to destabilize Nathan by stirring class-colored fears about his Jewish circulation among the British. It is not only that she accuses him of "hypergamy" in his relationship with Maria, of reaching sexually beyond his class, but also that she positions him as essentially errant, as by nature arrayed against the possibility of normativity; thrusting a mince pie in his face, she says, "Smell this. . . . Because it smells good. Don't be so defensive because you're in a church. Smell it. It smells like Christmas. I'll bet you have no smells associated with Chanukah" (279). If in but smelling a pastry she can pleasurably and properly feel her powerfully normative Christian affiliation, she suggests, he is as a Jew incapable of feeling normal, of feeling "affiliation" positively. Nowhere does she render this threat more explicitly than in the particular case of Mrs. Freshfield, Maria and Sarah's mother, whom Sarah informs Nathan is "terribly anti-Semitic, you know" (278) and whom she advises Nathan not to cross: "You will be making a mistake if, when this infant arrives, you try to stand in the way of a christening" (282). Thus, for Sarah, "Jewish," taken in the context of what the novel via Zionism describes as "normal," codes impropriety: "Well, if you are, as your work suggests, fascinated with the consequences of transgression, you've come to the right family. Our mother can be hellishly unpleasant when it comes to transgression. She can be hard like a mineral—an Anglo-Saxon mineral. I don't think she really likes the idea of her languid, helpless Maria submitting to anal domination by a Jew. I imagine that she believes that like most virile sadists you fancy anal penetration" (278). Another countertext: unlike for Henry, for whom "anal penetration" functioned as a sacrament, in Nathan's case, as the positive signifier of transgression, it therefore joins "Jewish" as the background against which "normal" projects its compelling self-evidentiary force—just as "gentile" constituted a similar normative background for the Agor settlers.[19]

Nathan parries a bit with Sarah but refuses, at least for now, to be provoked. Sarah seems a bit disappointed by Nathan's reserve, given the acerbic personality he projects in his books, and wonders why he is holding back. "Is that because you're in England and not in New York? Is that because you don't want to be confused with the amusing Jews you depict in your fiction? Why don't you go ahead and show some teeth? Your books do—they're all teeth. You, however, keep very well hidden the Jewish paranoia which produces vituperation and the need to strike out—if only, of course, with all the Jewish 'jokes.' Why so refined in England and so coarse in *Carnovsky*? . . . You look Jewish, unmistakably. You can't possibly hide that by not showing your teeth" (279). Reading "unpleasant" into the discursive cluster joining "Jewish" and "abnormal," Sarah imagines Zuckerman desiring to be free of the category—even, showing her essentialist hand, as she assures him that he can never escape it (though she does reassure Nathan that "the English are too polite for Pogroms" [279]). Zuckerman defies Sarah's narrative of Jewish abnormality and replaces it with what looks like an alternative normative narrative of Jewish identity, insisting, in an existential defense linked at once to his justification to the Chasid the night before that "That's the sort of Jew I am, Mac" and to Henry's explanation of how he initiated his affair with Wendy, that "I don't have to act like a Jew—I am one" (279). But by claiming the identity that Sarah tries to impose on him, by inscribing himself in what Sarah wants to read as an essentialist account of Jewish nature, Nathan destabilizes the normative force of Sarah's essentialist discourse. He does not propose an

alternative normative discourse of Jewish identity; rather, he counter-
normatively exposes the desire, and therefore artifice, underlying
Sarah's hegemonic appeal to essentialist self-evidence. Sarah can here
be grouped with Doctor Zuckerman and Judge Wapter in their shared
anxiety about literature, expressed in a reactionary violence against the
possibility of anything but a narrowly defined mimetic concept of documentary or positivist writing: if Nathan's elders were afraid that the
young author's readers would assume that his subjects were his actual
fellow Jews, so Sarah expects Nathan to be like the people he writes
about. In any case, Roth's deconstruction of this violent fear of literature
is ingenious: the normative desire to deny literature a nonmimetic or
nonrepresentational power testifies to nothing so emphatically as the
power of literature to create counternormative possibility.

Zuckerman's counterhegemonic move starts emerging about fifteen
pages earlier, when he admits that, instead of sending a letter he had written to Henry on the El Al flight back to England from Israel—neither
apology nor defense so much as an albeit inevitably infuriating attempt
at sympathetic appreciation—he had, after reading it to Maria, copied
it into his notes, "into that ever-enlarging storage plant of [his] narrative factory, where there is no clear demarcation dividing actual hap-
penings eventually consigned to the imagination from imaginings that
are treated as having actually occurred—memory as entwined with fantasy as it is in the brain" (264). Where "normativity" has emerged as an
epistemological frame in which what *is* is crossed by what *should be*,
now "narrative," or writing coded as "factory," emerges as an interpretive
space in which what *is* cannot be isolated from what is *not necessarily
not*, in which "actual[ity]" and "imagination" are not definitively demarcated. Where "Jew" in Sarah's or Lippman's mouths signals a normative
presumption that identity polices actuality, "Jew" as deployed by Nathan
will signal a desire that identity is continuous with possibility, a productivity that the book increasingly reads as a form of writing. In the unsent
letter, Nathan tries to understand why Henry has chosen to transform
himself under Lippman's wing, admitting to "a terrific weakness for
these showmen, too": "I asked, with excessive impatience, if your identity was to be formed by the terrifying power of an imagination richer
with reality than your own, and should have known the answer myself.
How else does it happen? The treacherous imagination is everybody's

maker—we are all the invention of each other, everybody a conjuration conjuring up everyone else. We are all each other's authors" (145). Israel is the perfect place for such transformation. Zionism's discourse of normalization allows Nathan to link this insight about inscription and the self with Israel, which Nathan describes in the letter as "a whole *country* imagining itself, asking itself, 'What the hell is this business of being a Jew?'—people losing sons, losing limbs, losing this, losing that, in the act of answering. 'What is a Jew in the first place?' It's a question that's always had to be answered: the sound 'Jew' was not made like a rock in the world—some human voice once said 'Djoo,' pointed to somebody, and that was the beginning of what hasn't stopped since" (145). The important thing is not whether Lippman is right that Jews should annex land in Hebron, whether Nathan is right to challenge the inevitable association of Jews and Israel, or whether Sarah is right to think Jews sexually transgressive because they are not Christians; the real issue here is the failure of a self-evident resolution of the problem of Jewish identification, which can finally reveal itself in none of these alternatives.

Nathan's "Jew" is therefore not the same kind of thing as Lippman's or Sarah's "Jew." For Sarah, the word *Jew* is as simple and referentially self-evident as the difference between English novels and American novels, Christmas and Chanukah, or normative vaginal sex and abnormal anal sex—likewise for Lippman, for whom the classification "Jewish" carries little in the way of existential, historical, or recognitive vexations. By contrast, Nathan's "Jew" looks far less self-evident. If Sarah and Lippman understand Jewish identity under the banner of representation—Jews are the representatives of a particular history that can be recognized—Nathan's Jew only gains referentiality in a complex historical crossing of bodies and codes and desires. Nathan suggests that Henry has derived from Lippman a too-simple, monumentalist concept of Jewish identity—a counterpart to Sarah's too-simple, degenerativist concept—"You know better than to swallow uncritically the big cliché they seem to cherish at Agor of American Jews eating greedily from the shopping-center fleshpots," one eye out for the "Gentile mob" even while "seething" with "self-hatred and shame" (146). As Nathan revises this "cliché," American Jews more accurately seethe with "confidence and success": "And maybe that's a world-historical event on a par with the history you are making in Israel. History doesn't have to be made the way a mechanic makes a car—one can play a role in history without its having to be obvious, even to oneself" (146). Here identity returns as performance, the performance of a role, moreover, that is not clearly articulated beforehand. To be Jewish for Nathan is precisely to find oneself in need of producing the terms in which one's identity can be legible—to oneself as much as to anyone else. "Jew" does not have to be imagined as a historical constant, Nathan cautions Henry, bravely fighting for what is self-evidently Jewish; it can also be a space of continuous, perilous, and exuberant inscriptive and reinscriptive performance: "It may be that flourishing mundanely in the civility and security of South Orange, more or less forgetful from one day to the next of your Jewish origins but remaining identifiably (and voluntarily) a Jew, you were making Jewish history no less astonishing than theirs, though without quite knowing it every moment, and without having to say it. You too were standing in time and culture, whether you happened to realize it or not" (146). The parenthetical "voluntarily," even as complicated by "whether you happened to realize it or not," is easily the key term in the book's critique of identity: to be Jewish is at least as much a function of desire as it is one of genealogy.

If Zionism initially allowed Nathan to realize the importance of normativity to any effort to think about identity, then this insight here allows Nathan to reinscribe Zionism's normalizing emphasis on what is properly Jewish—indeed, on Jewish proper-ty—within the text's emergent productivist paradigm of Jewish identification and thus to avoid the temptation to positivize, as the Agor Zionists do, the difference between Agor's Zionist Hanoch and South Orange's Diasporic Henry or, as Sarah does, that between a mince pie and, presumably, a latke or, perhaps, a sufganiyah.

> Zionism, as I understand it, originated not only in the deep Jewish dream of escaping the danger of insularity and the cruelties of social injustice and persecution but out of a highly conscious desire to be divested of virtually everything that had come to seem, to the Zionists as much as to the Christian Europeans, distinctively Jewish behavior—to reverse the very form of Jewish existence. The construction of a counterlife that is one's own anti-myth was at its very core. It was a species of fabulous

utopianism, a manifesto for human transformation as extreme—and, at the outset, as implausible—as any ever conceived. (147)

Nathan performs a deexceptionalization of Zionism—of Zionism both as a historical phenomenon and as a specific, and privileged, version of Jewish being. If Jews have historically suffered definition of a decidedly unflattering and disenfranchising variety at the hands of the dominant gentile cultures among which they existed (and still suffer, as evinced by Sarah, even if this ongoing definition, at least in Great Britain, will not be accompanied by pogroms), then Zionism merely reverses this function without in any way overturning it by vesting this agency or subjectivity of definition in the hands of the community that had been the erstwhile object of definition—and continues to be the object of definition. As Nathan explains to Henry, "At any rate, that you should be mesmerized by the Zionist laboratory in Jewish self-experiment that calls itself 'Israel' isn't such a mystery when I think about this way. The power of the will to remake reality is embodied for you in Mordecai Lippman" (147–148). If this explanation allows Nathan to justify Henry's actions, it is guaranteed to alienate Henry. Nathan applauds Henry's "courage at forty to treat himself like raw material" (148) far more than he can Henry's "trying to lock [himself] into a piece of history that [he is] simply not locked into" (149)—a construction, incidentally, that reads in this novel as a more justified way of getting at what the Agor settlers' word "authenticity" tried to get at. In Nathan's revisionary model, which the Foucauldian paradigm of the reversibility of power can perhaps illuminate a bit, "Zionism" loses its self-evident historical specificity and is no more or less than another means of self-creation, a process in which "imagination," in the form of the production of counterlives but pointedly *not* in the form of the self-evident positivist opposite of "actual," scripts narratives.

Identity as Polemic

With "voluntary," with the help of "playacting" and "pretending," joining "authenticity" and "normativity" in marking the problem of identity in the displacement of sociological positivism's provision of security, the peculiar insistence of Nathan's "I don't have to act like a Jew—I am

one" becomes conspicuous. Jewish identification here is less a function of representing a genealogical essence than it is of expressing a
desire to inscribe oneself in a genealogy that can only proleptically be
authoritative. Provoked by Sarah despite himself, at dinner with Maria
after the church choral service, Nathan resolves not to tell her about
Sarah's harassment. But after a short time, he finds he cannot help himself. He tells Maria he does not think he can break through with her
mother. When Maria tells him that she has talked to her mother about
how much difference she and Nathan have "traversed" (Mrs. Freshfield's word), how much they have in common, including, Maria adds
half jokingly, language and literature—in an earlier scene, taking place
before Nathan's trip to Israel, Maria and Nathan go to visit Mrs. Freshfield, and Nathan, having been coached that Maria's mother reads Jane
Austen, initiates a conversation about literature that ends very close
to where it began, with Mrs. Freshfield insisting decisively and unen-
couragingly on the unbridgeable gap between English and American
sensibilities—Nathan quite unjokingly responds, "But she's not talking
about my Americanness" (286). Further producing distance between
them, he then suggests that Mrs. Freshfield is concerned about what
Maria's "group" will think of her associating with him because he is Jewish (287). A few pages later, Nathan hears an old woman a few tables
down from where they are sitting complain about the stink in the res-
taurant and explains to Maria, "I am that stink" (291). Maria assures
him that "that woman is crazy" or "drunk" and then suggestively adds,
"Or maybe you are." Nathan responds that although maybe she is one
or both, "inasmuch as she continues looking at me, or me with you, I
have to assume that I am that stink. . . . It is a racial insult, it is intended
to be that, and if she keeps it up, I am not going to remain silent, and
you should be prepared" (291–292). Regardless of whether the old lady
intends anti-Semitism, Nathan and Maria are now largely in agreement:
Nathan is insisting on his Jewishness. As he narrates, "From down
the banquette, I heard the woman saying, 'They smell so funny, don't
they?' whereupon I raised my hand to get the headwaiter's attention"
(292). Nathan's "I" is at least as conspicuous an agent as "the woman": "I
heard," preceding "the woman saying," suggests also its subjective pre-
cedence. Narrating the scene, and echoing the problem suggested by
Roth's previous chapter, in which he was revealed as a possible writer of

our experience of the book, Nathan's construction inaugurates a doubt about whether his *hearing* the woman say to her husband "They smell funny, don't they" necessarily depends on her really having *said* it—given, that is, the incontrovertible fact of the anti-Semitic image of Jewish identity that authorizes both her having said it and his having heard it, to say nothing of Agor's Zionist paranoia and Sarah's anal fantasies. In locating an implied Jewish referent in the woman's statement, therefore, Nathan reveals his desire to produce, too, his own legibly Jewish identity. Earlier the object of reactionary anxiety about the accuracy of representation, writing here begins to resolve as context for the production of the terms in which experience becomes subjectively legible.

To what extent is Nathan, the Jewish writer, writing the Jewishness of this book? Demonstrating the normative alliance between England's soft-spoken anti-Semitism and the West Bank's militant Zionism, Maria complains to Nathan, "You simply cannot start putting everything in a Jewish context. Or is this what comes of a weekend in Judea?" (299). When asked vituperatively by Nathan what the English think of Jews, she "sharply" ventriloquizes, "'Why do Jews make such a bloody fuss about being Jewish?'" (300). Maria proclaims her "object[ion] to people clinging to an identity just for the sake of it" (301) and says, "'identity' is just where you decide to stop thinking, as far as I can see" (301). It is hard to know if we are supposed to view Nathan favorably here in his oppositional inhabitation of what is increasingly a polemical form of identity. What is more certain, however, is that earlier intimations of a link between identity and normativity, of identity's role as the agent of normativity, are beginning to take on a more distinct form. The novel does not necessarily have to agree with Nathan here—who, it pays to point out, is in fact essentially doing what Maria accuses him of doing—for it to endorse the mechanism of his offense and anger. Indeed, Maria is right that identity is where thinking stops—but not in the way she believes to be the case. Nathan's conduct, far from really contradicting her (despite the argument that is rising here and that will doom their relationship in the next few pages), seems to suggest that identity is a compulsion and that, in a sense, Maria was right in her implication, that what is "Jewish" here is indeed dependent on Nathan and his desire. So the difference between Nathan and Maria is that here in England, Maria feels no need to cling to an identity, while Nathan does. In explaining her distaste for identity claims, Maria admits, "I don't like going to north London, to Hampstead or Highgate, and finding it like a foreign country, which it really does seem to me" (301); used to feeling the privileges and prerogatives of citizenship, Maria insists that she feels "like an alien": "being there makes me feel left out and it makes me feel that I'm better off somewhere I feel more normal" (302). This is precisely how Sarah's gentile expects Nathan's Jew to feel in Christendom, and it is also how Lippman's Jew expects to feel outside Judea in Christendom, as well. We recall that for Nathan, Christianity is "foreign," which he glosses with "inappropriate," while the "consolations" of Christian religious practice transform "unattached" Christians "on their own" into a unified "battalion," allowing them to feel "normal," which is to say "delightful[ly]" and "indispensibl[y]" part of something that is beyond question. To feel "normal," then, is to feel the pleasure of recognizing one's own propriety, one's own appropriateness; it is to feel a kind of comfort born of recognizing the familiarity of being proper to or the property of, and it is also to feel the comfort in being recognized as both familiar and appropriate. Nathan, having the protocols of normativity exposed for him, articulates his nonnormative abnormality.

Though Maria all the while tries to put a stop to this conversation— "Look, is this a good thing, this kind of talk?"—Nathan keeps forcing the issue and in the process articulates a new paradigm for identification: "Sure. It gives me a foothold in a foreign land" (287). Maria fears, wisely, that talk about identity and identification will ultimately drive them apart, but for Nathan talk of identity orients. One of the problems articulated by this book is that these two possibilities do not exclude each other. If, as Maria suggests, identity talk inevitably normalizes and administers positive differences and therefore undercuts the links, or at least accentuates the divisions, between people who are identified differently, it also can be, as Nathan suggests, productive of the coordinates by which to map one's own foreignness. Maria's reaction, at least in what she has come to recognize as her legitimate homeland, to feeling foreign—to feeling made to feel foreign—is to displace the threat of abnormality through the reinscription of normativity: she reassures Nathan that she does not find the Jews of north London "distasteful" but that among them—people who she says "are my generation, who are my peers—they have the same sort of responses, they probably went to the same sort of schools, generally they'd have similar kinds of education, forgetting religious education, but they all have a different style form me"—she does feel circumscribed by an ineluctable difference she does not feel elsewhere. "I feel alien among them—being there makes me feel left out and it makes me feel that I'm better off somewhere I feel more normal" (302). What bothers Maria about Jewish difference is that civil-society-based citizenship is powerless before it; sharing the same "responses," the same "schools," the same generational frame, the most she can find that separates her from Jews is a different "style," a "tribalism" (Nathan's word; 301), that she reads reductively as a frustratingly self-referential and circular, but therefore inescapable and irremediable, insistence on difference. Maria may embrace more of a liberal multiculturalism than does Sarah, but the Freshfield sisters share a dedication to comprehending difference solely in positivized, representational terms.

What Maria experiences as self-evident and self-referential, however, Nathan will experience as an overdetermined compulsion. What most shocks Nathan about his argument with Maria is not that, "even after Hitler might have been thought to have somewhat tarnished the Jew-hater's pride" (306), there should still exist people in England who "harbored a profound distaste for Jews," nor that Maria tolerates her mother as much as she does, nor even that she "should have been naïve enough to believe that she was averting a disaster by pretending that there wasn't that kind of poison around" (307). Rather, he says, "The unpredictable development was how furious it all made me." Nathan wonders if he suffers from the "classic psychosemitic ailment" (307), paranoically normalizing his Jewish identification by imagining himself the Jewish victim of persecution wherever he looks. Though he had written his fiction "in the knowledge of" what he calls "the wounds that Jews have had to endure," he insists, "down to tonight, the experience of it had been negligible in my personal life. Crossing back to Christian Europe nearly a hundred years after my grandparents' westward escape, I was finally feeling up against my skin the outer reality which I'd mostly come to know in America as an 'abnormal' inner preoccupation permeating nearly everything within the Jewish world" (307). "Abnormal" is the word the militant Zionist settlers at Agor used to describe the deformed and degraded state of Diaspora Jews under gentile religious and social hegemony. "Abnormal" is the word Maria used to describe how she feels—or is made to feel—among the Jews of north London. And abnormal is what Sarah reckons Jews for their opposition to Christmas, to christening, and to sexual activity purged of "anal domination." And now here is Nathan, claiming for himself an affect he had heretofore considered an abnormal "preoccupation." Jewishness and normativity are intractably crossed in this book; no less than West Bank militancy and British anti-Semitism, as much as Hanoch's Zionism in Hebron and Maria's discomfort in north London, Nathan's psychosemitism shows how identity and normativity are two sides of the same coin, how identity serves as the agency of normalization.

Nathan wonders why he pursued this fight even as Maria implored him against it, and he realizes that in "talking about it, going on about it, mercilessly prolonging that discussion," he is responsible for driving toward the breakup of their marriage. While in America, "where people claim and disown 'identities' as easily as they slap on bumper stickers," he tells us that he could act like a "reasonable fellow" when Maria had distinguished Jews from Caucasians during their courtship in New York (she and her husband had lived in the apartment upstairs from Nathan), here in England, "where you are swathed permanently in what you were born with, encased for life with where you began," he "couldn't let the insult pass" (308). If the bumper-sticker comment suggests that Nathan might have wanted to believe that an understanding of identity as practice makes it harder to adopt the normative essentialism shared by the Gloucestershire Freshfields and the Agor Zionists, he instead finds himself compelled into an identification administered by that same kind of authoritative normalization. He inscribes himself into the very genealogy he resists being read into—in the very act of resisting. As he leaves Maria and their temporary apartment after their argument to alone tour the riverfront house in Chiswick that they are renovating for their new life together—"the house that was being transformed into ours and that represented my own transformation—the house that represented the rational way" (309)—Nathan realizes that "all [his] efforts" go against the attempt "to accede"; instead, he says, "the past, the unevadable past, had gained control and was about to vandalize our future" (309). Asking himself how he could have let this happen, he finds, "What had overcharged the rhetoric and ignited the resentment was of course her role of mother's daughter rubbing against mine of father's son—our first fight hadn't even been ours" (310). If identity is something one is compelled to accede to ("where you decide to stop thinking," as Maria would have it), then the agency by which one accedes is not completely one's own. In coordinating identity with normativity, with the powerfully, paradoxically self-affirmative experience of being recognized, of recognizing that one is recognized—familiarity as a function of being recognized as familiar—this book arrays identity *against* normalized self-possession via the defamiliarizing concept of the counterlife's contestatory deployment of desire against itself. One's identity is *always* a counterlife.

It is at this point that Nathan imagines that Maria, fancying herself a narrative construction of Nathan's, decides to will herself out of the book he is writing about her; when he returns home, Nathan worries, Maria will not be there. Everyone may be a conjuration conjuring everyone else, but that does not mean that anyone is the final author of the narratives he or she writes. She tells him in the note that he imagines he will find, "I'm leaving the book"; as he elaborates, "She conceives herself as my fabrication, brands herself a fantasy and cleverly absconds" (312). She blames his "Jewish hang-up" (313) and insists, as "disgusting as you've discovered my Englishness to be, I'm really *not* wedded to it, or to any label, in the way that most of you Jews do persist in being Jewish" (314). This seems to be the key difference that the book is concerned with presenting between identity as Maria conceives it and identity as Nathan conceives it. For Maria, identity may indeed be where thinking ends: it instantiates itself compellingly and authoritatively precisely where she does not have to think about it. Though she thinks she is using "identity" pejoratively, only to describe something that other, non-"English" (or non-"Caucasian") people have, in her articulation it just as forcefully refers to herself—that is, where and when she is among those whom she recognizes as recognizing her as normal—and she finds it acutely unpleasurable to find herself in a circumstance in which she has to think about her identity—that is, where and when she is among those whom she recognizes as recognizing her as abnormal. In articulating the concept of the counterlife, Roth's novel displaces the gravity of the familiarity of the discursive terms that enable self-recognition precisely in rendering their own illegibility, displaces—in pointing out the attraction of—the compensations of being addressed as normal. The desire that believes it is normal to be normal—like Maria's or Sarah's or Lippman's, but also like Doctor Zuckerman's and Judge Wapter's conviction that it is important to represent Jews being normal, which in their case is also to say acceptable according to gentile cultural protocols—normalizes desire and engages an aspiration to be normal that dislocates the authorizing legitimacy of normality.[20] Nathan does not transform this normative paradigm but rather transvalues it: identity only instantiates itself under the sign of "abnormality," in the disputation of counter-lives, but this is just another way of formulating its compelling force. It takes Maria to articulate Nathan's drive to write the conditions of this emergence; his "talk," twinned with his "persist[ence] in being Jewish," is the form taken by self-reinscription in this book. Indeed, identity is a species of reinscription: conjurations conjuring everybody else, we all are writers who, under the sign of "identity," narrate the emergence of the terms of our self-recognition.

In Maria's letter of abdication, she reveals herself as most Nathan's construction when she adumbrates the central role of desire in Nathan's oppositional Jewish self-relation. She claims to stand for "tranquility," a standard she admits is "disquieting" for Nathan (317). "The pastoral is not your genre, and Zuckerman Domesticus now seems to you just that, too easy a solution, an idyll of the kind you hate, a fantasy of innocence in the perfect house in the perfect landscape on the banks of the perfect stretch of river." Maria opines to Nathan, "Your chosen fate," by contrast, "is to be innocent of innocence at all costs, to not let me, with my pastoral origins, cunningly transform you into a pastoralized Jew" (318). But here Maria—indeed, precisely as Nathan's written creation, a turn Maria calls "diabolical" of him (319)—misses the mark. It is not that Nathan the Jew wants to avoid pastoralization; it is that for Nathan, who increasingly appears in psychosemitic—indeed, semitic—charge of the scene, the Jew can never be pastoralized. Maria admits that she should have seen this break coming "all the way back on page 73" (314), where Nathan, just arrived in Israel and before going off to Agor to find Henry, meets with his old friend Shuki, a jaded, secular, leftist journalist in Tel Aviv, and talks about circumcision. Surprised that Nathan, at forty-five, is "finally" to be a father (but not surprised that Nathan is married again), Shuki asks whether, if it is a boy, his "English rose will consent to circumcision" (73). To Nathan's oppositional retort,

"Who says circumcision's required?" Shuki responds, "Genesis, chapter 17." Nathan informs Shuki that he has "never been completely sold on biblical injunctions," to which Shuki responds, "Still, it's been a unifying custom among Jews for rather a long time now. I think it would be difficult for you to have a son who wasn't circumcised. I think you would resent a woman who insisted otherwise." They share a laugh, and Shuki comes back with something conspicuously close to what Sarah will say two hundred pages later, where she reads Nathan through *Carnovsky* and stimulates a reaction that proves Shuki remarkably prescient about Nathan's Jewish commitment (and where, again "diabolical[ly]" of author Nathan—or, to use terminology Roth introduced a handful of years later in *Operation Shylock*, "mischievously" of him—Sarah and Shuki can be seen banding together to answer Henry's implication, voiced on page 138, that Nathan's Jewish commitment in his books, which focus on "the kitchen table in Newark," is insufficient): "Why do you pretend to be so detached from your Jewish feelings? In the books all you seem to be worrying about is what on earth a Jew is." Nathan responds by invoking one of the novel's keywords: "Chalk it up to Diaspora abnormality," and Shuki reverses the polarity in which that opposition will be presented at Agor: "You think in the *Diaspora* it's abnormal? Come live here. This is the *homeland* of Jewish abnormality" (73). Shuki is quick to recognize what has happened with Nathan's brother, who is following a standard script.

> Henry must find it very romantic [at Agor]. The American Jews get a big thrill from the guns. They see Jews walking around with guns and they think they're in paradise. Reasonable people with a civilized repugnance for violence and blood, they come on tour from America, and they see the guns and they see the beards, and they take leave of their senses. The beards to remind them of saintly Yiddish weakness and the guns to reassure them of heroic Hebrew force. Jews ignorant of Islam and the Middle East, they see the guns and they see the beards, and out of them flows every sentimental emotion that wish fulfillment can produce. A regular pudding of emotions. The fantasies about this place make me sick. (75)

Among the militant nationalist theocrats of Agor, abnormality is the condition of assimilation, of appealing to nonproper modes of authority; among the spent cosmopolitan civil-socialites of Tel Aviv, abnormality is the condition of equating life with a sentimental fantasy born of resentment. But for Nathan, abnormality and normality lose their referential historical grounding. And yet Shuki's word "fantasy" ends up powerfully glossing "identity."

Maria should have seen as a warning the specter of circumcision 240 pages earlier; but what Nathan tries to dismiss as an unpersuasive "injunction" returns in Shuki's reintroduction precisely as an authoritative "unifying" force. Maria, herself rewriting the anxiety of Nathan's father in *The Ghost Writer*, resents Nathan's desire "to play reality-shift" (318) in his writing: to rewrite as characters inside his fiction actual people who really exist outside fiction. Nathan's "only defense," he responds in a letter addressed to his character Maria that ends the book, is, "[If] it can be said that I do sometimes desire, or even require, a certain role to be rather clearly played that other people aren't always interested enough to want to perform," nevertheless "I ask no less of myself"; as he elaborates, "Being Zuckerman is one long performance and the very opposite of what is thought of as being oneself. In fact, those who most seem to be themselves appear to me people impersonating what they think they might like to be, believe they ought to be, or wish to be taken to be" (319). With what people do understood no longer as "being oneself" but instead recast or reinscribed as "impersonation"— which constellates with Shuki's "fantasy" and Nathan's earlier "conjuration"—the "self" as identitarian bedrock or normative infrastructure, such as might underlie Maria's umbrage, is a "joke" that Nathan is "unwilling or unable to perpetrate upon [him]self" (320); "I am a theater and nothing more than a theater" (321). In this theater, the fantasized, conjured, impersonating self, "Homo Ludens," writes "the imperfect future" (321), "imperfect" inaugurating its own lexical counterdiscourse: not just the lack of perfection but also a grammatical form denoting uncompleted action: identity is produced out of the future of an unresolved desire.

"Being oneself"—self-evident security both on the West Bank and in Christendom—is the hegemonic desire that Nathan alone resists in this his book. It is the identitarian normal that orients Maria just as much as it orients Lippman, Henry-Hanoch, and Shuki, who each in his or her own way reveals, and revels in, the normative expectation that certain spaces and practices correspond with certain selves: it is the comforting reassurance of the proper, of recognizing that one belongs. "Being oneself" belongs to the pastoral, the genre that houses "those irrepressible yearnings by people beyond simplicity to be taken off to the perfectly safe, charmingly simple and satisfying environment that is desire's homeland" (322). The pastoral's proleptic original is the womb, and its despairing projection from a disappointed consciousness of exile from that origin reinscribes as normative the erasure of its own historical bad conscience. Nathan, however—through this book—reintroduces this guilty consciousness; as he writes in his letter to Maria,

> Do you remember the Swedish film we watched on television, that micro-photography of ejaculation, conception, all that? It was quite wonderful. First was the whole sexual act leading to conception, form the point of view of the innards of the woman. They had a camera or something up the vas deferens. I still don't know how they did it—does the guy have a camera on his prick? Anyway, you saw the sperm in huge color, coming down, getting ready, and going out into the beyond, and then finding its end up somewhere else—*quite* beautiful. The pastoral landscape par excellence. (322)

The book offers two opposed figurations of identity. On the one hand is identity as a normalizing interlock between "being oneself" and the compensated act of recognizing oneself in doing so. This identitarian machinery operates via the pastoral as a normative genre, at whose heart "is the idyllic scenario of redemption through the recovery of a sanitized, confusionless life. In dead seriousness, we all create imagined worlds, often green and breastlike, where we may finally be 'ourselves'" (322). Nathan calls the pastoral "therapeutic" (323) and a species of "fleeing" (322): its imagination of a regime of normality amounts to an escape at once from disappointment and the uncertainty of enjoying no proper recognition, an escape from the difficult awareness "that that is the womb and this is the world" (322). Judea to Henry and the Lippman crew is a revisionary Zionist name for this pastoral retreat (as he puts it in his letter responding to Maria's fleeing the book) "back to day zero and the first untainted settlement—breaking history's mold and casting off the dirty, disfiguring reality of the piled-up years" (322). And Nathan reminds his epistolary Maria of the choral service where all this began: "Think of all those Christians, hearty enough to know better, piping out their virginal vision of Momma and invoking that boring old Mother Goose manger" (322)—rather, for example, than thinking about how (to requote Nathan) Christianity has "been beyond Western society's serious challenge for a hundred generations." And he admits that his imagination of fatherhood with Maria in the Christendom that claims her in her claiming it once meant the same thing to him. Pastoral identity reimagines history as a species of recognition: it offers up a narrative in which the historical subject can normatively know itself as the one justified and proper protagonist.

"Jewishness," not as it has been invested by Lippman but as it is unendingly reinscribed in "history," becomes a name for the counterpastoral—not an escape from pastoral normalization but the failure of the pastoral illuminated by the pastoral's promised "confusionless[ness]." Just as Doctor Zuckerman and Judge Wapter get it wrong when they worry about whether Nathan's early stories are bad for the Jews (as many readers worried that Roth's first two decades of writing were bad for the Jews), so Maria and Henry get it wrong when they worry about what is normal and what is not: identity is the furthest thing from being a matter of mimesis, of coordination with something positive that can be represented or documented. Shuki's question about circumcision and Maria's anxious citation of this discussion, like Sarah's provocations about the fate of Nathan and Maria's imaginary child, suggest another paradigm of identification. If the identitarian pastoral articulates identity as a machine that situates the subject properly in history, circumcision suspends this normalization. "The pastoral stops here and it stops with circumcision" (323). Where we are all conjurations conjuring everybody else, circumcision writ large emerges as an admonition, a disruption or irruption preventing resentment's desire from overwriting history with an imperial sentimentality. The pastoral resolves as a kind of historicism: through its lens, history is legible as the narrative of its proper, representable subject, itself already recognized as the legitimate and original subject of history. "Circumcision" emerges as the displacement of this paradigm, where identity can only be recognized in the "imperfect future" of a contested series of reinscriptions of the subject of a narrative that has no originary legitimacy.

Circumcision is startling, all right, particularly when performed by a garlicked old man upon the glory of a newborn body, but then maybe that's what the Jews had in mind and what makes the act seem quintessentially Jewish and the mark of their reality. Circumcision makes it clear as can be that you are here and not there, that you are out and not in—also that you're mine and not theirs. There is no way around it: you enter history through my history and me. Circumcision is everything that the pastoral is not and, to my mind, reinforces what the world is about, which isn't strifeless unity. Quite convincingly, circumcision gives the lie to the womb-dream of life in the beautiful state of innocent prehistory, the appealing idyll of living "naturally," unencumbered by man-made ritual. To be born is to lose all that. The heavy hand of human values falls upon you right at the start. (323)

Norman Finkelstein calls this a "genuine modern midrash" and a "clear" example of "the ritual of new creation," what he describes as the act of finding new meaning in an established or traditional rite—in Nathan's case, a meaning "commensurate with the circumstances of his ceaselessly destabilized existence."[21] Finkelstein reads Nathan's concept of circumcision as a mode of resecuring Jewish identity (and the Jew!) in a coherent and self-evident Jewish tradition, just as Finkelstein historicizes modern Jewish literature itself as a cultural resource produced and consumed by Diasporic Jews; if it reaffirms the exile in which it is written, Jewish literature also provides the means by which Jews can read themselves back into a secure Jewish identification. But such historicism overwrites and suppresses Zuckerman's critical irruption here. As Daniel and Jonathan Boyarin point out, circumcision can otherwise be understood "precisely as the cultural construction of a genealogical differentiation, as a diacritic that symbolizes the biological status of Jewishness—not in the sense of a biological difference between Jews and others but in the sense of the biological connection that filiation provides."[22] Nathan is precisely not "one of those Jews who want to hook themselves up to patriarchs or even to the modern state" (324); he understands that there is no self-evident Jewish "we" to which he seeks to relate his Jewish "I," as Henry seeks. If identification is glossed in this book by impersonation, another term for which Roth's post-Zuckerman oeuvre might resolve as "writing," then the particular paradigm of inscription announced by the act of circumcision suggests that identity writing is an activity that does not have a self-evidently legitimate subject. "Circumcision confirms that there is an us, and an us that isn't solely him and me" (324), but it is a difficult, differentiated, and critically proleptic "us" that lacks a secure sociological referent, an "us" that cannot be taken for granted and that can never hold up a mirror for the self, an "us" that is never situated in the normalized fantasy promised by the pastoral. The same operation that allows Henry to fuck his assistant by pretending to fuck her compels Nathan to claim a Jewish identification that he has also spent his career disclaiming.

"Only a few hours ago, I went so far as to tell Shuki Elchanan that the custom of circumcision was probably irrelevant to my 'I.' Well, it turns out to be easier to take that line on Dizengoff Street that sitting here beside the Thames. A Jew among Gentiles and a Gentile among Jews" (324). Maria asked in her letter, "Can't you ever forget your Jews?" (314)—assumedly in the manner in which she can in Christendom forget both his Jews and her Britons (but only by taking for granted the normality of her Britons)—but Nathan, try as he might, cannot. Unlike the pastoral's confident historicist recognition, circumcision offers an alternate take on identity: a necessary impersonation, a fantasy and an act of conjuration, identity is at once man-made and intractable. Nathan is "a Jew without Jews, without Judaism, without Zionism, without Jewishness, without a temple or an army or even a pistol, a Jew clearly without a home, just the object itself, like a glass or an apple" (324). But the inscriptive substance of this "object itself" is precisely not the substance of Mrs. Freshfield's "Anglo-Saxon mineral," whose confident, definitive, positive "hard[ness]" is a universe away from the constitutively critical indefinition of Nathan's impossible Jewish identification, and it is not the surfaceless self-sufficient substance of the "rock" that Nathan contrasts to the interminable and uncontainable history of ceaseless reinscription that began when some schmuck said "Djoo." Nathan is also a Jew only as the contested and fantasized, simultaneous subject and object of a writing he is fated to project back from his own "imperfect future." The pastoral promises the self normalization, but here Nathan voices the displacement of this dream of self-recognition: the contested site where counterlives cross each other, identity is the counterdiscourse of normativity. Identity is not a function of recognition; it is what happens when recognition fails, as it will, to recognize its necessary or national propriety. The importance of the book's deconstruction of the boundary between "writing" and "reality" is not encapsulated in some banal platitude about postmodern textuality or the fictionality of the self; rather, it displaces the historicist expectation that Jewish literature represents an already-legible Jewish subject, exuberantly and "treacherously" drawing our attention to the emergent future production of the Jew's recognition. At the end of *The Counterlife*, where Zuckerman *decides*, despite his lack of identitarian confidence, to mark himself (through his unborn son) as Jewish by insisting on circumcision, a new means of Jewish self-recognition becomes available: he represents himself as a Jew by *desiring* a Jewish identification that seeks critical legitimacy in the future rather than by *indicating* actual evidence of a Jewish identity that expects historicist legitimacy in the past. When we redirect our analysis, away from an ethnographically legible Jewish subject assumed to underwrite representationally a canon of Jewish American literature and toward an anxiety about Jewish identification that is as much a characteristic of our critical practice as it is a phenomenon in the texts we take to be proper to that practice, we reimagine too the temporality of Jewish identity: no longer anchored in the stable coherence of a Jewish past, identity-based literary criticism can derive its sanction from an as-yet-undiscerned future of Jewishness. To Maria the pastoralist's foolish dream of fleeing Nathan's writing, Nathan asks, "To escape into what, Marietta?" Roth ends their book: "this life is as close to life as you, and I, and our child can ever hope to come" (324).

5

9/11's Stealthy Jews

Jonathan Safran Foer and the Irrepresentation of Identity

In this book's interest in thinking about Jewish literature outside of a normative and inevitably nationalist anthropological paradigm that takes for granted that texts represent, express, or otherwise bear the legible traces of a biologistically legitimized historical population—whether through the proxy of already-identifiable authorship, content, or practice—it has located itself in the difficult region where the doubled subject of an identity-based canon is recognized—both the historical subject whom literary history recognizes as responsible for the literature and the historical subject whom literary history recognizes as represented in the literature. As Michael Kramer has helped us understand, identity in this sense is a normative concept that, while frequently coordinated by such terms as "culture," "tradition," "archive," "religion," and "history," literary history in its current state all but inevitably imagines as categorical and heritable, buttressed and mapped, whether avowedly or not, by the logic of "race" (or, perhaps more vaguely, "ethnicity"). Kramer calls this structure the "casuistry of metonymical ethnicity," a structure that relies for its coherence on the identity it purports to ground. "While the metonym represents the text, it is premised upon the identity of the writer. The part stands in for the whole because—the ethnicity of the author being known or supposed—the whole has already been identified as appropriate to the part."[1] It has been my goal in this book to open up space for the articulation and employment of a concept of identity, or perhaps of historical categoricality more generally, that is not based in a fiction about blood, what Jonathan Arac glosses as the filiative structure of ancestry and descent that forms the armature around which so much racialist argument wraps itself.[2] We need to displace the hegemonic temptation to read identity as the authorization machine of a biologistic nationalism: though it may for now be

all but impossible to disengage the thought of Jewish American literature as a field (like other identity-based literatures) from the biologistic
thought of the genealogy or heritable cultural identity of the author as
he or she stands as proxy for a categorically recognized historical subject, a responsible identity-based criticism must work to denormalize
that linkage. In the face of this elision, I suggest that we conceptualize
Jewish literary study (and Jewish studies more generally) not as part of
a history of Jews (or, more perniciously, as part of a history of an even
more fictitious category, The Jew) but as part of a history of the idea
of the Jew, a history of a concept whose referent does not exist in any
essential or historically self-evident way but only catachrestically, in a
variety of practices, including literary historical practices, that resolve
and administer the vocabularies in which we can limn its recognizability. The argument of this book has been that the Jewish American literary canon should be considered an archive attesting not to a Jewish
American subject but to a desire for Jewish American differentiation.
The difficulty lies in freeing our literary critical practices from the burden that our knowledge and knowledge practices necessarily carry positivistic or documentary authorization.

Part of the effort of trying to critically displace the hegemonic power
of our biologistic concept of identity is to ask, specifically and particularly, what we are really doing when we mark the Jewishness of a text
in terms of a categorical historicist identity that anthropologizes and
nationalizes, that simultaneously focuses, by determining, an array of
knowledge practices, including historical, sociological, ethnographic,
biographical, and literary critical vocabularies (for example). I am hoping to be able to move away from an identity-based literary criticism
that at least implicitly, but necessarily, links to a presumed transhistorical Jewish subject that, if not self-evident, is certainly taken for granted.
More legitimate than a positivist program that takes for granted a categorically "Jewish" literary canon and that, at least implicitly, expects
to be able to representationally locate something unifying or coherent
inhering in all those texts, I claim, is a critical program that questions
how and why our scholarly discourses thematize a categorical identity. Such a program, which this final chapter aims to outline, would
question too the political itineraries that engage and are engaged by
these discourses. The urgency of such a program is highlighted by the

paradox of identity's rise as a critical value in the wake of the poststructuralist critique of the subject—what I discussed in chapter 1. On the one hand, identity as a positive, interpretively self-evident, and historically coherent value has been exposed to a far-reaching critique, and we can no longer verify a dependent relationship between the inside of a text and an essential, extratextual concept of identity. And yet, on the other hand, the rise of identity-politics-based and ethnicity-centered literary studies during the same period—an explosion that shows little sign of burning out—suggests a more fundamental interpretive self-evidence, that the rise of critically sanctioned rhetoric about diversity and historical multiplicity is in fact leveraged by a foundational assumption that a categorical inscription (of a group, a culture, a text, etc.) can always be recognized as such, and it indicates the persistence of identitarianism's hold on critical discourse despite the deconstructive critique of the subject. If the self-evidence of the bourgeois subject was challenged because of its claim to timeless universality, then there is likely a contradiction in the wide appeal to so-called minority identity (i.e., as an anchor and/or warrant for representation in both its aesthetic and political sense) that has rushed in to fill the gap left by that subject's retreat in post-Vietnam critical discourse. This contradictory appeal to universality housed in an appeal to the specificity of a recognizable identity suggests the need to rethink the role and function of identity in literary study. Rather than trivializing the literary historical category of identity by ghettoizing it, by assuming the self-evidence of something called "Jewish identity" and then looking for its representation in literature, *The Impossible Jew* proposes reorienting literary study of identity around the possibility that literature is one place (among a multitude of places) where identity is in the making, precisely where the contradictions of recognizable identities—between universality and particularity, for example, or between inheritance or givenness and practice—are most conspicuously marked.

Some words about the lexical invention in this chapter's title, "irrepresentation," will help clarify my goal here in this final chapter. One of the key axes of contradiction I have been investigating, obviously, is representation: on the one hand, an identitarian concept of representation can no longer be justified as the thing that literature does, while on the other hand it is difficult to imagine ethnicity- and identity-based literary history that does not understand a "blood"-based or filiative, biologized or racialized concept of identity, in the pernicious sense that Arac has marked, as the representational key to a particular, identifiable body of literature. The problem with the representational model, with presuming that literature (among its other capacities) represents an identifiable "ethnic" positivity that exists self-evidently and independently of it, is a function of desire: at the end of the day, we find identity represented in a text because we want to find it there, because we are already expecting to recognize its documentary effects there. While I am largely convinced by the deconstructive challenge to representation, I am also quite persuaded by the critical productivity of an identity-centered literary history. This is where "irrepresentation" comes in. Relying on its prefix's multivalent etymology, I am hoping the term does two things. First, with the help of *ir-*'s meaning of *non-*, *un-*, or *not*, "irrepresentation" is meant to suggest that identity is not where we want it to be, that the text expected to represent identity in fact does not unequivocally do so. Second, with the help of *ir-*'s meaning of *in, within,* or *into,* the term is meant to suggest at the same time that even as identity is not where we desire it, it irrupts out of— and into—this displacement. Mapped by this term's multivalence, I argue here that Jonathan Safran Foer's second novel, *Extremely Loud and Incredibly Close* (2005), stages literary criticism's escape from the nationalist paradigm by defying the filiatively deterministic expectations of a positivist, biologistic concept of identity. That a novel by one of the most acclaimed Jewish novelists of his generation should lack any decisively "Jewish" content, and more specifically that a novel as interested as Foer's is in the panoply of the twentieth century's worst historical traumas should refuse to decisively mention the Holocaust (and this especially in the wake of the intense focus of his first novel, *Everything Is Illuminated,* on the Holocaust),[3] do not of course in themselves present any significant problem. But considered in the context of the literary criticism of identity, of the academic politics of canonicity, and of Foer's placement in a newly vibrant Jewish American canon, they together provide a productive occasion to reconceptualize the foundation of Jewish American literary history, away from a confident *presumption of* represented identity and toward a fraught *desire for* identity's categorical coherence.

Through the mediation of the critical trope of "trauma," *Extremely Loud and Incredibly Close* affords an opportunity for literary criticism to confront the agency of its own historicist desire to read texts for narratives of what it already wants to recognize. As I have been suggesting throughout this book, the register that authorizes this redemptive agency—and the mechanism that administers it—is the machine called "identity." And it is on this point that I want to read Foer's novel within but also against the identitarian machinery of Jewish American literary history, given both Foer's status as one of the major Jewish novelists of his generation and a prevailing identitarian literary historical interest in constitutively reading literature for represented signs of Jewish American history, signs of some categorical, racialized element common to the people, cultures, traditions, histories, archives, and so on that we call "Jewish." A central premise of *The Impossible Jew* is that Jewish American literary study has in the aggregate inadequately theorized its labor; when engaged by the problem of identity, the field is characterized by repeated deferrals of the critical question "What makes a Jewish (American) text Jewish?" in pragmatic performances of a historicism that takes for granted the categorical recognizability of Jewish identity. The categorical problem of Jewish identity, of course, has no simple solution; as Nathan Zuckerman, Jewish American literature's second-most-infamous Jew—after, and as a kind of final cause of, his progenitor, Alexander Portnoy—wrote in a letter to his newly Zionist brother Henry in Philip Roth's *The Counterlife*, " 'What is a Jew in the first place?' It's a question that's always had to be answered: the sound 'Jew' was not made like a rock in the world—some human voice once said 'Djoo,' pointed at somebody, and that was the beginning of what hasn't stopped since."[4] The problem that Zuckerman distinguished is only amplified when this questionable identity is used to secure the categorical legibility of a field of literary historical practice: we are left wondering how a recognizable Jewish historical subject's Jewish identity "gets into" (for lack of a better term) a text or canon, how we establish the categorical connection between the "Jewish identity" classification and the "Jewish American literature" classification. The urgency of some critics to argue, presumably against the positivism that takes for granted the structure by which Jewish writers produce Jewish literature, that Jewish literature does something Jewish or Jewishly—an iconic example is Cynthia Ozick's claim that Jewish literature worthy of the name is "liturgical," and Julian Levinson (among others) has more recently claimed that "it is possible to discern signs of distinctly Jewish creativity in the realm of imaginative literature. Such writing would be Jewish not merely because it might occasionally refer to the Bible or because it might depict characters eating bagels or complaining to their *zaydes*, but because it would truly ruminate upon, engage, and contest traditions that are central to Jewish self-definition. The Jewish novel might then be a new midrash"[5]—commits the fallacy of Kramer's "casuistry of metonymical ethnicity"; it is the already-determined identity of the writer that metonymically authorizes the search for categorical Jewish functionality. The critical urgency enacted in *Extremely Loud and Incredibly Close* provides an occasion, not least in the form of a summons, to reimagine the ground of the Jewish American literary canon free from inevitably biologized—or racialized—nationalist protocols. The book is relevant to the critique of Jewish American literary study not because its author is Jewish (he is, and has won a National Jewish Book Award to prove it)[6] nor because it represents self-evidently Jewish material (it does not) but because it compels a literary historical desire for Jewish identification to proclaim itself.

Traumatic Identification

Unsurprisingly, trauma studies has been the prevailing critical approach in the growing scholarship on Foer's book—as it has been in scholarship on 9/11 literature more generally. A frequent touchstone in trauma-studies-based 9/11 literary historical scholarship, Slavoj Žižek offers much to an intelligent critique of such work; he limns the ambivalence between negation and inhabitation that I hope to evoke by my term "irrepresentation." In his great book on the attacks, *Welcome to the Desert of the Real!*, he reminds us that the usual alternative offered apropos of historical traumas—between remembering them and forgetting them—is a false one; just as some forms of remembering actually amount to forgetting, so to really forget an event, it is necessary to remember it properly. Doing so, he helps us move past what John Duvall and Robert Marzec have called a "truism of trauma studies—the notion that trauma is unknowable."[7] As Žižek explains, "we should bear in mind that the opposite of *existence* is not nonexistence, but *insistence*: that which does not exist, continues to *insist*, striving toward existence. . . . When I miss a crucial ethical opportunity, and fail to make a move that would 'change everything,' the very nonexistence of what I *should have done* will haunt me forever: although what I did not do does not exist, its spectre continues to insist."[8] The opposition between existence and insistence active in the concept of the "specter" is particularly relevant in considering Foer's *Extremely Loud and Incredibly Close*, which, with its interest in a constellation of historical catastrophes orbiting around the precocious nine-year-old Oskar Schell, represents trauma in precisely these terms. Oskar's father, Thomas, has died in the World Trade Center on 9/11—he had a breakfast meeting at Windows on the World—and Oskar, definitely his father's son,[9] has predictably had a hard time of it since then. As he tells his mother, with a touch of hostility, "I'm not trying to find ways to be happy, and I won't" (171). Indeed, he resists his mother, both in her efforts to help him and in her own struggle with loss, and he has limited his social world almost exclusively to his paternal grandmother, who lives in the apartment building across the street. Oskar's traumatic secret is that on being sent home from school on the morning of the attacks and after listening to a series of distressed messages on the home answering machine from his father, who is trapped at the top of the North Tower (but claims to be fine), he lets the machine pick up when the phone rings, incapable of answering, and listens as his father leaves what will be a final message, a single, desperate question, "Are you there?," asked eleven times over a period of one minute and twenty-seven seconds, against, as Oskar tells it, a background of "screaming and crying" and "glass breaking, which is part of what makes me wonder if people were jumping" (301–302); the phone cuts out at 10:28 a.m., when the building starts coming down. Part of the novel's denouement involves Oskar discovering that his father had called his mother, as well, telling her that he was fine and that she should not worry, implying that the excuse Oskar has been relying on for maintaining his emotional hermeticism, the nontransferability manifested in his presumed secret, can be broken down in preparation for his eventual social reengagement.

The novel's front story follows Oskar as he searches New York City for the lock that will fit a key he finds in a vase he discovers (about a year after what he repeatedly refers to as "the worst day") on a shelf in his father's closet, assuming the discovery will reveal something significant about his father that will presumably allow him, in Žižek's terms, to "remember" his trauma "properly." He finds the key in an envelope with the word "Black" written on it, which Oskar determines must be a name, so he endeavors to alphabetically visit every person in the city with the last name Black. When (through a bit of what might defensibly be called novelistic contrivance) he finally finds William Black, whose dead father's safe-deposit box is the match for Oskar's key (and whose first name locates him near the bottom of Oskar's alphabetical list, after the point at which Oskar gives up hope), he finds someone who is only accidentally associated with his father (Oskar's father had bought a vase at an estate sale from William Black, who had not known the key was in it, shortly before 9/11, as an anniversary gift for Oskar's mother) but who has experienced his own traumatic losses: the estrangement from and then death of his father and his own divorce (from Abby, the second Black on Oskar's list; her call after Oskar's early visit, recorded on the Schells' answering machine but which Oskar only receives months later, on the day he gives up his search in despair [we assume Oskar's mother, who has been secretly sanctioning his search, has left Abby's message there for him to hear], redeems the possibility of communication from the void to which Oskar's inability to pick up the phone when his father called consigned it). Empathetic connection between individuals is provisionally barred in this book.

A primary condition of trauma is represented in this book as a failure of communication, in the form of messages rarely making their way to their intended or proper recipients. We get an important early preview of this trope, for example, in the story Oskar's grandmother tells of receiving as a child back in Dresden a very sad—dare I say "traumatic"?—letter from a detainee in a Turkish prison camp who has no apparent connection to her family (75–76). That the letter has presumably only mistakenly arrived at her family's house is the least of it; the geographical and temporal gap instantiated in the letter—not only has it made its way across Europe, but it had been sent fifteen years before it arrived—and the near-total excision of specific, identifying information from the letter (presumably by prison authorities) do nothing to attenuate its affective hold. Also previewed in this anecdote, incidentally, is the book's solution to trauma: in the wake of the flood of questions that press on Oskar's grandmother in response to the letter, she asks everybody she knows to write her a letter, in the hope of gaining triangulated knowledge from "comparisons" (78) and "connections" (79) between the "one hundred letters" she in the end compiles. Though she never learns anything about the detainee or the mystery of his letter—"I wanted to understand" (79)—she ultimately does learn about "everybody [she] knew." Thus the traumatic rupture of the letter's origin is displaced into empathetic intersubjectivity. But if trauma appears initially as a failure of communication, it is important that communication in the book is often so conspicuously a matter of interpretable mediated representation rather than self-evident immediate presentation, of writing and recordings rather than of speech; what Žižek allows us to understand as the reclaiming of the existence of trauma from its insistence is instantiated in moments when the normalized possibility of communication's rightful circuit between addresser and addressee is reinscribed.

Oskar, however, is not the novel's only victim, nor does 9/11 dominate the novel's concern with historical trauma; indeed, 9/11 often recedes behind other, more intensively represented traumas. Besides the Blacks, there is Oskar's paternal grandmother—who remains nameless—who survived the firebombing of Dresden, as did her husband, Oskar's grandfather, named, like his son, Thomas. As we come to learn, grandfather Thomas had been in love with grandmother's sister, Anna, back in Dresden, but Anna, carrying grandfather Thomas's unborn child, was killed in the Allied bombing. When grandfather Thomas and grandmother run into each other in New York after the war, the sole survivors of their respective families, Anna—or rather her loss or absence—is the unspoken basis of their relationship. By this time, grandfather Thomas has already lost his voice, having begun to lose it during "one of [his] first meals in America," when he had wanted to tell the waiter serving him that the way he had handed him the knife reminded him of Anna but found himself incapable of saying her name. After "Anna," he loses "and," then "want"—ancillary losses that stand as clear proxies for the animating structure of desire—and then all his remaining words, until finally he loses his last word, "I," eventually communicating solely with gestures and writing (16–17). Shortly before father Thomas is born, grandfather Thomas, unable to make peace with the fact that the present is now only secondary, an always-inadequate replacement for what was lost with Anna, disappears, abandoning grandmother to raise their about-to-be-born child. We can read as a comment[10] on this impasse grandmother and grandfather Thomas's "rule" of marking out "Something" and "Nothing" places in their apartment, about which we learn a bit later: Something places are those where life is presumed to be normal, but Nothing places are preserves to which the couple can retreat when they "need" or sometimes (and indeed increasingly) just "want" to disappear—from life in general but more specifically from each other. Not only do the number and size of Nothing places grow, to the point where their "apartment was more Nothing than Something," but "a friction began to arise between Nothing and Something," as when light from a room spills under a Nothing door into the Something hallway or when "the Nothing vase cast a Something shadow, like the memory of someone you've lost. . . . It became difficult to navigate from Something to Something without accidentally walking through Nothing" (110–111). That the vase in this passage repeats the one Oskar finds in his father's closet emphasizes precisely Žižek's tension between existence and insistence manifested in Oskar's traumatic experience of his father.

Though grandfather Thomas writes his son a letter every day after his departure, he only ever sends one to its intended recipient (the novel shows this letter, dated 12 April 1978, to its readers; it is marked everywhere with the characteristic red pen of Oskar's father, constituting a kind of barred record of the meeting that grandfather Thomas could not let happen—a proscription in which Oskar's father is shown to be complicit in the scene in which he seeks out and finds grandfather Thomas in Dresden following his receipt of this 1978 letter, a scene in which neither Thomas lets on to recognizing the other and in which we are forced to face the possibility of a recognition that must be read as spectrally insistent rather than self-evident insofar as neither has ever been immediately present to the other). Just as Oskar cannot bear to face his father before the imminence of his death, so grandfather Thomas cannot bear to face his son before the imminence of his own social death; both imminences signal the impossibility of the only legible future. That it is the same person who occasions, in Žižek's words, the "miss[ed] . . . crucial ethical opportunity" for both Oskar and his grandfather emphasizes their parallel trauma. Neither the attacks on the

World Trade Center nor the firebombing of Dresden (nor the atomic bombing of Hiroshima, for one other notable example, which the novel adds to the traumatic mix on the occasion of a rather harrowing report Oskar presents to his class) is really the issue here; rather, what is really traumatic—what makes all the ethical difference—is failing to face and voice one's feelings for, and therefore connection to, another at a moment of crisis.[11] As Oskar describes the final message from his father, "Why did he keep asking? Was he waiting for someone to come home? And why didn't he say 'anyone'? *Is anyone there?* 'You' is just one person. Sometimes I think he knew I was there. Maybe he kept asking it to give me time to get brave enough to pick up. Also, there was so much space between the times he asked. There are fifteen seconds between the third and the fourth, which is the longest space" (301).[12] Neither Oskar nor his grandfather is able to communicate across this "space" of a suspended present that demands a response: as grandfather Thomas writes of the Dresden bombing in the 12 April 1978 letter, "Sometimes I think if I could tell you what happened to me that night, I could leave that night behind me, maybe I could come home to you, but that night has no beginning or end" (208), and Oskar admits that he has avoided "the truth . . . That he's [i.e., his father's] dead" (321). The insistent specter of an alternative past denied a future—a claim that repeats the traumatic moment neither can traverse—haunts all these characters.

That the first word grandfather Thomas loses is "Anna" and the last is "I" insists on this problem of communication: his immobility positions him before a void that communication cannot cross. As he explains in his first letter to his son, "the distance that wedged itself between me and my happiness wasn't the world, it wasn't the bombs and burning buildings, it was me" (17). Similarly, Oskar makes bead jewelry for his mother that spells out in Morse code his father's final answering-machine messages—precisely that about which he finds himself incapable of straightforwardly telling his mother or grandmother (35). For both characters, the failure to communicate, sharpened by the unforgiving specter of successful communication, parallels their inability to narrate themselves out of this suspended, voided present. A shared action—Oskar and grandfather Thomas digging up father Thomas's empty coffin on the second anniversary of his death, filling it with all the thousands of grandfather Thomas's unsent letters, and reburying it—will allow them each to, in Žižek's vocabulary, "remember" their respective traumas "properly" in order "to really forget" them. Though Oskar does not, finally, learn anything about his father or his death, he is, finally, able to confess—and ask for forgiveness—"for not being able to tell anyone" (302) that he could not speak to his father as the North Tower collapsed. If in doing this he is able to assert the fact of his connection to his father, the agency through which this becomes possible is that he is finally able to face his inability to face the fact of his father's death. Trauma is experienced as the failure to experience the traumatic event.

Thus, if trauma had been characterized by a failure of communication *haunted* by the specter of successful communication, then here in this therapeutic reversal the failure is now *displaced* by the specter of successful communication. Philippe Codde, a recent critic of Foer's novel, points out another example of the novel's elevation of a kind of restorative communication that, even as it is deferred, nonetheless gestures toward salutary remediation: in the one letter grandfather Thomas sent to his son (the one dated 12 April 1978), he, in describing the Dresden carnage, explains that, in the confusion following the bombing, "I looked for my parents and for Anna and for you" (214), eliding the difference between the unborn child he had fathered with Anna and the living son he has fathered with Anna's sister.[13] Though his inability to communicate with the first child is repeated in his (different) inability to communicate with the second child, we see the haunting possibility—however displaced, from the nonexistent child to Oskar's father—of successful communication. As though marking this unstable, pregnant transposition, father Thomas, with his ubiquitous red pen, has circled "you."[14]

We can read trauma in Foer's novel, therefore, as a problem of forestalled narrative. In Oskar's failing to pick up the phone and in grandfather Thomas's failing to face the son he has fathered (after establishing a rule with grandmother when they decide to get married that they will have "no children" [85]), the two characters similarly foreclose the possibility of narrating themselves out of the suspension of their respective losses and therefore into a history of themselves with futurity. Each is unable to recognize a future. This discloses another, perhaps more grave, dimension of historical trauma. Žižek's book is probably best known for his claim that we already recognized what happened on 9/11 from the movies we watch: "the landscape and shots of the collapsing towers could not but be reminiscent of the most breathtaking scenes in big catastrophe productions. . . . The unthinkable which happened was the object of fantasy, so that, in a way, America got what it fantasized about, and that was the biggest surprise."[15] For Žižek, 9/11 is such a salient event (especially for criticism) because it shows us that getting what is already the object of desire is the most disturbing and anxious possibility of all. As he casts the problem, we get it wrong when we adopt the clichéd presumption that 9/11 forced America to see the reality that our imperial consumerist fiction had allowed us for so long to ignore; in fact, what 9/11 did—and we are still reeling from the shock— is force us to see the fantasy that structures reality. "Much more difficult than to denounce/unmask (what appears as) reality as fiction is to recognize the part of fiction in 'real' reality."[16] That is, the trauma of 9/11 is its direct display of fantasy, its revelation to us of our desire; what is really traumatic is the discovery that we experience the historical-identitarian fantasies we impose on experience. If Oskar and his grandparents are denied a chance to narrate the futures of their respective histories, then the really disturbing, traumatic, part of this, we might say, following Žižek, is that this failure discloses history's dependence on its imagined—its fantasized, its desired—futures. Insofar as the critical interest in "trauma" in fact anchors—by figuring—the historiographic search for a recognizable narrative, Žižek allows us to see how 9/11 occupies compelling ground in a critique of identity. In disclosing to us the imperious agency of our own desire, the trauma of 9/11 provides us an occasion to reformulate the literary critical concept of identity: we can now think of it not primarily as something represented in narrative but more fundamentally as a specter haunting the narrative place where it is desired, supporting through the agency of recognition the fantasies used to navigate—and narrate—historical experience. Thought of in this way, identity—such a powerful and pervasive literary historical instrument—can be retained as a useful critical term.

One of the problems with talking critically about 9/11 literature is that we are still witnessing a proliferation of attempts to inscribe this event in recognizable terms—and in a variety of registers, including (in no particular order) literature, politics, architecture and urban design, psychoanalysis, citizenship, economics, film, ethics, nationalism, and religion, to name some of the more conspicuous ones. Part of the horror for Americans in 9/11, surely, is that no definitive narratives of its beginning, middle, and end have yet presented themselves.[17] One could add to an accounting of 9/11's traumatic impact—add to the loss of life and the threat to US citizens' nationalized sense of security, for example—its having effected an uncomfortably insistent awareness of our demand that experience be recognizable.[18] Thus the trauma of 9/11 is that the event is not where we want it to be, its meaning's place taken by our failure to definitively understand it. That 9/11's overdetermination destabilizes the normalizing function of understanding, destabilizes our attempt to redeem its horror and violence, may help account for why criticism of 9/11 literature—and of *Extremely Loud and Incredibly Close* in particular—is so interested in the idea of trauma, as an expanding host of scholarly books, journal articles, and special issues (such as the Fall 2011 issue of *MFS: Modern Fiction Studies* edited by Duvall and Marzec, timed to coincide with the tenth anniversary of the attacks) attest. By focusing less on the unavailability of a traumatic event itself and more on the tensions through which trauma is represented or manifested or accessed in literature, trauma theory names an attempt to identify history's relevance, to continue to be able to talk about history; it remains attractive, presumably, because it proposes a hermeneutic for reading apparently destabilizing manifest cultural content for an identifiable, potentially normative latent content. Indeed, it can be seen as one of the few ascendant secular methods of talking about redemption in critical terms—regardless of whether critics want to talk about an individual, collective, or national subject. "Trauma" names the desire (and provides some tools) to recast something anxiously incoherent as something identifiably coherent.

An analysis of this productivist interest in recovering from the past's traumatic displacement of meaning a pragmatic—and interpretive—agency narratively useful to a history of a self-evident subject can be useful to a critique of identity-based literary scholarship. Too frequently the trauma-studies tack takes form in a therapeutic drive to reclaim narrative coherence, and through it subjective coherence, from trauma's offending incoherence; the frequency with which one comes across vague bromides such as "come to terms" and "work through" in recent literary scholarship is pretty surprising. For Ilka Saal, for example, the reconstructed ability to communicate one's tragic past is coincident with a regained, if untheorized, "sense of self": "Trauma, in order to be communicated and integrated into one's personal knowledge of the past as well as that of the collective, must be narrativized."[19] Trauma disrupts a cogent social arrangement and thus destabilizes the subject's ability to narrate his or her self and world; the drama of literature concerned with trauma is the search for the means to revive this narrative capacity. For Saal, the particular interest of *Extremely Loud and Incredibly Close* is its enactment of what she terms "trauma transfer," a "prominent narrative strategy emerging in US literature in the wake of September 11" that she describes as "the reading of the current trauma through the lens of a previous one"[20]—specifically, Saal focuses on how Foer's novel refracts 9/11 through World War II atrocities in order to pave the way for a decentered intersubjectivity attuned to the open possibilities of multiple and possibly discontinuous voices and discourses. Despite such rhetoric, however, this kind of work takes for granted a more or less consistent transhistorical subject whose human being is cemented in an empathetic capacity to be similarly traumatized across history; it presumes the spectral community whose "coherence" it claims to be endangered. The implication of this literary historical project's expectation of a "constructive solution"[21] to trauma is that through trauma studies literature can provide positive knowledge about how to be human (not least in providing positive knowledge about how to narrate that capacity). More fundamentally, literature in this literary historical context is valued for its documentary capacities.

Cathy Caruth is widely cited in a lot of 9/11 literary history for recommending trauma as a powerful critical rubric for allowing us to theorize history as a densely ethical modality rather than simply an epistemological one. The point of thinking about trauma as a methodology is not to reveal or discover an occluded but self-evident traumatic origin that, once uncovered, will serve as interpretive key to a significant, but interrupted, history. On the contrary, in trauma "we can begin to recognize the possibility of a history which is no longer straightforwardly referential. . . . Through the notion of trauma . . . we can understand that a re-thinking of reference is not aimed at eliminating history, but at resituating it in our understanding, that is, of precisely permitting *history* to arise where *immediate understanding* may not." As Caruth explains, the traumatic scenario is characterized not so much by a period of forgetting that occurs after a traumatic event but rather by the fact that the victim was never fully conscious during the event, that the traumatic event is in fact never fully experienced. Caruth insists that the "historical power of the trauma" derives not simply from the fact that the experience is repeated after its forgetting but that "it is only in and through its inherent forgetting that it is first experienced at all." And since the trauma "is not experienced as it occurs, it is fully evident only in connection with another place, and in another time"; it is precisely—paradoxically—the unconsciousness of the event that preserves the event "in its literality. For history to be a history of trauma means that it is referential precisely to the extent that it is not fully perceived as it occurs. . . . History can be grasped only in the very inaccessibility of its occurrence." Because it is justifiable to speak of trauma in terms of epistemological accuracy only in the absence of any such content of the traumatic experience as might make accuracy an analytical virtue, Caruth turns to focus on the ethical framework in which trauma and its analysis also operate. Caruth enables an understanding of trauma as a displacement in a something and a somewhere else; and *history* names the condition of this displacement or narrative reinscription of a recognizable subject. Thus, as Caruth goes on to suggest, "the traumatic nature of history means that events are only historical to the extent that they implicate others"; "history, like trauma, is never simply one's own. . . . History is precisely the way we are implicated in each other's traumas."[22]

Understandably, Caruth—with her interest in reformulating the ground of a collective subject—is a frequent point of reference in the growing scholarship on *Extremely Loud and Incredibly Close*, which characteristically tends to make trauma productive, to use it as a means to reinscribe the possibility of communication and narration that crisis has suspended.[23] This criticism casts Oskar's trauma as linking him—necessarily—to others who have experienced trauma; on the one hand isolating the individual, trauma also creates a space of common experience for its disparate victims, a collective subject of grief, and consciousness of this commonality—as a modality of community—is cast as beneficial. Thus a productive reinscription of identity (taking form in what has been variously termed "communication," "traumatic solidarity," or "global community," for example) is the instrumentalist-positivist fantasy largely through which literary criticism has read—has desired—the trauma of 9/11.[24] But if trauma provides a potentially powerful method to critique an event's overdetermination by already-recognizable identity categories, at the same time the dominant direction taken by trauma-based readings of Foer's 9/11 novel—namely, using trauma to restabilize an ethical communitarian identity secured by the promise of positivity[25]—is troubling, precisely by shortchanging this critique of identity in the interest of narrating a recognizable redemption. The problem, as Žižek allows us to understand, is desire: the desire of Oskar for determinacy and certainty and relief repeated in the desire of the novel's critics for an ethically useful or productive representational or documentary reading. While I would not go so far as to say that it is disingenuous to narrate 9/11 as a story about redeemed loss and bereavement, I think it probably *is* disingenuous to ignore the role of our own literary critical desire—a desire that, being born *of* recognition, is necessarily also *for* the recognizable—in constituting it as such.

I think part of the problem may be that Caruth's focus on "ethics," reproduced but not sufficiently criticized or theorized in so much of the scholarship on Foer that cites her, might tend to privilege an ethnical agent or subject. Michael Rothberg, another perceptive critic of "trauma," though one who for some unaccountable reason has not achieved the citational prestige that Caruth has, argues for a concept of "traumatic realism" as a way of contending with the epistemological problems of analyzing representations of trauma that Caruth displaces with her concern with ethics. "Traumatic realism develops out of and in response to the demand for documentation that an extreme historical event poses to those who would seek to understand it." But Rothberg cautions that "documentation" has two elements—"reference and narrative"—that demand careful attention. "On the one hand, the demand for documentation calls for an archive of facts or details referring to the event. On the other hand, the active sense of documentation indicates the need for the construction of a realistic narrative that would shape those details into a coherent story." Traumatic realism is a "productive" rather than passively "mimetic" mode of representation or documentation "beyond direct reference and coherent narrative" that at the same time does "not fully abandon the possibility for some kind of reference and some kind of narrative." Moreover, as productive, it seeks also to "transform its readers" in their relationship to "post-traumatic culture." Traumatic realism "seeks both to construct access to a previously unknowable object and to instruct an audience in how to approach that object."[26] Emphasizing the need—the desire—for a documentary archive and a narrative to describe it, Rothberg offers critics a way of maintaining the critique of identity without recognitively normalizing it. The short literary history of Foer's book certainly suggests a desire to read the book as redeeming loss, as a story of bereavement and forgiveness and therefore of Oskar's—and the US's—ability to redemptively reinscribe 9/11 in a narrative with a future. But this desire—subtended as it is by the expectation of an identity interdependent with the possibility of such a narrative—displaces this goal, and the book is well aware of this disturbingly counternormalizing fact.

Jewish Stealth

By the time we meet Oskar, his trauma takes the form of a self-destructive compulsion to invent (and reinvent) the scene of his father's death, attesting to Caruth's tension between epistemology and ethics: he confesses to the "renter" who came to stay with his grandmother after 9/11, who is in fact his returned grandfather, though Oskar does not yet know this, "I need to know how he died. . . . I want to stop inventing. If I could know how he died, exactly how he died, I wouldn't have to invent him dying inside an elevator that was stuck between floors, which happened to some people, and I wouldn't have to imagine him trying to crawl outside of the building, which I saw video of one person doing on a Polish site, or trying to use a tablecloth as a parachute, like some of the people who were in Windows on the World actually did. There were so many different ways to die, and I just need to know which was his" (257).[27] As Oskar admits of the photograph he keeps of a man falling from one of the Twin Towers (a single frame from a "Portuguese video" he found on the Internet), "There's one body that could be him. It's dressed like he was, and when I magnify it until the pixels are so big that it stops looking like a person, sometimes I see glasses. Or I think I can. I probably can't. It's just me wanting it to be him" (256–257). It is this desire that knows itself to be ungrounded, vain, impossible, and therefore really just a desire (only when Oskar magnifies the image beyond the threshold of recognition does he imagine that he recognizes his father's glasses) that, precisely in figuring the recognition-based reclamation of loss that "traumatic" literary criticism demands of the book, positions the book as a powerful tool in the critique of identity.[28] If the engagement with the trope of trauma in Foer's novel enables critical investigation of a pervasive literary historical investment in normalizing categorical identity as a legitimizing interpretive tool, then the book also offers a powerful tool to the critique of specifically Jewish American literary study. My point here is not to argue that *something* literary historically Jewish is somehow present in the novel, that the Jewish American canon is enacted in a reading that finds—by interpreting—a Jewish presence in its putative absence. That said, the Holocaust (which, whatever else it may be, can probably with some justification be called a Jewish metonym) recommends itself as a relevant approach into a discussion of such concealment, as its absence from a book that cites so many historical traumas is conspicuous. But in that case, we again return to the problem of desire and must accept that the search for Jewish identity determines the products of this inquiry (midrashic or not) and their categorical relevance; that is, we can find the Holocaust, and through it Jewish categoricalness, because we are looking for it, because we have already marked the text as Jewish.

I am certainly not alone in noting the conspicuous absence of the Holocaust in the book. Though Saal claims that the "primary" trauma transfer in the book is from Dresden onto 9/11, which "serves to elevate the latter to the level of the mythical and sacred," even more important for her is "the spectral reference to the Holocaust contained in the Dresden analogy."[29] However, there is an obvious (and curious) tension between the referential instability brought to mind by Saal's central trope of spectrality and the referential certainty secured by her verb "contained"; or, rather, any instability conjured by her invocation of the specter is decisively exorcised by the documentary positivism summoned by the metaphorology of containment. Indeed, "while evoked only indirectly and in spectral form, the Holocaust serves as a key traumatic reference, haunting and complicating Foer's text."[30] Saal's argument here understandably relies on the circulation through Foer's book of the Simon Goldberg figure, a man living in Dresden about whom we hear in two of grandfather's letters. Goldberg, we gather from the first of these letters, written (but not posted) on 21 May 1963, is an intellectual and a friend of grandmother's father. In a second letter—the one dated 12 April 1978, the only one Oskar's grandfather actually sent to Oskar's father—we learn that Oskar's great-grandfather hid Goldberg, presumably during the war (we hear in this letter also of nightly air-raid sirens in Dresden) and presumably from anti-Jewish policies. Later in this same letter, we learn that Goldberg had sent a letter to grandfather Thomas, care of Oskar's great-grandfather (i.e., Anna and grandmother's father), from "Westerbork transit camp in Holland," which, grandfather Thomas writes, is "where the Jews from our region were sent, from there they went either to their work or to their deaths" (215). The important thing here is that the reader's belief that Goldberg is Jewish is proportional to how easily he fits—how easily we can fit him—into a network of hermeneutic associations: Goldberg is often a Jewish name, Jews living in Germany in the '30s and '40s were subject to increasing legalized persecution to the extent that if they were going to stay and survive, they would need to be hidden, and Goldberg is eventually interned at a transit camp known for its Jewish population, an associational power amplified by its being itself associated with—in serving as the transit point for—the most famous Jew since Moses. For Saal, "Goldberg's spectral haunting of the grandfather's narrative," while not necessarily mattering greatly on the "diegetic level," prompts pressing "speculative questions" for interpretation of the book; the issue, for Saal as much as for anyone reading Foer's novel, is that if Goldberg is a Jew, then we must wonder about the implications of his telling grandfather Thomas, in a letter that grandfather Thomas tells father Thomas about in his own letter, "For obvious reasons that need not be explained, you made a strong impression on me."[31] Could Oskar's grandfather be Jewish? (And therefore could there be Jewish content in the book, could it be a Jewish book?) This is a question that Saal admits the novel "refuses" to answer, but her argument is grounded in overwriting this supposed deferral in a definitive declaration that the novel is about the Holocaust, one she is able to make only by leveraging a positivization of Goldberg's Jewish identity, closing her essay by claiming that "Oskar's voice might sound loudest at the end, but underneath it we can—if we choose to—still decipher those other voices haunting the text, defying closure and facile appropriation: the distant voices of Grandma and Grandpa Schell and, above all, the muted voice of Simon Goldberg."³² Saal is on to something important when she admits—parenthetically—that we can discover the Holocaust's presence in the novel "if we choose to" find it there, but she pulls back from this significant insight; the Holocaust for Saal can only "haunt" Foer's novel, that is, because Saal has already decided that the novel, to invoke her keyword, in fact positively "contains" the Holocaust. And she can make this determination only because of her certainty that Goldberg is Jewish—an identification she has already insisted the novel "refuses." Saal allows us to understand the relevance to a consideration of Foer's novel of the Holocaust and Jewish stealth, but she does not adequately show the way. In order to take up such a consideration, I want to turn to Isaac Bashevis Singer, as he brings down a powerful midrash (as I am sure many scholars of Jewish American literature would agree) not merely on the Holocaust but more fundamentally on the critically fraught intersection of identity, desire, and representation.

Toward the end of *Enemies, a Love Story*, Singer's protagonist, Herman Broder, articulates a theory of Jewish identity. Admitting to himself—or perhaps trying to convince himself—that "we're not really alive anymore,"³³ Broder's evasion is of course an attempt to escape responsibility, an abdication before what in the book is an incontrovertible failure of history, certainly after the Holocaust, to align with human desire. Broder has carried on an elaborate deception for a number of years in order to maintain at least two lives—one in Coney Island with Yadwiga, the simpleminded Polish peasant girl who had been his well-off family's servant before the war, who hid him in her own Jew-hating family's hayloft during the war, and who immigrated with him to America after the war, and one in The Bronx with Masha, the sexy, already-married nihilist he met in a DP camp at the war's close. And this is to say nothing of his day job with the morally dubious and entrepreneurial Rabbi Lambert. But now he finds himself disclaiming both choice and desire: "Herman no longer felt that he was in control of things, nor did he want to be. He had become a fatalist in practice as well as in theory. He was willing to let the Powers lead him" (245). When the lie that he has perpetuated with Yadwiga in Coney Island as cover for his visits to Masha in the Bronx—namely, that he is a traveling book salesman—finally takes on an air of reality after Tamara, the wife he had thought to have been murdered in Poland, returns, exhumed from the past to which Broder had thought he lost her (and to which he left her), and asks him to help her run her uncle's Jewish bookstore, he is convinced that nothing "wasn't a game. Nowhere could he find anything that was 'real,' not even in the so-called 'exact sciences' " (247). One night in the Catskills, Herman "imagine[s]" hearing the screech of a chicken or duck and, prompted by his recent experience in Europe, thinks of slaughter: "Treblinka was everywhere" (112). Here is a great example of what Žižek is on to when he writes that historical trauma should be understood not as the Real intruding into an illusory sphere but rather precisely as the fantasmatic entering reality: "It is not that reality entered our image [i.e., on 9/11]: the image entered and shattered our reality."[34] When the Holocaust, dislodged from what might have been thought to be its historical specificity and rendered a universal metaphor or fantasmatic specter, overdetermines all experience by overwhelming any other interpretive paradigm, there can be no hope of any kind of determinate or determining, normative, "real" history. Though in our literary historical practice we may want to invest the Holocaust with the power of categorical Jewishness, this desire threatens to trump any possibility of collective identity.

Broder's attempted evasion is relevant to a discussion of representation and identity insofar as it functions as a literary critical cautionary tale about how identity's categorical fixity deconstructs on the desire for its self-evidence:

In Herman's private philosophy, survival itself was based on guile. From microbe to man, life prevailed generation to generation by sneaking past the jealous powers of destruction. Just like the Tzivkever smugglers in World War I, who stuffed their boots and blouses with tobacco, secreted all manner of contraband about their bodies, and stole across borders, breaking laws and bribing officials—so did every bit of protoplasm, or conglomerate of protoplasm furtively traffic its way from epoch to epoch. It had been so when the first bacteria appeared in the slime at the ocean's edge and would be so when the sun became a cinder and the last living creature on earth froze to death, or perished in whichever way the final biological drama dictated. Animals had accepted the precariousness of existence and the necessity for flight and stealth; only man sought certainty and instead succeeded in accomplishing his own downfall. The Jew had always managed to smuggle his way in through crime and madness. He had stolen into Canaan and into Egypt. Abraham had pretended that Sarah was his sister. The whole two thousand years of exile, beginning with Alexandria, Babylon, and Rome and ending in the ghettos of Warsaw, Lodz, and Vilna had been one great act of smuggling. The Bible, the Talmud, and the Commentaries instruct the Jew in one strategy: flee from evil, hide from danger, avoid showdowns, give the angry powers of the universe as wide a berth as possible. The Jew never looked askance at the deserter who crept into a cellar or attic while armies clashed in the streets outside.

Herman, the modern Jew, had extended this principle one step: he no longer even had his faith in the Torah to depend on. He was deceiving not only Abimelech but Sarah and Hagar as well. Herman had not sealed a covenant with God and had no use for Him. He didn't want to have his seed multiply like the sands by the sea. His whole life was a game of stealth—the sermons he had written for Rabbi Lambert, the books he sold to rabbis and yeshiva boys, his acceptance of Yadwiga's conversion to Judaism, and Tamara's favors. (247–248)

What is Herman's self-justification if not an attempt—albeit a perverse one, perhaps—at what we might call midrashic identification? But the Jewish paradigm surviving here, even if grounded in "the Bible, the Talmud, and the Commentaries," in fact subverts any secure (and securely Jewish) bedrock that we might initially expect to desire from such grounding. Broder displaces categorical Jewish content with a kind of tactics that, if apparently specifically *Jewish*, unfortunately (i.e., for those interested in a literary historical category of Jewish identity) are shared by "microbes," "protoplasm," and "bacteria" that probably are not. In the passage's opposition between what it labels "certainty" and the act of "smuggl[ing]" or "st[ealing] across borders," and specifically in its indictment of "certainty" as the vainly foolhardy pole of that opposition, we get a possible counterimage of the traumatic ethics so characteristic of recent criticism of Foer's novel: here, cutting across legible identity categories is far more disruptive to the possibility of solidarity than productive of it. Thus, if the passage initially looks (at least to a certain kind of desire) to be engaged in a reinscription of the possibility of Jewish identity, instead, or rather at the same time, in its narrative of Jews surviving by smuggling themselves into history and sneaking past the "angry powers of the universe" (through "crime," "madness," "flight," and "stealth"), the "borders" of Jewishness become so unsettled that there is no longer a stable distinction between inside and outside, between "Sarah" and "Abimelech." If we are attracted by the possibility of a "midrashic" reading that finds Jewishness by interpreting the Holocaust in literary texts, we stand warned that such a project proceeds on the categorical failure of Jewish self-evidence. We remain in need of a way to justify the categorization of "Jewish" literature.

As the discussions throughout *The Impossible Jew* attest, I see the value of identity in the study of Jewish American literature, but I am worried about how to retain this valuable concept as something critically relevant to the literature without at the same time reinscribing an unjustified and politically dubious nationalism that inevitably grounds itself in an assertion of biologistic self-evidence. Foer's *Extremely Loud and Incredibly Close* is part of this project not because the novel theorizes or normalizes a concept of identity outside an identitarian or nationalist rubric but because it mercilessly toys with our literary historical *desire for* identity—and in so doing forces it to proclaim itself precisely at the point of its normalization. The one site of promise for the critic seeking to justify the book's inclusion in the Jewish canon by way of Jewish content is the briefly mentioned Simon Goldberg. But it is the specter of mere metonymical affiliation's displacement of self-evident definitiveness, far more than the specter of the Holocaust, that hangs over every attempt at categorical Jewish identification in and of Foer's text. The book's front story certainly is set in what could easily be found to be a Jewish context. Oskar Schell—bearing what could be a Jewish name,[35] in an association pregnant with the potential stoked by Goldberg's letter—lives on the Upper West Side of Manhattan and sees a psychiatrist named "Dr. Fein" (43). His dead father was a jeweler who dealt with diamond merchants (36).[36] In grandfather Thomas's unsent 1963 letter, we learn that Oskar's great-grandfather (i.e., Anna and grandmother's father) buries old books and kisses books that fall on the floor, practices that are ascribed to the fact that "literature was the only religion her [Anna's] father practiced" (114) but that also repeat traditional Jewish practices. Grandfather Thomas writes in his letter of 11 September 2003, this one unsent because it is written two years after its addressee's death, about father Thomas's having tracked him down in Dresden, after which visit, he says, "I stopped eating, I got so skinny that the bathwater would collect between my bones" (278), a description that, given a Jewish context, could be found to suggest a concentration-camp victim. In a dream related to Oskar by his grandmother (again in a letter—communication in this book is so often written),[37] a dream whose salient feature is time's spinning backward from catastrophe to wholeness, from buildings collapsing and families torn apart to love's ability to unify, we are told, "My dream went all the way back to the beginning. / The rain rose into the clouds, and the animals descended the ramp. / Two by two" (312); indeed, in one of Oskar's grandmother's earlier narratives, she describes the apartment that Oskar's grandfather lived in when she met him again in New York as so full of animals and birdcages and fish tanks that it was "like Noah's ark" (82).[38] Again it is an image that, given a desire to find Jewish content, can certainly be made to yield Jewish content. And in Oskar's final triumph over despair, initiated by the clever trick of rearranging a series of photographs showing a body falling from one of the Twin Towers so that when he flips through them, the body is seen to rise up to its life rather than fall down to its death, a trick extended by his imagining what he could do with more pictures, extending life's dominion further into death—in this triumph over despair, he imagines seeing his father on the morning of September 11 moving farther and farther from the World Trade Center and his breakfast meeting at Windows on the World and closer and closer to home, including a scene on the IRT, traveling uptown rather than downtown: Oskar imagines his father backing up through the turnstile and walking home backward "as he read the *New York Times* from right to left" (326).

In fact, if we consider the novel's motif of reorienting history—of reimagining its direction—as more than merely clever but rather as a significant part of the work Foer's book does, it discloses a further turn of the novel's engagement with an important critique of identity. In one of grandmother's narratives, she writes of the evening of 9/11, when she had Oskar with her at her apartment because Oskar's mother had gone downtown to put up posters. After Oskar fell asleep on her lap, she put on the TV with the volume turned down, watching repeated images:

> The same pictures over and over.
> Planes going into buildings.
> Bodies falling.
> People waving shirts out of high windows.
> Planes going into buildings.
> Bodies falling.
> Planes going into buildings.
> People covered in gray dust.
> Bodies falling.
> Buildings falling.
> Planes going into buildings.
> Planes going into buildings.
> Bodies falling.
> People waving shirts out of high windows.
> Bodies falling.
> Planes going into buildings. (230)

Repetition is so often a mechanism of traumatic suspension in this book. When grandfather Thomas sees the attacks on the World Trade Center (again on TV—on a grid of screens in the front window of an electronics store back in Dresden, where he fled from a future with Oskar's grandmother and a child whose mother was not Anna), he describes watching "the same images over and over, as if the world itself were repeating" (272), a structure itself repeated in the bank of TV screens, all repeating the same image; this construction simultaneously suggests Oskar's inability to move outside the suspended moment of his father's death and attests that New York in September 2001 repeats Dresden in February 1945, confirming also grandfather Thomas's inability to move outside the suspended moment of his own loss. Back in grandmother's living room, Oskar's mother's terrible chore has repeated grandmother's abandonment by grandfather Thomas, which had been signaled by his leaving for the airport so many years earlier with a heavy, filled suitcase instead of the light, empty one he usually took (i.e., so that he could fill it with the magazines and newspapers he would bring back so that grandmother could learn idiomatic English, in service to her unful-filled desire to erase the traces of the German loss of her family): "She took the posters downtown that afternoon. She filled a rolling suitcase with them. I thought of your grandfather. I wondered where he was at that moment" (229).

The static repetition on grandmother's TV articulates trauma's structure of inescapability. But this is precisely the problem with a literary critical preoccupation with "trauma," oriented, as it is, around the recognition—or, more tendentiously, the identification—of a determining narrative it posits. To emphasize—to look for—this traumatic machinery is to overdetermine historical narrative: the fixation on the past, the orientation backward, demanded and operated by the critical trope of "trauma" already identifies history as the history of a subject whose agency or proper narrative we expect to recognize. Indeed, it is impossible to avoid this overdetermination if history is directed backward. But Foer's novel imagines an escape from this nationalist trap by reorienting history forward, toward the future. For grandmother, the inescapability of the catastrophe replaying itself endlessly on the screen repeats her own trauma, her own degrading suffering: "I didn't want to get up. I wanted to lie in my own waste, which is what I deserved. I wanted to be a pig in my own filth. . . . I wanted so much for it to be me under the rubble" (231–232). And yet, in contrast to her husband-manqué and anticipating her grandson, grandmother in fact *can* imagine an escape. As she writes to Oskar, "When I looked at you, my life made sense. Even the bad things made sense. They were necessary to make you possible / . . . / My parents' lives made sense. / My grandparents'. / Even Anna's life. / But I knew the truth, and that's why I was so sad. / Every moment before this one depends on this one" (232). Grandmother's theory of history as proleptic dependency will anticipate the personal response that Oskar finally receives from Stephen Hawking, in which the physicist, to whom Oskar has written at least five letters since 9/11,[39] writes, "I'm sure I don't have to tell you that the vast majority of the universe is composed of dark matter. The fragile balance depends on things we'll never be able to see, hear, smell, taste, or touch. Life itself depends on them. What's real? What isn't real? Maybe those aren't the right questions to be asking. What does life depend on? / I wish I had made things for life to depend on" (305). Thinking about history as dependency allows grandmother, and now, more significantly, Oskar, to imagine a future that had up to this point been impossible. The problem with trauma is that it is directed toward the past: it is a past-oriented history that operates primarily, as the scholarship on Foer's novel has shown, through the mechanics of recognition, by shoring up categorical identities that function fundamentally through being known in the sense of being documented. By looking backward in order to account for the already recognizable, the orientation around trauma operates under the umbrella of identity. Foer's novel, however, reconceptualizes history. Hawking's gloss on grandmother's idea of "dependency" alters the terms of historiography: rather than using knowledge to contain an identifiable history through the restrictive and categorical operation of a determining subject, *Extremely Loud and Incredibly Close* offers a theory of history that, resituating its origin in a future on which historiographic narrative depends rather than a past for which historiographic narrative accounts, is not so much known as made, produced in thought and activity. If the turn from an epistemological question to an ethical one here recalls Caruth's reinscription of a collective subject, this displacement in fact operates quite differently. In Foer's novel, identity—that is, that machine that categorically underwrites history—is displaced from a secure past that should be *known* to a possible future that can be *desired*.

My argument here, I want to emphasize, is neither that Foer's book lacks Jewish content nor that it has Jewish content; the point is precisely not to displace the book's invocation of this problem about categoricality and identification in the reactionary positivism of an alternative between its being a Jewish book and its not being a Jewish book. Rather, it is that the book's Jewishness is dependent on our desire to find it there. More to the point, Foer's novel seems to articulate this fact and make it an object of critical focus: in a book that mentions so many of the twentieth century's catastrophes (the firebombing of Dresden, Hiroshima, the 9/11 attacks [let us call it the long twentieth century], "the Spanish Civil War, and the genocide in East Timor, and bad stuff that happened in Africa" [154], not to mention Kent State, apartheid, and the Bay of Pigs), the absence of the Holocaust—at once the synecdoche of modern catastrophic historical trauma in general and a particular catastrophic historical trauma that is identifiably (if met-onymically) *Jewish*—screams out. But this scream, which we might want to read as representing identity's scream for recognition, is in fact already recognized—it has been marked by the machine of our liter-ary historical desire for identity, a desire that transposes identity from the positive representation where it had in fact only been presumed to be secure to the negative space of its own deferral. No longer adminis-tered by the protocols of documentary positivism, Jewishness in Foer's novel proclaims a categorical recognizability that constitutively eludes the critical literary historical desire for it and in doing so is liberated from the nationalistic expectation of self-representation: Jewishness is not the kind of something that gets represented, or gets to represent itself, here. The particularity of Jewishness becomes legible only in this abandonment of particularistic self-evidence and categorical belonging, only in this irruptive emergence of universality. It is Jewish categorical-ity, not Jewish historical specificity, that haunts this book. If Herman Broder has made possible a redefinition of Jewishness as stealth, offer-ing perhaps a literary historical hermeneutic for which Jewish pres-ence is announced by its apparent absence, in doing so he in fact points toward an alternate path for Jewish American literary study: rather than being located where we recognize its appearance, literary history's Jew is displaced from the representational site of its concrete exposition by the specter of a nationalist desire.

Conclusion

Minority Report

As I suggested at the outset, I am aware of—and a bit anxious about—the fine line I am trying to walk in *The Impossible Jew*. On the one hand, this book is a polemic, full of vitriol and bile, but on the other hand, in attacking the current arrangement I am trying to justify myself to others and convince them to join forces. *The Impossible Jew* is directed at anyone who thinks that the status quo between Jewish American literary study, Jewish studies, "ethnic" or multicultural studies, and English and American literature is unsatisfying; but it is also aimed at those who might read—and look at the current state of Jewish studies and critical identity formations more generally—with an open mind. I hope I am not playing the Pollyanna in assuming that one does not have to work in Jewish American literature to be unsatisfied. Which is to say that while I list the relative lack of interest in talking about Jewish identity on the part of other fields such as American studies and comparative ethnicity studies as one of the axes of Jewish American literary study's professional alienation, I also trust any reader of this book to recognize that I am the farthest thing from interested in rehearsing a kind of resentful "Why Won't They Accept Us Jews" line; my book aims squarely at critiquing the nationalist mode of Jewish studies from within. I think we can all agree that *The Impossible Jew* intervenes in a very complicated, fraught, and overdetermined space. In choosing to contest Jewish criticism from the inside, I open myself to attack (or risk neglect) at once from critics outside Jewish studies for maintaining an exclusionist bias and from critics within Jewish studies for betraying conventional patterns of practice. But the critique of the crossing of Jewish studies, ethnicity studies, multicultural studies, and American studies likely calls for more than one tack; my hope is that *The Impossible Jew*, as a single book sized to sell, can aid the process of clarifying our thinking about identity.

In this book, I have eschewed sweeping claims about what Jewish American literature is in favor of sweeping claims about what Jewish American literary study can and should do with and say about that literature. I worry that once the decision is made to focus primarily on a presumed body of literature to the exclusion of how critical practices and habits take hold of that literature and make it available, we set in motion biologistic processes of reification and positivization that, authorized by the hegemonic self-evidence of a transhistorical Jewish subject, reproduce nationalistic patterns of thought. An anthropological historicism is dominant in Jewish studies formations to the extent that opportunities to delink work pursued under the Jewish studies rubric from the expectation that it contributes to an archive of positive knowledge of a historical Jewish subject are institutionally suppressed. Indeed, we now largely lack a way of imagining Jewish studies work without normalizing reference to a recognizable Jewish subject (which is to say a population or linked group of populations) as bearer or agent of the welter of histories, cultures, practices, and so on that Jewish studies sets itself to study. Much of my discussion and polemicizing here constitutes a response to the fact that Jewish studies and Jewish American literary study have often avoided a sustained critique of the mutual articulation of identity and normalization; as such, *The Impossible Jew* is also committed to the possibility that comparative approaches to the problem of ethnic legibility, where, to be sure, there has been a great deal of critical vibrancy lately, need not be the only solution. Identity—as a constitutive problem for scholarship—needs to retain a greater hold on critics and the institutional formations through which their work circulates. A critical Jewish studies will reconceptualize itself as the history of a desire for a concept of Jewish identity rather than as the history of Jews, displacing the Jewish subject from the site where it is recognized.

Jewish studies faces a constitutive problem. In its currently dominant configuration, it often takes shape as a mode of sociologically or anthropologically minded history that locates its authorization or justification in the legibility of a population—that is, under the auspices of a historiography that can fairly directly and without too much complication trace its ancestry (both "historically" and "theoretically") to racialist nationalism. These days it is easy to assume that "Jewish studies" is in a fundamental sense a largely unproblematic term, meaning roughly, but self-evidently, the academic study of Jews, however diversely or multi-valently that term is defined—including "their" history, culture, litera-ture, religious practices, social practices, self-conception, and so on; this professionalized study is different from, but by no means antithetical to and often in fact complementary with, other extra-academic formations of ideologically coherent Jewish self-regard, including religious obser-vance, philanthropy, cultural identification movements, hipster Yid-dishism, sociological measures of identification,[1] Zionism, and so on. I should say that *what* gets to count as Jewish history, culture, literature, religious practices, social practices, self-conception, and so on is always very much up for debate; Jewish studies as an institutional formation exists precisely in the investment of these debates—often in an expand-ing, multiple or "diverse," inclusiveness. But *that* Jewish studies studies the history, culture, literature, religious practices, social practices, self-conception, and so on of Jews is, I contend, more often than not taken for granted. I marked the pronoun "their" two or three sentences ago, which one obviously wants to refer to "The Jews," with scare quotes; as this book has endeavored to argue, the possibility of this pronoun is precisely the point, because to use this pronoun is in fact to dismiss the very problem I am trying to suggest is constitutive of "Jewish studies." Once it is possible to use such a pronoun, one has already assumed the existence of a conceptual and historical unity of all "Jewish" phenom-ena, and one is therefore no longer in a position to entertain the pos-sibility that there is a real problem with how Jewish studies imagines itself and its function. For a constellation of reasons that I have analyzed here, most explicitly in chapter 1, it is very easy to perform the concep-tual maneuver signified by the ability to assume that this pronoun is self-evident, despite the ultimately nationalist-biologistic implications of this assumption—of assuming the coherent identity of a "people" (despite whatever historical, religious, geographical, etc. variation one cares to count) that authorizes, by investing, all the variety of "stuff" properly addressed by all these various disciplinary categories (such as "history," "literature," "religion"). While this imaginary unity is not nec-essarily a racial unity, I do want to suggest that its conceptual machinery is genealogically dependent on a racialization or anthropologization of thought. A Jewish studies critically configured as a postanthropologis-tic analysis of Jewish identity, of the production of categorical Jewish legibility, and of the disciplinary machinery of Jewish identification would be better situated to contest the easy, normalized elision of political and aesthetic forms of representation that so powerfully marks our identitarian occasion.

Far be it from me, occupier of a named professorship thanks to some exceedingly generous alumni, to argue that Jewish studies as an academic entity needs to absolutely decouple itself from nonacademic Jewish identity formations such as Jewish philanthropy, but there is no reason that scholarship produced under the Jewish studies rubric needs to normalize itself according to a restrictive identitarian logic. The responsibility of a critical Jewish studies is to displace this normalization and disrupt its easy replication at the level of scholarship. One of the problems I am trying to write around in this book is precisely that I do not think we have a persuasively coherent alternative means of conceptualizing the historical unity we intend when we use the term "identity," at least when we use it to invoke any or all in a constellation of senses including "ethnicity," "heritage," "culture," and so on, than is provided by "race" and/or the racialized practices and patterns of thought that have so successfully operated as its institutional deputies. Thus, the same thing that allows an American citizen born in America to American-born parents who themselves had American-born parents (in three cases out of four) who in turn were born to parents raised somewhere in Austria-Hungary to European-born parents to declare, even jokingly, there to be more at identitarian stake in the texture of bagels than in that of biscotti, for example, is the same thing that underlies my not needing to account to my university colleagues for my interest in Jewish American literature: it is an ethnic concept of cultural identity, the result of biologistic processes and procedures that function for us as a relay between a concept of "population" and a concept of "culture," lending the articulation of the two a coherence and self-evidence. Our current term "identity"—at least in contexts where so many people would be comfortable using a vocabulary of ethnicity, which notably includes our current context, namely, a concern with the institutional formation called "Jewish studies"—is as powerful and omnipresent as it has become because it is invested by precisely this kind of biologistic logic. This is why I have tried in this book to sketch instead a possible counterhegemonic way of referring Jewish literary practice to the institutional imperatives and compensations of resolving a Jewish historical subject and through that to the multilayered history of that subject's statist recognizability—rather, that is, than relying on that ostensible recognizability to resolve nationalistically limned questions about cultural generativity. Instead of expecting identity of the recognizable minoritarian populations we study, let us instead ground our scholarly practices in a critique of the ways in which identity operates as a machine that produces recognition. If chapter 3 articulates the dangers of linking Jewish literary criticism to a concept of a Jewish people, and chapter 4 analyzes normalization as the modality of the identitarian investment of thought, then in chapter 5's interest in a counteridentitarian concept of history-as-dependency, of a history oriented around the ineffable future, *The Impossible Jew* comes around to contesting the recuperative, generative history that chapter 2 shows to be so necessary to nationalistic anthropologism. The primary question for a critical Jewish studies to ask, rather than simply "*What* makes our archive Jewish?" would be "*Why* is our archive Jewish?": What does it mean for an archive to be Jewish, to become Jewish, or to be made Jewish? and How is the Jewishness of an archive produced by specific practices or reading and archiving?

Jonathan and Daniel Boyarin argue in their introduction to *Jews and Other Differences*—titled "So What's New?"—for the comparativist "cultural studies paradigm" because, to the extent that it "opens up to other groups doing cultural studies, it will have political and social effects": "Specifically, one of our main goals in promoting the rubric of Jewish cultural studies is to move toward the recognition of Jewish culture as part of the world of differences to be valued and enhanced by research in the university, together with the differences of other groups hanging onto cultural resources similarly at risk of being consumed by a liberal universalist ethos."[2] Now, for reasons that should be apparent to anyone who has read this far into my book, I tend to suspect such pronouncements as this one, for all its epiphenomenal antiessentialism and for all the good work it sponsored and otherwise underwrote, of a fundamentally, and borderline nationalistic, statist identitarianism, insofar as it never really critically destabilizes the coherence, recognizability, or subject status of "Jewish culture." That said, I hope readers and intellectuals in the Jewish studies, ethnicity studies, and literature establishments, inspired by the Boyarins' utopian optimism and realizing that my argument aggressively disrupts the possibility of ad hominem criticism, will see fit to imagine *The Impossible Jew* as contributing to the critique "of the world of differences to be valued and enhanced by research in the university," even as a resource, if not actually a "cultural resource," for any number of "other groups," that may or may not be "at risk"—with the proviso that it is not other groups or populations to which establishment criticism needs to open itself but other thought. It is certainly within their power to.

NOTES

INTRODUCTION

1. Except in my case we are talking about a couple of clubs. Come to think of it, I suppose that this perversion I am riding is where the other great Groucho Marx joke that everybody knows from Woody Allen, the one in which we complain about the small portions of bad food, locates itself.

2. Jonathan Rutherford, "A Place Called Home: Identity and the Cultural Politics of Difference," in *Identity: Community, Culture, Difference*, ed. Jonathan Rutherford (London: Lawrence and Wishart, 1990), 12.

3. For a couple of recent and well-noted analyses of what I mean by literary practices that span both the "creative" and "critical" sides of literature—that is, practices that traverse the literary field—see Mark McGurl, *The Program Era: Postwar Fiction and the Rise of Creative Writing* (Cambridge: Harvard University Press, 2009); and Loren Glass, *Counterculture Colophon: Grove Press, the Evergreen Review, and the Incorporation of the Avant-Garde* (Stanford: Stanford University Press, 2013). See also "By What Strange Channels: Assembling Contemporary Literature," the Ph.D. dissertation that Abram Foley, a graduate student at Penn State University, is writing.

4. One obviously does not take oneself entirely seriously when using a term like this, but then again, one may not be able to think of an unequivocally better alternative. "Jewishishness" carries certain advantages, but it is certainly ungainly. Maybe "Jew-ishness"? My colleague and friend Jon Abel suggested "Jewicity." In any case, my frolicsome attraction to these ridiculous terms is that they destabilize the implication that the Jewishness of a text is self-evidently that of, or proper to, an extant and recognizable historical subject or community. Incidentally, this is one of those moments in academic writing when confidence crosses paths with self-loathing.

5. When I hyphenate this term this way, I mean it to insist on the link between property and the proper name or label, emphasizing both the fact and the thinking of something that belongs, categorically, to a category or class. For the record, I will admit that I feel enabled in this invention by our post-"Theory" age; in any case, see note 4, above, on self-loathing.

6. Abdul R. JanMohamed and David Lloyd, eds., *The Nature and Context of Minority Discourse* (New York: Oxford University Press, 1990); David Palumbo-Liu, ed., *The Ethnic Canon: Histories, Institutions, and Interventions* (Minneapolis: University of Minnesota Press, 1995); Michael Omi and Howard Winant, *Racial Formation in the United States: From the 1960s to the 1990s* (New York: Routledge, 1994).

7. "But while the transformation of Jewish difference from being racial to being cultural is included in this history of social science [i.e., that Douglas has just been tracing—from Boasian anthropology to Parkian sociology], I do not examine Jewish American writers in its critical genealogy of literary multiculturalism because social science did not crucially provide them with the enabling concept of culture that it provided to the other racialized minorities"; Christopher Douglas, *A Genealogy of Literary Multiculturalism* (Ithaca: Cornell University Press, 2009), 327. Frankly, this strikes me, as it undoubtedly does you, as a dodge.

8. Here is some admittedly anecdotal evidence: in the most recent five issues (that is, two and a half years—since 2012) of *AJS Review*, the scholarly journal published by the Association for Jewish Studies and likely the most visible mainstream, general Jewish studies journal, not one of the thirty-four articles addressed North American English-language literature, and of the sixty-five reviews in those issues, only one, on two books about Broadway and musical theater, did (although there was a review essay in the April 2014 issue on cinema studies, which sometimes is categorized under literary studies, and if we go back further, to 2011, it is true that an issue included a symposium on the 2010 Coen brothers film *A Serious Man*—but nothing else). Moreover, the categories by which *AJS Review* classifies book reviews do not seem hospitable: "Jewish History and Rabbinic Culture in Late Antiquity," "Medieval and Early Modern Jewish History and Culture," and "Modern Jewish History and Culture." Going back more than two years, we can find other categories—"Modern Jewish Thought and Philosophy," "Gender Studies," "Biblical Studies," "Talmud, Midrash, and Rabbinics," and "Art"—but these seem no more felicitous. Unless we want to subsume without remainder the category of "Literature" under the "Culture" rubric and, therefore, it would seem, more often than not reduce literary studies to an arm of a particularly historicist form of culture studies (which plenty of people in English departments, I should admit, seem perfectly happy doing), AJS-sponsored Jewish studies does not seem to be an apposite home for Jewish American literary study.

9. The occasion of this discussion was the annual "Jewish American and Holocaust Literature Symposium," held in November 2012 in Miami Beach.

10. See Douglas's *Genealogy of Literary Multiculturalism* on how a liberal racialist concept of identity came to underwrite, and transform, US multiculturalist and minoritarian discourse during the Cold War; Douglas draws on Walter Benn Michaels's critique of the racial heritage of our concept of cultural identity in such works as *Our America: Nativism, Modernism, Pluralism* (Durham: Duke University Press, 1995) and *The Shape of the Signifier: 1967 to the End of History* (Princeton: Princeton University Press, 2004). See also Jonathan Arac's absolutely essential paper "Toward a Genealogy of the U.S. Discourse of Identity: *Invisible Man* after Fifty Years," *Boundary* 2 30.2 (2003): 195–216, on which Douglas draws. See my chapter 1 for more on the genealogy of literary historical identitarianism in the Jewish American context.

11. Michael Kramer, "Race, Literary History, and the 'Jewish' Question," *Prooftexts* 21.3 (2001): 336. I will return to Kramer's argument throughout the book, but again, see chapter 1 for more on Kramer.

12. Kandice Chuh, *Imagine Otherwise: On Asian Americanist Critique* (Durham: Duke University Press, 2003), 10–11.

13. Ramon Salidívar, "Historical Fantasy, Speculative Realism, and Postrace Aesthetics in Contemporary American Fiction," *American Literary History* 23.3 (2011): 575, 595.

14. Jonathan Boyarin, *Thinking in Jewish* (Chicago: University of Chicago Press, 1996); Ann Pellegrini, *Performance Anxieties: Staging Psychoanalysis, Staging Race* (New York: Routledge, 1996); Daniel Boyarin and Jonathan Boyarin, "Diaspora: Generation and the Ground of Jewish Identity," *Critical Inquiry* 19.4 (1993): 693–725; Jonathan Boyarin and Daniel Boyarin, eds., *Jews and Other Differences: The New Jewish Cultural Studies* (Minneapolis: University of Minnesota Press, 1997); David Biale, Michael Galchinsky, and Susannah Heschel, eds., *Insider/Outsider; American Jews and Multiculturalism* (Berkeley: University of California Press, 1998); Sander L. Gilman, *Jewish Frontiers: Essays on Bodies, Histories, and Identities* (New York: Palgrave Macmillan, 2003); Daniel Boyarin, Daniel Itzkovitz, and Ann Pellegrini, eds., *Queer Theory and the Jewish Question* (New York: Columbia University Press, 2003); Caryn Aviv and David Shneer, *New Jews: The End of the Jewish Diaspora* (New York: NYU Press, 2005); Vincent Brook, ed., *You Should See Yourself: Jewish Identity in Postmodern American Culture* (New Brunswick: Rutgers University Press, 2006); Jonathan Freedman, *Klezmer America: Jewishness, Ethnicity, Modernity* (New York: Columbia University Press, 2008).

15. This point was clarified for me by Daniel Itzkovitz in a conversation.

16. David Biale, "Confessions of an Historian of Jewish Culture," *Jewish Social Studies* 1.1 (1994): 41–43.

17. See Amos Funkenstein, "The Dialectics of Assimilation," *Jewish Social Studies* 1.2 (1995): 1–14. Funkenstein cites his student Biale in the essay—though not as frequently as Biale himself does in his own essay.

18. See William V. Spanos, *The Errant Art of Moby-Dick: The Canon, the Cold War, and the Struggle for American Studies* (Durham: Duke University Press, 1995), where the concept plays a major role throughout.

19. For this particular citation I happen to be looking at Ranen Omer-Sherman's *Diaspora and Zionism in Jewish American Literature: Lazarus, Syrkin, Reznikoff, Roth* (Hanover, NH: Brandeis University Press, 2000), 5. For another version of this move, one more defensively aligned with Wisse, we can look to the apologia in the editors' introduction to the festschrift in her honor, *Arguing the Modern Jewish Canon*, compiled by some of her ex-students, which, while suppressing a bit the "flawed" part of the articulation, reproduces the general effect: "Students often come to know Wisse first by reputation, as a teacher and scholar who does not march in step with the dominant ethos of the liberal academy. Though the passion and force of her ideas invariably generate heated reactions, students appreciate the competing perspectives she brings to campus. Those colleagues who casually dismiss her ideas invariably do a disservice to themselves by diminishing the culture of argument itself" (Justin Cammy, Dara Horn, Alyssa Quint, and Rachel Rubinstein, eds., *Arguing the Modern Jewish Canon: Essays*

on Literature and Culture in Honor of Ruth R. Wisse [Cambridge: Harvard University Press, 2008], 5).

20. Ruth R. Wisse, *The Modern Jewish Canon: A Journey through Language and Culture* (New York: Free Press, 2000), xv; further references to Wisse are to this work and will be cited parenthetically in the text. For a more nuanced, and critical, stab at this problem, see Hana Wirth-Nesher's engaging study of Jewish American literature's multilingual negotiations, in *Call It English: The Languages of Jewish American Literature* (Princeton: Princeton University Press, 2006).

21. See, on both counts, Kramer, "Race, Literary History, and the 'Jewish' Question," which informs my critique.

22. If only the two groups could agree that they share an obsessive and obfuscating identification of "Jewish" with "Israel," they might agree also to keep quiet. All this is to say that, for what is it worth, I am a bit anxious about how some readers might react to my use of the *tsadi*-word. But I will leave it at that.

23. See Eric Santner's *The Royal Remains: Two People's Two Bodies and the Endgames of Sovereignty* (Chicago: University of Chicago Press, 2011), which is helpful on this score. Particularly clarifying is his argument that biopolitics can be understood in terms of a disciplinary power that "underwrites" the legitimacy of sovereignty and government (xv), terms that form a cluster with my concept of the "national."

24. Michel Foucault, *The Birth of Biopolitics: Lectures at the Collège de France, 1978–1979*, ed. Michel Snellart, trans. Graham Burchell (New York: Picador, 2008), 22.

25. I expand on this concept of biologism or biologistic identitarianism, which I introduce here, in "Literary-Historical Zionism: Irving Kristol, Alexander Portnoy, and the State of the Jews," *Contemporary Literature* 55.4 (2014): 760–791. I actually wrote the article long after the bulk of the book, but because of the vagaries of book and journal publishing, the article gets to see the light of day first.

26. Judith Butler, *Bodies That Matter: On the Discursive Limits of "Sex"* (New York: Routledge, 1993), 228.

27. See José David Saldívar, *Trans-Americanity: Subaltern Modernities, Global Coloniality, and the Cultures of Greater Mexico* (Durham: Duke University Press, 2011).

28. Here, too, "essentialist" or "Zionist" might be useful terms, but see my earlier discussion of these terms.

29. See Boyarin, *Thinking in Jewish*.

CHAPTER 1: TOWARD A CRITICAL SEMITISM

1. See Michel Foucault, "'*Omnes et Singulatum*': Toward a Critique of Political Reason," in *The Chomsky-Foucault Debate: On Human Nature*, ed. John Rajchman (New York: New Press, 2006), 190.

2. See Michel Foucault, "Truth and Power," in *Power/Knowledge: Selected Interviews and Other Writings, 1972–1977*, ed. Colin Gordon (New York: Pantheon, 1980), 117.

3. See Jonathan Boyarin and Daniel Boyarin, eds., *Jews and Other Differences: The New Jewish Cultural Studies* (Minneapolis: University of Minnesota Press, 1997); and

David Biale, Michael Galchinsky, and Susannah Heschel, eds., *Insider/Outsider: American Jews and Multiculturalism* (Berkeley: University of California Press, 1998).

4. Sara R. Horowitz, "The Paradox of Jewish Studies in the New Academy," in Biale, Galchinsky, and Heschel, *Insider/Outsider*, 129, 120.

5. Paul Bové, *Mastering Discourse: The Politics of Intellectual Culture* (Durham: Duke University Press, 1992), xii, xi.

6. *MELUS*, notably, has long embraced this model of professionalization in critical practice. See, for example, the penultimate sentence of editor Martha Cutter's introduction to a recent issue, "Reading, Writing, and Recognition," which betrays a faith that literary language is valuable primarily for an unquestioned representational functionality: "If we are never quite 'outside' ideology and the technology of recognition, it may also be that we are also never quite 'inside' of them, either" (*MELUS* 37.1 [2012]: 13). Incidentally, it pays also to consider the article's conspicuous term "literal," which Cutter repeats six times, almost always as in "recognition in a literal sense" (6), for which Cutter's paradigmatic case here is the US government's recognition of Native American tribal sovereignty. For scholars who embrace this kind of critically neutered, nationalistic work, the all-important concept of literary recognition cannot be comprehended without the help of an allied concept of political recognition. Literature's job is to represent subjects who are already legible in currently dominant languages of political, cultural, and social administration, and the literary critic's job is to find those subjects in it. Unaccountability and difference are suppressed in this positivization of identity.

7. I think Marjorie Garber's idea of "discipline envy" can be pressed into service here. See her *Academic Instincts* (Princeton: Princeton University Press, 2001), 53–96.

8. Jacques Rancière, *The Politics of Aesthetics*, trans. Gabriel Rockhill (London: Continuum, 2004), 13, 12.

9. See my "Jew Historicism: Delmore Schwartz and Overdetermination," *Prooftexts* 27.3 (2007): 500–530.

10. Michael J. Kramer, "Race, Literary History, and the 'Jewish' Question." *Prooftexts* 21.3 (2001): 287–349.

11. Not that any of his respondents make the point, but I think it is fair to challenge Kramer's reification of race in the wake of his critique of how Jewish literary history handles the identity of Jewish literature—that is, that we moderns lack a coherent means of identifying a set of literature other than via the concept of race does not prove that "race" exists; what is missing from Kramer is a genealogy of our inability to imagine identity without the conceptual crutch of race. But the real strength of the article is the critique of identitarianism, not the single positive claim that Jewish literature is simply literature written by Jews.

12. Meditating on the modernist fact that the distance between a generative theory of art and a theory of degenerate art is likely not so great would not be such a bad idea either.

13. See not only Michael P. Kramer's "Race, Literary History, and the 'Jewish' Question" but also his "Beginnings and Ends: the Origins of Jewish American Literary

History," in *The Cambridge Companion to Jewish American Literature*, ed. Michael P. Kramer and Hana Wirth-Nesher (Cambridge: Cambridge University Press, 2003), 12–30, in which he writes, "To call modern Jewish literature Jewish is more often than not to speak metonymically, to substitute a discerned (or imagined) Jewish part for the complex cultural whole. To locate modern Jewish writing within the same history as, say, Rashi and Rabbi Isaac is to make a political assertion as much as a cultural observation, one that may obscure as much as it clarifies" (15). Adam Zachary Newton has received far less attention than his important work deserves; see *Facing Black and Jews: Literature as Public Space in Twentieth-Century America* (Cambridge University Press, 1999) and "Incognito Ergo Sum: 'Ex' Marks the Spot in Cahan, Johnson, Larsen, and Yezierska," *Race and the Modern Artist*, ed. Heather Hathaway, Josef Jařab, and Jeffrey Melnick (Oxford: Oxford University Press, 2003), 140–183, for his careful work on ethnic recognition, where ethnic American literary texts become "allegories of entanglement" that find "in language another rehearsal of transcendental homelessness rather than a respite or solution to it" (140–142). Dean Franco's *Ethnic American Literature: Comparing Chicano, Jewish, and African American Literature* (Charlottesville: University of Virginia Press, 2006) situates literature within a canonizing project to chart cultural histories whose very administrative energies "undermine concrete determinations of group boundaries" (12). "My interest in 'ethnicity,' then, springs from the insight that cultural contingency and geohistorical contiguity end up so muddying the waters of identity that any account of where cultural identities come from and how they function must necessarily be one that favors impurity over purity, dissonance and a bit of chaos over harmony and order" (22–23). See also his "Rereading Cynthia Ozick: Pluralism, Postmodernism, and the Multicultural Encounter," *Contemporary Literature* 49.1 (2008): 56–84; and "Portnoy's Complaint: It's about Race, Not Sex (Even the Sex Is about Race)," *Prooftexts* 29.1 (2009): 86–115, both of which laid the groundwork for his recent book *Race, Rights, and Recognition: Jewish American Literature since 1969* (Ithaca: Cornell University Press, 2012). Caroline Rody's *The Interethnic Imagination: Roots and Passages in Contemporary Asian American Fiction* (Oxford: Oxford University Press, 2009) likewise encourages critical thinking across purportedly self-evident ethnic boundaries. Few critics have been more incisive on the destabilizing role of language in Jewish literature than Hana Wirth-Nesher; see *Call It English: The Languages of Jewish American Literature* (Princeton: Princeton University Press, 2005). Joshua Miller's *Accented America: The Cultural Politics of Multilingual Modernism* (Oxford: Oxford University Press, 2011) extends Wirth-Nesher's critique of translational excess in important ways. Julian Levinson's *Exiles on Main Street: Jewish American Writers and American Literary Culture* (Bloomington: Indiana University Press, 2008) is eloquent: "My hope is to move from the idea that Jewish writers have some inherent or given 'Jewish experience' to express and toward the idea that a new version of Jewishness can be formed in dialogue with American literary culture, its vocabularies, conceptual categories, and implicit politics. . . . We gain a picture of Jewish writers actively engaged in the process of recreating the framework through which identity and the world is perceived" (2–6). I will say more on Jonathan Freedman's

Klezmer America: Jewishness, Ethnicity, Modernity (New York: Columbia University Press, 2008) shortly.

14. Freedman, *Klezmer America*, 12, my emphasis.

15. Freedman, *Klezmer America*, 9, 18, 332.

16. Franco, "Rereading Cynthia Ozick," 57–58.

17. See, for a famous example, Norman Podhoretz's "My Negro Problem—and Ours," *Commentary* 35.2 (1963): 93–101.

18. Franco, "Rereading Cynthia Ozick," 60.

19. See Bové, *Mastering Discourse*, 171, for more on this process in the academy in general (but not in the specific area of ethnic studies). Incidentally, consideration of this point and the preceding discussion suggest that talk of a Cold War social or cultural settlement or consensus is probably more obfuscating than it is helpful. Obviously, those terms are usually used in reference to the 1950s rather than the 1960s, but what we see here is that the model of institutional academic and professional investment shifted sometime in the late 1950s or early 1960s, certainly by Vietnam. The more important point, likely, is not so much an objective transformation in American identity but rather a shift in what it makes sense—indeed, what it pays—to recognize and talk about in academic and professional contexts. And in any case, it is clear that there was no unitary, settled or consensual, mode or set of procedures by which identity was marked before this era.

20. Mark McGurl, *The Program Era: Postwar Fiction and the Rise of Creative Writing* (Cambridge: Harvard University Press, 2009), 333.

21. Franco, "Rereading Cynthia Ozick," 68, 70. Attention to this series of transformations likely involves an account of the relocation of the thinking of identity from a Marxist terrain articulated by a concept of radical culture commonly associated with the early history of the New York intellectuals to a neoliberal terrain articulated by a consumerist concept of the market. That some of the important intellectual infrastructure of this latter system was erected by converted architects of the former system certainly demands sustained examination, probably in the form of a historical analysis of American liberalism in the twentieth century. Needless to say, I am not prepared to pursue that history here.

22. See Walter Benn Michaels, *Our America: Nativism, Modernism, and Pluralism* (Durham: Duke University Press, 1995); and Michaels, *The Shape of the Signifier: 1967 to the End of History* (Princeton: Princeton University Press, 2004).

23. Christopher Douglas, *A Genealogy of Literary Multiculturalism* (Ithaca: Cornell University Press, 2009), 157, 250, 254, 298, 306, 320, 322, 9.

24. From the relative safety of a note, I will admit that I have long been curious about Michaels's conspicuous eschewal of matters Jewish, given his otherwise far-reaching interest in identity. Though my Jewdar is not similarly triggered by Douglas's largely steering clear of Jewish identity and literature (with some exceptions, including a few references to Boas's heritage), circumstantial concerns render it notable.

25. Gilles Deleuze and Félix Guattari, *Kafka: Toward a Minor Literature*, trans. Dana Polan (Minneapolis: University of Minnesota Press, 1986), 16.

26. Deleuze and Guattari, *Kafka*, 19.

27. As Dana Polan warned in his 1986 introduction to Deleuze and Guattari's *Kafka*,

> Already, some of the American critical adulation of other Deleuze-Guattari texts, especially *Anti-Oedipus*, suggests how quickly a politics of the rhizomatic can assuage the unhappy guilty conscience of the depoliticized intellectual by offering him or her the alibi of a process in which everything one does can be something that one can pretend is politically engaged. . . . Dangerously, despite all the efforts of Deleuze and Guattari to deconstruct hierarchies, American literary criticism may treat them . . . not as theorists of the ties of collective enunciation and minor literature but as aesthetes of a high-culture avant-garde closed in on its own fetishes of interiority. Deleuze and Guattari themselves admit that there is a fine line between territorializing and deterritorializing processes, and it is easy for their work to be appropriated to the most divergent and even contradictory of ends.

Dana Polan, "Translator's Introduction," in Deleuze and Guattari, *Kafka*, xxvi.

28. Deleuze and Guattari, *Kafka*, 18.

29. Deleuze and Guattari, *Kafka*, 18–19.

30. Chana Kronfeld, "Beyond Deleuze and Guattari: Hebrew and Yiddish Modernism in the Age of Privileged Difference," in *Jews and Other Differences: The New Jewish Cultural Studies*, ed. Jonathan Boyarin and Daniel Boyarin (Minneapolis: University of Minnesota Press, 1997), 258, 259, 260, 270.

31. As Bové has written in discussing Stanley Aronowitz, "since capital can subvert the margins by making them fashionable, marginality should not be valorized per se as a form of subversion" (*Mastering Discourse*, 100).

32. McGurl, *Program Era*, 56–57.

33. Alain Badiou, *Saint Paul: The Foundation of Universalism* (Stanford: Stanford University Press, 2003), 10–11.

34. Badiou, *Saint Paul*, 6.

35. Abdul R. JanMohamed and David Lloyd, "Introduction: Toward a Theory of Minority Discourse: What Is to Be Done?," in *The Nature and Context of Minority Discourse*, ed. Abdul R. JanMohamed and David Lloyd (New York: Oxford University Press, 1990), 1, 4; David Palumbo-Liu, "Multiculturalism Now: Civilization, National Identity, and Difference before and after September 11," *Boundary 2* 29.2 (2002): 127.

36. Badiou, *Saint Paul*, 6–7, 10.

37. Daniel O'Hara, "'The Cry of Its Occasion': On the Subject of Truth; or, The Terror in Global Terrorism." *Boundary 2* 34.2 (2007): 57.

38. Badiou, *Saint Paul*, 12.

39. Incidentally, the key figure for Badiou's critique of identitarianism is Saint Paul, whose universalist theorization of identity, situated at the threshold of Jewishness, beyond both group particularism and statist authority, stands at the horizon of categorical recognition. While there is a danger that Pauline Christianity's universalizing emphasis potentially produces a positive Jewish difference, or ethnicity, that

can in turn be invested by anti-Semitism—well, any kind of racism—I think Badiou's interpretation aims to prevent any such reactionary positivistic reification. That said, I might editorialize that I suspect that only a Christian living under Christian hegemony could see Paul as Badiou does, valuing pure subjectivity thus; I cannot help seeing Badiou's figuration of Paul, as valuable as it is to my task, as effected from a hegemonic position. In any case, thanks to Matt Biberman, long ago, for pointing me in the direction of Paul.

40. Mark Chiang, *The Cultural Capital of Asian American Studies: Autonomy and Representation in the University* (New York: NYU Press, 2009), 10. I think these critical moves can be traced with early New Americanist gestures in Chicano studies, such as in the 1990s work of José David Saldívar, to articulate a counternationalist concept of the "border" in place of the nationalized "frontier": a canon that opens itself to writers of the borderlands, sensitive to the "terrors of border-crossing and diaspora amid the debris of . . . the cultures of U.S. imperialism," cannot be used to construct a "smoothed-over" image of "ethno-racial wholeness" because such writers "operate at other levels than those constructed by national borders" (José David Saldívar, *Border Matters: Remapping American Cultural Studies* [Berkeley: University of California Press, 1997], 197). A formulation like this is certainly susceptible to the kind of ethnographic or anthropologistic, nationalizing impulses that I am diagnosing here, but it is at the same time directed precisely at disrupting those energies. In any case, it likely belongs in a genealogy of the kind of energies that *The Impossible Jew* is trying to vivify for Jewish studies.

41. Edward W. Said, *Beginnings: Intention and Method* (1975; repr., New York: Columbia University Press, 1985), xiv.

42. Sander Gilman might support this project in places: "The links between questions of identity, identification and history, and historiography rest on the construction of organizational categories by the authors and readers of texts. We inscribe who we believe ourselves to be and where we believe we came from in these texts we call history. Identity is what you imagine yourself and the other to be; history and historiography is the writing of the narratives of that difference" (Sander Gilman, *Jewish Frontiers: Essays on Bodies, Histories, and Identities* [New York: Palgrave Macmillan, 2003], 3). Gilman's account, however, elides occasions when one's identity is defined by another.

43. I owe a lot of this discussion to conversations with Dean Franco, who knows a lot more about this stuff than I do and who therefore deserves no blame for any errors I may be introducing in this very quick sketch of a complex history.

44. Neil Jumonville has argued that Jews were helped in part by the 1944 GI Bill, which "pried open" what had been a "highly elitist" "American university system" (Neil Jumonville, introduction to *The New York Intellectuals Reader*, ed. Neil Jumonville [New York: Routledge, 2007], 2), though we would want to specify, of course, that to the extent that this "open[ing]" benefited Jews more than it did others, this account really just punts an explanation of the difference. See Susanne Klingenstein's two accounts of the entrance of Jewish scholars into the American academy in the early twentieth century: *Jews in the American Academy, 1900–1940: The Dynamics of*

Intellectual Assimilation (1991; repr., Syracuse: Syracuse University Press, 1998) and *Enlarging America: The Cultural Work of Jewish Literary Scholars, 1930–1990* (Syracuse: Syracuse University Press, 1998). These books are dedicated to a distracting philo-Semitic program—I wonder if it originates in their author's neoconservative politics—but there is some value in their breadth (if not in their lack of critical depth).

45. Kandice Chuh, *Imagine Otherwise: On Asian Americanist Critique* (Durham: Duke University Press, 2003), 6.

46. Caryn Aviv and David Shneer, *New Jews: The End of the Jewish Diaspora* (New York: NYU Press, 2005), 12.

47. Benedict Anderson, "Exodus," *Critical Inquiry* 20.2 (1994): 327; Norman G. Finkelstein, *The Holocaust Industry: Reflections on the Exploitation of Jewish Suffering*, 2nd paperback ed. (London: Verso, 2003). On the matter of the Holocaust and Jewish studies discourse, it might pay also to examine the subtle relays by which the Holocaust provides an occasion for the mourning of a lost object to become a site of meaning production. Relevant is not so much the Holocaust's role as an explicit focus of Jewish literary practice—though it obviously can and does fill that role—but a structure, perhaps first announced in the wartime wave of immigrant European Jewish intellectuals who taught in American universities but revised and enlarged frequently since (it links, for example, to the history of the Zionist eruption of neoconservatism from the political belly of the New York intellectuals), that indicates or makes available a "Jewish" ground paradoxically through the Jewish object's absence: thus the traumatic loss of Jewishness underwrites "Jewish" critical and cultural production. See my chapter 3 for a consideration of this idea; but in any case, this cannot be the place for full exploration of this idea. Thanks to Jonathan Eburne for initially pointing me in the direction of the displaced European Jewish intellectuals teaching in the US.

48. Jonathan Boyarin, *Thinking in Jewish* (Chicago: University of Chicago Press, 1996), 172, 170.

49. Boyarin, *Thinking in Jewish*, 172, Boyarin's emphasis.

50. Boyarin, *Thinking in Jewish*, 170.

51. David Biale, Michael Galchinsky, and Susannah Heschel, "Introduction: The Dialectic of Jewish Enlightenment," *Insider/Outsider: American Jews and Multiculturalism*, ed. David Biale, Michael Galchinsky, and Susannah Heschel (Berkeley: University of California Press, 1998), 4–7.

52. Biale, Galchinsky, and Heschel, "Introduction," 8.

53. Biale, Galchinsky, and Heschel, "Introduction," 9.

54. If it were still the 1990s and I were still in graduate school, I would format this word with the "strikethrough" feature.

55. Again, I would make an appeal to the relevance of Anderson's "long-distance nationalism" here ("Exodus," 327).

56. I use "capture" deliberately—and critically—to avoid a stronger verb such as "create"; while it is important to submit recognition that presumes its own self-evidence to the counternormative force of genealogy, it is equally obvious that an identity criterion that simply proclaims itself will not do.

57. I suppose in this context I can point out that this looks like a particularly literal manifestation of *teshuva* (or "return"). A "semitic" question to ask, however, is whether we would make this connection if we were not operating in the context of Jewish literary history or more generally in a context in which we can take for granted the historicist availability and/or coherence of a Jewish identification.

58. Bernard Malamud, *The Assistant* (1957; repr., New York: Farrar, Straus and Giroux, 2003), 121. Further references to this book will be cited parenthetically in the text.

59. Earlier, Frank's gnawing guilt about robbing Morris constitutes a threat to his subjectifying ability to envision himself and his future: "He was afraid to look into the mirror for fear it would split apart and drop into the sink" (85).

60. I am tempted to say *avant la lettre*, but in 1957 it is barely *avant*. Maybe *sans la lettre*?

61. Bernard Malamud, *Conversations with Bernard Malamud*, ed. Lawrence Lasher (Jackson: University Press of Mississippi, 1991), 30.

62. Malamud, *Conversations with Bernard Malamud*, 146.

63. Robert Alter, *After the Tradition: Essays on Modern Jewish Writing* (New York: Dutton, 1969), 129.

64. Alter, *After the Tradition*, 120.

65. Leslie Fiedler, *Fiedler on the Roof: Essays on Literature and Jewish Identity* (Boston: David R. Godine, 1991), 66.

66. Fiedler, *Fiedler on the Roof*, 59. No need to cite Irving Howe's unfortunate 1977 pronouncement that Jewish American literature was past its prime!

67. Fiedler, *Fiedler on the Roof*, 60. John Murray Cuddihy has also discussed this symbolic phenomenon in Jewish writing; he describes a "Christian 'definition of the situation'" and writes of a drama "played out before a Gentile status-audience, for a symbolic cultural good—a crown of thorns—first worn by that Supreme Victim from whom our civilization takes it name" (John Murray Cuddihy, *The Ordeal of Civility: Freud, Marx, Lévi-Strauss, and the Jewish Struggle with Modernity*, 2nd ed. [Boston: Beacon, 1987], 212).

68. Fiedler, *Fiedler on the Roof*, 65.

69. Fiedler, *Fiedler on the Roof*, 68–69, 71.

70. Fiedler, *Fiedler on the Roof*, 65, 71.

71. Fiedler, *Fiedler on the Roof*, 66.

72. Michael Gold, *Jews without Money* (1930; repr., New York: Carroll and Graf, 1984), 50

73. Gold, *Jews without Money*, 309.

74. Fiedler, *Fiedler on the Roof*, xii

75. Alter, *After the Tradition*, 10–11.

76. Daniel Boyarin, *A Radical Jew: Paul and the Politics of Identity* (Berkeley: University of California Press, 1994), 8. We can turn also to Gayatri Spivak: "when the Western European intellectual defines the universal intellectual and then says I am specific as opposed to that universal, what he doesn't see is that the definition of that universal is itself contaminated by a nonrecognition of a specific production"

(Gayatri Spivak, "Criticism, Feminism, and the Institution," in *Intellectuals: Aesthetics, Politics, Academics*, ed. Bruce Robbins [Minneapolis: University of Minnesota Press, 1990], 159).

CHAPTER 2: AGAINST THE DIALECTIC OF NATION

1. For an obvious example, see Ruth Wisse's nationalism in *The Modern Jewish Canon: A Journey through Language and Culture* (New York: Free Press, 2000) and my discussion of it in the introduction. "Zionism" used as I am proposing may be a blunt term, but it can also be quite productive (in a clearing-the-decks sort of way) in the literary historical context.

2. Jonathan Boyarin, *Thinking in Jewish* (Chicago: University of Chicago Press, 1996), 158, 163, 170, 161, 162.

3. Caryn Aviv and David Shneer, *New Jews: The End of the Jewish Diaspora* (New York: NYU Press, 2005), 2–3.

4. Joseph N. Riddel, "To Perform—A Transitive Verb?," in *America's Modernisms: Revaluing the Canon, Essays in Honor of Joseph N. Riddel*, ed. Kathryne V. Lindberg and Joseph G. Kronick (Baton Rouge: Louisiana State University Press, 1996), 25.

5. Abraham Cahan, *The Rise of David Levinsky* (1917; repr., New York: Penguin, 1993), 525. Further references to this book will be cited parenthetically in the text.

6. Though I cannot establish intentionality in the connection, it does not seem at all accidental, at least from my perspective, that "the faith of our fathers" is an important phrase in Herzl's *The Jewish State*; see, for example, one of the more well-quoted passages: "We have honestly endeavored everywhere to merge ourselves in the social life of surrounding communities and to preserve the faith of our fathers. We are not permitted to do so" (Theodor Herzl, *The Jewish State* [1896; repr., Mineola, NY: Dover, 1988], 76).

7. Thanks to Adam Zachary Newton for pointing out that this gentile woman who focuses Levinsky's anxiety about identity also tells him about "the good novels she had read" and got him "interested in good, modern fiction" (528), suggesting that Cahan shares my larger interest in theorizing the link between questions about identity and questions about canon formation.

8. Julian Levinson, *Exiles on Main Street: Jewish American Writers and American Literary Culture* (Bloomington: Indiana University Press, 2008), 13.

9. Stephanie Foote, "Marvels of Memory: Citizenship and Ethnic Identity in Abraham Cahan's 'The Imported Bridegroom,'" *MELUS* 25.1 (2000): 34, 51.

10. Isaac Rosenfeld, "The Fall of David Levinsky," in *Preserving the Hunger: An Isaac Rosenfeld Reader*, ed. Mark Shechtner (Detroit: Wayne State University Press, 1988), 152–153.

11. Amos Funkenstein, "The Dialectics of Assimilation," *Jewish Social Studies* 1.2 (1995): 4, 8, 9, 10–11. See also my introduction and chapter 1 for my critique of such Jewish cultural studies approaches as Funkenstein's.

12. Rosenfeld, "Fall of David Levinsky," 155, 157.

13. Abraham Cahan, "The Russian Jew in America," *Atlantic Monthly* 82 (July 1898): 138.

14. Abraham Cahan, "The Late Rabbi Joseph, Hebrew Patriarch of New York." *American Monthly Review of Reviews* 26.3 (1902): 313–314.

15. Jules Chametzky, *From the Ghetto: The Fiction of Abraham Cahan* (Amherst: University of Massachusetts Press, 1977), vii–viii.

16. Chametzky, *From the Ghetto*, 26, 83–84, 127.

17. Phillip Barrish, "'The Genuine Article': Ethnicity, Capital, and *The Rise of David Levinsky*," *American Literary History* 5.4 (1993): 643–644.

18. Sara Blair, "Whose Modernism Is It? Abraham Cahan, Fictions of Yiddish, and the Contest of Modernity," *Modern Fiction Studies* 51.2 (2005): 259, 264, 261, 266, 272.

19. In this figuration, incidentally, Blair follows my grandmother ע"ה, who (like so many of her generational cohort) almost always referred to Yiddish simply as "Jewish."

20. Philip Joseph, "Literary Migration: Abraham Cahan's 'The Imported Bride-groom' and the Alternative of American Fiction," *MELUS* 27.4 (2002): 4–5.

21. Joseph, "Literary Migration," 24–25, 28–29.

22. As I have already argued earlier in the book, Michael Kramer has shown how this perspective is often supported by a mostly untheorized concept of race that does the heavy lifting for such apparently respectable unifying metonyms as culture, tradition, or language. Indeed, it would be productive to examine how the concept of race is imbricated with a specific understanding of the temporality of identity; that is, "race" is a name for a constellation of procedures by which identity is secured in the past. Though I make gestures toward such an analysis in the introduction and chapter 1, a full elaboration is beyond the scope of this book; that said, I think the work of Walter Benn Michaels would be a logical place to look for support for such a critique. In any case, see both Kramer's article and his response to the waspish "responses" to it in the same issue of *Prooftexts* 21.3 (2001). See also my "Jew Historicism: Delmore Schwartz and Overdetermination," *Prooftexts* 27.3 (2007): 500–530, in which I mount a friendly critique of Kramer's argument that cautions against assuming that race exists because of the helpful critical solution its existence would offer.

23. Abraham Cahan, *"Yekl" and "The Imported Bridegroom" and Other Stories of the New York Ghetto* (New York: Dover, 1970), 98. Further references to this book will be cited parenthetically in the text.

24. In fact, the scene of the attic salon looks a lot like an earlier scene in which Asriel visits his synagogue's study rooms. There, we see a motley group poring over the Mishnah instead of Comte, but the groups look nearly the same: "There were about a dozen of them, mostly poor peddlers or artisans—a humble, seedy, pitiable lot, come after a hard day's work or freezing, to 'take a holy word into their mouths'" (144). Likewise, when Shaya in the attic "became engrossed in the reading" (160), he looks a lot like he does when engaged in Talmudic study—rocking back and forth, gesturing, making arguments with his hands, and so forth. I thank a great student, Alex Weisler, for pointing out this repetition.

25. Any surviving possibility of representation can now only be radically contingent, arising in specific occasions wherein specific articulations of canonical material, interpretive desire, and critical self-definition are produced; such contingent representation is therefore fatally hostile to the protocols of identity politics. For more on this idea of contingent representation, see Daniel O'Hara, *Empire Burlesque: The Fate of Critical Culture in Global America* (Durham: Duke University Press, 2003), especially chapter 2.

26. One can find a gendered critique of the patriarchal circulation of women here, a critique supported by a reading of the text pitying Flora here and throughout for the fact that in her case agency is dependent on getting men to act. Thanks to Chris Reed for pointing this out.

27. I suppose "Jewishist" could replace the more polemical "Zionist" (see note 1 to this chapter and my discussions of this problem earlier in the book), but it risks occluding the field-organizing racialist statism of so much American literary criticism carried out under the Jewish identity rubric (and occluding more specifically the powerful American tendency, both inside and outside the academy, to link discussion of Jewish identity to the Israeli state).

CHAPTER 3: THE NEGATIVE DESIRE OF JEWISH REPRESENTATION

1. Irving Howe, "The New York Intellectuals: A Chronicle and a Critique," *Commentary* 46.4 (1968): 29.

2. Just as, not entirely unrelatedly, the University of Illinois's decision to unhire (after first deciding to hire) Steven Salaita in the mid-2010s is widely accounted a significant moment in the institutional acceptance of the privatization of speech and knowledge.

3. Sidney Hook, "Anti-Semitism in the Academy: Some Pages of the Past," *Midstream*, January 1979, 51–53.

4. Diana Trilling, "Lionel Trilling: A Jew at Columbia," *Commentary* 67.3 (1979): 44–45.

5. Mark Krupnick, "Lionel Trilling, 'Culture,' and Jewishness," *Denver Quarterly* 18 (Autumn 1983): 118–119.

6. Krupnick, "Lionel Trilling, 'Culture,' and Jewishness," 119.

7. The word ("underwrites") is Eric Santner's, from *The Royal Remains: Two People's Two Bodies and the Endgames of Sovereignty* (Chicago: University of Chicago Press, 2011), xv.

8. See, for example, David Suchoff, who, while having done much to advance understanding of the New York critics, nonetheless throws up the critical white flag when he writes that "the cultural ascent of figures such as Trilling depended, as his 1925 story 'Impediments' already suggests, on escaping from Hettner, the 'scrubby little Jew' from the working class. Trilling's narrator fears that the Jewish Jew might 'break down the convenient barrier I was erecting against men who were too much of my own race, and against men who were not of my own race and hated it'" (David Suchoff, "The Rosenberg Case and the New York Intellectuals," in *Secret Agents: The Rosenberg Case,*

McCarthyism, and Fifties America, ed. Marjorie Garber and Rebecca L. Walkowitz [New York: Routledge, 1995], 157). See also Morris Dickstein, who argues that Jewishness persists as the key to Trilling's writing—as outward theme in his early fiction and as implicit problematic in his later criticism:

> Once Trilling had used fiction to dramatize his own inner dialectic, his buried feelings of attraction and repulsion toward characters outwardly different from himself, like Hettner, the "scrubby little Jew" in "Impediments," Tertain, the mad and brilliant young student of "Of This Time, Of That Place," and the charismatic Gifford Maxim, the Whittaker Chambers figure in *The Middle of the Journey*. But Trilling's modest fictional gifts, like Matthew Arnold's poetic powers, were gradually sublimated into the drama of his critical voice, and he published no more fiction after the success of *The Liberal Imagination*. Trilling's constitutional ambivalence is related to his ordeal of being a Jew in a gentile world, teaching English literature in a gentile university.

Morris Dickstein, *Double Agent: The Critic and Society* (New York: Oxford University Press, 1992), 80. I hope it is not vainly unrealistic to expect more from an analysis of Trilling's work than evidence that he did not want to be identified as a "scrubby little Jew." After all, who but a heroic few would?

9. As, we should admit, Suchoff is trying to suggest.

10. Daniel O'Hara, *Lionel Trilling: The Work of Liberation* (Madison: University of Wisconsin Press, 1988), 6, 8, 44, 63, 66.

11. For more on this concept of revisionary critical parody as I am employing it here, see O'Hara not only in the Trilling book but also in *Radical Parody: American Culture and Critical Agency after Foucault* (New York: Columbia University Press, 1992).

12. Alan Wald, *The New York Intellectuals: The Rise and Decline of the Anti-Stalinist Left from the 1930s to the 1980s* (Chapel Hill: University of North Carolina Press, 1987), xv, 6–10.

13. Milton Himmelfarb, as author of the quip that Jews earn like Episcopalians and vote like Puerto Ricans, certainly gives Kristol a run for the money as leading Jewish aphorist. Neoconservatives get all the good epigrams.

14. Let us recall the terms of Podhoretz's own "Issues" column advocating for Nixon's reelection in 1972, in which he noted (not entirely accurately) that observers across the political spectrum were predicting that Jews were abandoning George McGovern and the Democrats in favor of Nixon. It is not that "Jews are beginning to move into the Republican party" but rather "a steadily mounting Jewish uneasiness over McGovern" that Podhoretz attributes in part to worry about McGovern's attitude toward "Israel" (Norman Podhoretz, "Issues: Between Nixon and the New Politics," *Commentary* 54.3 [1972]: 4). This was of course an early example of a long chain of rightist prognostication, which intensified through the '80s and which is by no means over, that the Jews were becoming a more conservative, Republican-friendly voting bloc.

15. John J. Mearsheimer and Stephen Walt, "The Israel Lobby and U.S. Foreign Policy" (Kennedy School of Government Working Paper RWP06-011, March 13, 2006). It was later published as a book: John J. Mearsheimer and Stephen Walt, *The Israel Lobby and U.S. Foreign Policy* (New York: Farrar, Straus and Giroux, 2007).

16. Susanne Klingenstein, "Town Whores into Warmongers: The Ascent of the Neoconservatives and the Revival of Anti-Jewish Rhetoric in American Public Discourse, 1986–2006," in *The New York Public Intellectuals and Beyond: Exploring Liberal Humanism, Jewish Identity, and the American Protest Tradition*, ed. Ethan Goffman and Daniel Morris (West Lafayette, IN: Purdue University Press, 2009), 276, 294; see also an earlier version of Klingenstein's essay, "'It's Splendid When the Town Whore Gets Religion and Joins the Church': The Rise of the Jewish Neoconservatives as Observed by the Paleoconservatives in the 1980s," *Shofar* 21.3 (2003): 83–98.

17. "Under Forty: A Symposium on American Literature and the Younger Generation of American Jews," *Contemporary Jewish Record* 7.1 (1944): 3–36. Hereafter cited parenthetically in the text.

18. I use this preposition deliberately for its ambiguity, to mark, and ride, the line between an existential or ethical sense of *faced by* and the more definitional or epistemological sense invoked by *belonging to the category*.

19. Indeed, it may be worth noting here that she came from a different, and higher, socioeconomic location than did many of the other symposium participants.

20. Nathan Glazer, "Discussion Forum," in *The New York Public Intellectuals and Beyond: Exploring Liberal Humanism, Jewish Identity, and the American Protest Tradition*, ed. Ethan Goffman and Daniel Morris (West Lafayette, IN: Purdue University Press, 2009), 160.

21. Glazer, "Discussion Forum," 161.

22. Glazer, "Discussion Forum," 160–161.

23. Nathan Glazer, "*Commentary*: The Early Years," in "*Commentary*" *in American Life*, ed. Murray Friedman (Philadelphia: Temple University Press, 2005), 49.

24. Glazer, "*Commentary*: The Early Years," 50.

25. Glazer, "*Commentary*: The Early Years," 49–50.

26. Rebecca L. Walkowitz, "Introduction: Secret Agents," in *Secret Agents: The Rosenberg Case, McCarthyism, and Fifties America* (New York: Routledge, 1995), 3.

27. It is not for nothing that the book that Walkowitz's essay introduces, on the Rosenbergs and 1950s America, is titled *Secret Agents*, emphasizing the importance of agency in the critique of intellectuals.

28. Edward Said, *Representations of the Intellectual* (New York: Vintage, 1994).

29. Alexander Bloom, *Prodigal Sons: The New York Intellectuals and Their World* (New York: Oxford University Press, 1986), 4.

30. Terry Cooney, *The Rise of the New York Intellectuals: "Partisan Review" and Its Circle, 1934–1945* (Madison: University of Wisconsin Press, 1986), 229, 245.

31. Harvey M. Teres, *Renewing the Left: Politics, Imagination, and the New York Intellectuals* (New York: Oxford University Press, 1996), 5.

32. Howe, "New York Intellectuals," 44.

33. Howe, "New York Intellectuals," 30.

34. Howe, "New York Intellectuals," 30.

35. Howe, "New York Intellectuals," 30–31. It pays to keep in mind that we are talking 1968 here, still a year before *Portnoy's Complaint* was published and four years before Howe reversed course on Roth, decreeing that the novelist suffers from a "thin personal culture"—that is, that Roth has not simply *chronicled* in Jews "leav[ing] behind the bonds of Jewishness entirely" the enervation of the Jewish heritage but has himself actually betrayed that heritage.

36. Howe, "New York Intellectuals," 31.

37. Incidentally, Allen Guttmann, who seems to have fallen out of favor, is subtly perceptive on this score, focusing on the unsettled crossing of biology—as he writes, "In the beginning, or what will have to serve as the beginning, Jews defined themselves as a biological group, as the seed of Abraham"—with the problem of conversion, with the fact that people can convert to Judaism and with the concomitant problem introduced by this fact of possible conversion *from* Judaism. Guttmann does not want to say simply that any literature written by the seed of Abraham is Jewish literature; his criterion, ultimately but possibly vaguely (though probably not incorrectly), is that Jewish literature worthy of the name must "deal significantly with the process of assimilation and resultant crisis of identity." See Allen Guttmann, *The Jewish Writer in America: Assimilation and the Crisis of Identity* (New York: Oxford University Press, 1971), 4–5, 13.

38. Howe, "New York Intellectuals," 42.

39. Howe, "New York Intellectuals," 42.

40. Howe, "New York Intellectuals," 42.

41. Howe, "New York Intellectuals," 43.

42. Howe, "New York Intellectuals," 43.

43. As many people know, this is Philip Rahv's term, from his contribution to the 1952 *Partisan Review* symposium "Our Country and Our Culture." See "Our Country and Our Culture," *Partisan Review* 19.3–5 (1952): 306.

44. Much as the word "snake" would, for example, when Trilling was a child first reading for pleasure; like "snake," "Jew" was a word that, as he describes it, "would leap magnetically to my eye from the page before I had reached [it] in the text" (15).

45. This argument is largely formulated in the context of an attack on Ludwig Lewisohn, whom Trilling accuses of precisely this kind of small-mindedness. Incidentally, it is an argument that Ruth Wisse challenges. She wonders (rhetorically) why Trilling chose Lewisohn as representative of contemporary Jewish writing rather than, say, the Zionist magazine *Jewish Frontier*, whose militant nationalism, Wisse points out, could not have led Trilling to his regrettably mistaken belief that twentieth-century Jews manifested a "willingness to be provincial and parochial" (Ruth R. Wisse, "The New York (Jewish) Intellectuals," *Commentary* 84.5 [1987]: 35).

46. Note, please, that he has spelled "micromillimetre" with the British ending,

perhaps suggesting his own success in traversing the provincial and parochial nature of his American Jewish peers.

47. Ruth R. Wisse, "The Jewishness of *Commentary*," in *"Commentary" in American Life*, ed. Murray Friedman (Philadelphia: Temple University Press, 2005), 69.

48. Wisse, "The Jewishness of *Commentary*," 70.

49. Wisse, "The Jewishness of *Commentary*," 53–54.

50. Wisse, "The Jewishness of *Commentary*," 54.

51. Wisse, "The Jewishness of *Commentary*," 54; see also Elliot E. Cohen, "An Act of Affirmation: Editorial Statement," *Commentary* 1 (1945–1946): 1.

52. Wisse, "The Jewishness of *Commentary*," 58. Fiedler, it bears emphasizing, is of course after a far more cosmopolitan outcome in this essay than Wisse seems willing to grant him—certainly more than she is willing herself to advocate; see Leslie Fiedler, "What Can We Do about Fagin? The Jew-Villain in Western Tradition," *Commentary* 7 (1949): 411–418. If one so desired, one could see in Wisse's recuperation here a perverse, parodic repetition of the Mormons' posthumous conversions of Jewish Holocaust victims.

53. Wisse, "The Jewishness of *Commentary*," 58–59.

54. Wisse, "The Jewishness of *Commentary*," 63. At some risk, I suppose, I will quote Scott McConnell, from the pages of the *American Conservative*, in which he calls Norman Podhoretz, who "could well be counted the most influential American intellectual of the postwar era," "a talented and pugnacious ideologue with control of a nicely subsidized magazine" (Scott McConnell, "Thought Leader," *American Conservative*, August 1, 2011, 45).

55. Wisse, "The Jewishness of *Commentary*," 63.

56. Wisse, "The Jewishness of *Commentary*," 64.

57. Indeed, one sometimes gets the *unheimlich* feeling that Wisse—presumably unintentionally—is arguing on behalf of those anti-Semitic wingnuts who saw in the second Iraq War, and specifically in Paul Wolfowitz, Richard Perle, and Douglas Feith's chicken-hawk war council, evidence that George W. Bush's foreign policy had been hijacked by Zionists to unduly benefit the Jews—that is, Israel. What makes the feeling uncanny more than simply perverse is that Wisse seems quite deliberately to agree with the anti-Semites that "Israel" and "The Jews" should without remainder map each other. One might be willing to call this a characteristic move of neoconservative Zionist criticism: see my discussion of Susanne Klingenstein, earlier in this chapter.

58. Irving Kristol, we recall, was always a bit suspicious of calling neoconservatism anything more than this: insofar as "it was never really a movement, . . . since no organizational efforts were made or even thought of," he preferred terms such as "impulse," "persuasion," and, even, "generational phenomenon." See Irving Kristol, "An Autobiographical Memoir," in *Neoconservatism: The Autobiography of an Idea* (1995; repr., Chicago: Ivan R. Dee, 1999), 31, 40.

59. Wisse, "The Jewishness of *Commentary*," 67. Podhoretz, for notable example, uses the term "neoconservative" as early as 1961, in the introduction to *Commentary*'s symposium dedicated to "Jewishness and the Younger Intellectuals" (31.4 [1961]: 309).

See also Lionel Trilling, *Beyond Culture: Essays on Literature and Learning* (1965; repr., New York: Harcourt, Brace, Jovanovich, 1978).

60. Wisse, "The Jewishness of *Commentary*," 67.

61. Wisse, "The Jewishness of *Commentary*," 67.

62. Wisse, "The Jewishness of *Commentary*," 68.

63. Wisse, "The Jewishness of *Commentary*," 71. As Wisse has more recently written, on the occasion of the posthumous publication of the Irving Kristol essay collection *The Neoconservative Persuasion*, edited by his widow, Gertrude Himmelfarb, "As far as the Jews were concerned, Kristol thought that the encounter between the worst of European weakness and the best of American power ought to have wised them up politically, making them vigilant against declared enemies; he was disappointed to find how keen they remained to ignore history's teachings. In later decades, those same teachings were what prompted Kristol's definition of a neoconservative as 'a liberal who has been mugged by reality': that is, someone essentially hopeful of human progress who—however reluctantly—musters the ability to confront the forces that would thwart it." Wisse says of Kristol's term "neoconservative" that it

> spoke for those who in the late 1960s and early 70s were sobered up by aggressions against the American democratic order, and against Israel and the Jews, and by the failure of so many to stand up to them: from without, Soviet expansionism, Arab revanchism, and other cold-war dangers; from within, New Left violence and the anti-American excesses of the accurately-named counterculture. Kristol marveled that the liberalism of Jews, who ought to have been the first to rally in defense of the goodness of American society and its values, remained "especially rich in illusions." How could Jews, of all people, fail to appreciate the justice of Israel or the force of the enmity against it; how could they blithely continue to support socialist, quasi-socialist, or left-liberal positions that demonstrably threatened the social and economic health of the United States?

In this unequivocal environment, Wisse argues,

> Norman Podhoretz, the longtime editor of *Commentary* and, with Kristol, the most powerful voice of neoconservatism, has held up his late friend and colleague as "a great warrior on the battlefield of ideas and a great general in the political and cultural wars of our time." The military metaphor is apt—there was, and there continues to be, a great battle of ideas over the essential worth of our civilization, and great battles require great leaders. In the struggle for the minds of American Jews in particular, Kristol's leadership was of a special kind. To him, the reflexes of American Jews had atrophied; over-habituated by too many centuries of accommodation to power, they had become unable or unwilling to recognize where their true friends lay, and who were now their true enemies. He encouraged them to consider afresh what it meant, and what it would take, to persevere as a minority in a primarily Christian country—without obsolete fears of religious persecution.

Ruth R. Wisse, "The Conscience of a Jewish Conservative," *Jewish Ideas Daily*, January 21, 2011, http://www.jewishideasdaily.com/content/module/2011/1/21/main-feature/1/the-conscience-of-a-jewish-conservative/.

64. "Editorial Statement," *Partisan Review* 4 (December 1937): 3–4; *Partisan Review* editors, "Editorial Statement (1934)," in *The New York Intellectuals Reader*, ed. Neil Jumonville (New York: Routledge, 2007), 56.

65. Wisse, "New York (Jewish) Intellectuals," 33.

66. Wisse, "New York (Jewish) Intellectuals," 34.

67. Wisse, "New York (Jewish) Intellectuals," 34.

68. Wisse, "New York (Jewish) Intellectuals," 34.

69. Wisse, "New York (Jewish) Intellectuals," 34. Wisse does not cite Isaac Deutscher here, but she does put the term in quotation marks, so it is quite possible she means to reference him. Moreover, Alan Wald, whose book is one of those that Wisse's 1987 *Commentary* piece, ostensibly a review essay, takes up, cites Deutscher (and his compelling catchphrase) in describing the rationalist disdain of Judeo-centrism among Jewish intellectuals in early twentieth-century New York. Wald's interest in Deutscher's Jewish humanism and internationalist concern with world culture, as apart from both assimilationism and separatist nationalism, no doubt further fuels the indignant fire of Wisse's nationalist pique. See Isaac Deutscher, *The Non-Jewish Jew and Other Essays*, ed. Tamara Deutscher (Oxford: Oxford University Press, 1968).

70. Wisse, "New York (Jewish) Intellectuals," 34.

71. Wisse, "New York (Jewish) Intellectuals," 34–35. Incidentally, as I suggested earlier, this line of argumentation arises in intimate conjunction with Wisse's elevating of the Zionist magazine *Jewish Frontier*, whose militant nationalism, she points out, Trilling could have turned to instead of to Ludwig Lewisohn as the paragon of contemporary Jewish writing, from whose example Trilling derived his regrettably mistaken belief that twentieth-century Jews manifested a "willingness to be provincial and parochial" (35).

72. Wisse, "New York (Jewish) Intellectuals," 34.

73. Wisse, "New York (Jewish) Intellectuals," 38.

74. Wisse, "The Jewishness of *Commentary*," 54.

75. Wisse, "The Jewishness of *Commentary*," 55.

76. Wisse, "The Jewishness of *Commentary*," 55.

77. Wisse, "The Jewishness of *Commentary*," 54–55.

78. Norman Podhoretz, introduction to "A Symposium: Jewishness and the Younger Intellectuals," *Commentary* 31.4 (1961): 306–310.

79. Podhoretz, introduction, 306.

80. Podhoretz, introduction, 307.

81. Podhoretz, introduction, 306.

82. Podhoretz, introduction, 307–308. The Kazin quote is cited on 307; Kazin's phrase from the original was actually "Babbitt-warrens," as I quote it earlier, but

Podhoretz cited it without the hyphen. It might be salutary to remember Irving Howe's words on alienation, from the later *Partisan Review* "Our Country and Our Culture" symposium:

> This word has a curious history. As used by Marx, it suggests the psychic price of living in a society which resolves "personal worth into exchange value" and in which the worker's "deed becomes an alien power." The subdivision of labor makes the worker "a cripple . . . forcing him to develop some highly specialized dexterity at the cost of a world of productive impulses. . . ." Certain writers therefore have a point when they attack the notion that intellectuals are alienated and insist, rather, that intellectuals are among the few who can achieve an organic relation to their work—but it is a scholastic point. For it must by now be clear that the word "alienation" has at least two distinct uses. When the worker, because of his place in production, is alienated from his capacities, that is a social evil; when the intellectual, because of his spiritual independence, becomes alienated from bourgeois society and its values, that is something else again.

"Our Country and Our Culture," 575. Then again, in Podhoretz's defense (perhaps?) in his indignation at Kazin, it might be salutary to quote Arthur Schlesinger, Jr., from the same symposium: "Next to Himmler, even Babbitt began to look good" (591).

83. Podhoretz, introduction, 307.

84. Wisse, "New York (Jewish) Intellectuals," 36.

85. Wisse, "New York (Jewish) Intellectuals," 35.

86. Podhoretz, introduction, 307.

87. Podhoretz, introduction, 308.

88. Wisse, "The Jewishness of *Commentary*," 69.

89. Wisse, "New York (Jewish) Intellectuals," 36.

90. Wisse, "The Jewishness of *Commentary*," 55.

91. Incidentally, the essay's indictment of Trilling's snobbery is still largely standard.

92. Delmore Schwartz, "The Duchess' Red Shoes," in *Selected Essays of Delmore Schwartz*, ed. Donald A. Dike and David H. Zucker (Chicago: University of Chicago Press, 1970), 205–206; Schwartz is here quoting Lionel Trilling, from "Manners, Morals, and the Novel," in *The Liberal Imagination: Essays on Literature and Society* (New York: Harcourt Brace Jovanovich, 1978), 198, 199.

93. Trilling, "Manners, Morals, and the Novel," 194.

94. Schwartz, "The Duchess' Red Shoes," 208.

95. See, for example, Trilling's spelling of "micromillimetre," earlier.

96. Schwartz, "The Duchess' Red Shoes," 222.

97. Schwartz, "The Duchess' Red Shoes," 211.

98. Schwartz, "The Duchess' Red Shoes," 212.

99. Norman Finkelstein, *The Ritual of New Creation: Jewish Tradition and Contemporary Literature* (Albany: SUNY Press, 1992), 144.

CHAPTER 4: WHY JEWS AREN'T NORMAL

1. Philip Roth, *The Counterlife* (1986; repr., New York: Vintage, 1996). Further references to the book will be cited parenthetically in the text.

2. It is notable that Roth's so-called Roth Books—that is, the novels featuring a character named "Philip" or "Philip Roth," such as *Deception*, *Operation Shylock*, and *The Plot against America*, which are conspicuously grouped with ostensibly nonfiction books such as *Patrimony* and *The Facts* on the "Books by Philip Roth" page of the paratext of recent editions of books by Philip Roth—seem to have escaped some of the more egregious varieties of reductive documentary positivism to which the Zuckerman books are routinely subjected in the scholarship.

3. Philip Roth, *Zuckerman Bound: A Trilogy and Epilogue, 1979–1985* (New York: Library of America, 2007), 66–67.

4. Roth, *Zuckerman Bound*, 257.

5. As much as I respect Irving Howe's work outside the self-righteous pontification in which he occasionally engaged, such as in "Philip Roth Reconsidered," part of me persists in the hope that he will be discovered to have secretly put out a heretofore unknown publication that any number of Roth's readers will be able to analogize to *Lickety Split*.

6. That the expectation of such an algorithm may be an increasingly dominant characteristic of the corporatist university's take on the humanities does not make it a good one.

7. As Roth's readers know, *My Life as a Man* is the novel in which a character named Nathan Zuckerman first appeared, though I think it would be difficult to show that this Nathan Zuckerman is the same character who emerged five years later in the first of the so-called Zuckerman books.

8. Roth, *Zuckerman Bound*, 59.

9. Dean J. Franco, *Race, Rights, and Recognition: Jewish American Literature since 1969* (Ithaca: Cornell University Press, 2012). Christopher Douglas, in his *Genealogy of Literary Multiculturalism* (Ithaca: Cornell University Press, 2009), follows Walter Benn Michaels's persuasive critique (in books such as *Our America: Nativism, Modernism, Pluralism* [Durham: Duke University Press, 1995] and *The Shape of the Signifier: 1967 to the End of History* [Princeton: Princeton University Press, 2004] and, more popularly, *The Trouble with Diversity: How We Learned to Love Identity and Ignore Inequality* [New York: Holt, 2006]) of the racialist heritage of currently ascendant ideas about culture and ethnicity but also like Michaels relies on an overly simplistic notion of authorial agency, reducing the problem of identity, in the last instance, to a stance adopted by an author.

10. Chantal Mouffe, "Democratic Politics and the Question of Identity," in *The Identity in Question*, ed. John Rajchman (New York: Routledge, 1995), 36, 38.

11. Jacques Rancière, "Politics, Identification, and Subjectivization," in Rajchman, *The Identity in Question*, 65–69.

12. "Discussion" section in part 1, "Debate," in Rajchman, *The Identity in Question*, 129.

13. See Benjamin Schreier, "The Failure of Identity: Toward a New Literary History of Philip Roth's Unrecognizable Jew," *Jewish Social Studies: History, Culture, Society* n.s. 17.2 (2011): 101–135. Some of the discussion to follow in the next two pages is derived from this article.

14. Philip Roth, *Operation Shylock: A Confession* (New York: Vintage, 1993), 130; ellipses and emphasis in original.

15. Philip Roth, *American Pastoral* (1997; repr., New York: Vintage, 1998), 3–4.

16. Roth, *American Pastoral*, 20.

17. We can see this paradox as a kind of perverse parallel, perhaps, of what Andrew Ross has analyzed as an (earlier) Cold War paranoia about Communist infiltration in US society. If in the leftist 1930s *real* Communists were easy to distinguish, by the postwar years signs of normality and of social conformity could be regarded (by alert neighbors and friends) as the most insidious signs of treachery. For Ross, the Rosenbergs stand as the paradigmatic example: they could be presented as a social threat not because they harbored subversive or violently revolutionary ideas but precisely because they were so much like an ordinary, patriotic American couple. See Andrew Ross, *No Respect: Intellectuals and Popular Culture* (New York: Routledge, 1989), 20–22.

18. In later chapters, "Maria" will be a married British woman with whom a sexually disabled Nathan has an affair in New York and, as we have already seen, the wife with whom Nathan lives in England.

19. Leo Bersani's famous explication of how nonnormative difference is coded as transgressiveness in the normative image of a self is helpfully illuminating here; see "Is the Rectum a Grave?," *October* 43 (Winter 1987): 197–222.

20. See on this point Michael Warner, *The Trouble with Normal: Sex, Politics, and the Ethics of Queer Life* (Cambridge: Harvard University Press, 1999), 69.

21. Norman Finkelstein, *The Ritual of New Creation: Jewish Tradition and Contemporary Literature* (Albany: SUNY Press, 1992), 140.

22. Daniel Boyarin and Jonathan Boyarin, "Diaspora: Generation and the Ground of Jewish Identity," *Critical Inquiry* 19.4 (1993): 705.

CHAPTER 5: 9/11'S STEALTHY JEWS

1. Michael Kramer, "Race, Literary History, and the 'Jewish' Question," *Prooftexts* 21.3 (2001): 336–337. I do not think the recent renascence of literature by religiously observant Jews in America alters this literary historical problematic much. Modern Judaism's difficult categorical status, with feet in both consent- and descent-based logics, demands that even if we seek a specific kind of doctrinal or practice-based knowledge from literature, the warrant for such searching often arises in the assumption that identity is descent based.

2. Jonathan Arac, *"Huckleberry Finn" as Idol and Target: The Functions of Criticism in Our Time* (Madison: University of Madison Press, 1997), 216.

3. *Everything Is Illuminated* is a novel, incidentally, that I find to be unreadable in its self-satisfied posturing—at least in the Trachimbrod sections. Again incidentally, I feel bound to note that an anonymous reviewer commented—piercingly—that my

aversion to *Everything Is Illuminated* must be an example of the narcissism of small differences, given my book's "mile-a-minute referentiality and its concern with high-stakes intellectual and moral questions," which I *suppose* could come across as "self-satisfied posturing." I of course prefer to—must—disagree with this judgment, but due diligence demands I cite it.

4. Philip Roth, *The Counterlife* (New York: Vintage, 1996), 145. See my discussion of this passage in chapter 4.

5. Julian Levinson, review of *Singing in a Strange Land: A Jewish American Poetics*, by Maerra Y. Schreiber, *American Jewish History* 94.1–2 (2008): 135. Ozick famously wrote in 1970,

> Nothing thought or written in Diaspora has ever been able to last unless it has been centrally Jewish. . . . By "centrally Jewish" I mean, for literature, whatever touches on the liturgical. Obviously this does not refer only to prayer. It refers to a type of literature and to a type of perception. There is a critical difference between liturgy and a poem. Liturgy is in command of the reciprocal moral imagination rather than of the isolated lyrical imagination. A poem is a private flattery; it moves the private heart, but to no end other than being moved. A poem is a decoration of the heart, the art of the instant. It is what Yehudah Halevi called flowers without fruit. Liturgy is also a poem, but it means not to have only a private voice. Liturgy has a choral voice, a communal voice, the echo of the voice of the Lord of History. Poetry shuns judgment and memory and seizes the moment. In all of history the literature that has lasted for Jews has been liturgical.

Cynthia Ozick, "America: Toward Yavneh," in *What Is Jewish Literature?*, ed. Hana Wirth-Nesher (Philadelphia: JPS, 1994), 27–28. The point, of course, is that such a liturgical literature necessarily demands a midrashic reading communally grounded in commentary.

6. Of course, so did John Hersey, for *The Wall*, and he was the son of missionaries, so I guess winning that award does not *actually* prove anything.

7. John N. Duvall and Robert P. Marzec, "Narrating 9/11," *MFS: Modern Fiction Studies* 57.3 (2011): 396.

8. Slavoj Žižek, *Welcome to the Desert of the Real!* (New York: Verso, 2002), 22. This strikes me as largely persuasive: only something recognized as possible—that is, bearing some kind of potential, some kind of legibility, even if a negative, excluded one—can be nonexistent; it simply does not make sense to talk about that which has no possibility, and we certainly cannot talk about its being nonexistent, as it is unmarked.

9. We recall that A. R. Black's one-word biography card of Oskar reads "Son" (Jonathan Safran Foer, *Extremely Loud and Incredibly Close* [2005; repr., Boston: Mariner, 2006], 286; further references to the book will be cited parenthetically in the text); only an acrobatically tendentious reading of the book could support a claim that Oskar earned this judgment for his relation with his mother.

10. Can one fairly call a "midrash" a comment about characters who are not Jewish? In any case, the irruption of the word "midrash" here is clearly part of the field of literary semitism's operation.

11. Oskar's grandmother asks Oskar in a letter, "how can you say I love you to someone you love?" adding that "it's always necessary" (314).

12. Indeed, Oskar's mother's admission late in the novel that Thomas called her from the tower, and that she told him that Oskar was home, adds to the sustainability of Oskar's self-traumatizing suspicion here—though proleptically so.

13. Philippe Codde, "Philomela Revisited: Traumatic Iconicity in Jonathan Safran Foer's *Extremely Loud and Incredibly Close*," *Studies in American Fiction* 35.2 (2007): 251.

14. Incidentally, and I note this with no more than half a mind to burnish the Holocaust bona fides of Foer's book ("no more than half" because I think one *cannot* ultimately or definitively link the book to the Holocaust), this move repeats Art Spiegelman's gesture in the final frame of *Maus*, in which Vladek, having just narrated his reuniting with Anja after the liberation—the furthest thing from the end of story, as far as Spiegelman's book is concerned—and requested that Artie turn off the tape recorder, refers to Artie as Richieu, Vladek and Anja's first son, who died during the war, in one of *MAUS*'s more horrific scenes (Art Spiegelman, *Maus: A Survivor's Tale*, vol. 2, *And Here My Troubles Began* [New York: Pantheon-Random, 1991], 136).

15. Žižek, *Welcome to the Desert of the Real!*, 15–16. This of course echoes—I would be surprised if Žižek in fact had not seen and was not inspired by—the *Onion*'s famous headline of 26 September 2001 (from its "Holy Fucking Shit: Attack on America" issue): "American Life Turns into Bad Jerry Bruckheimer Movie" (*Onion*, September 26, 2001, http://www.theonion.com/articles/american-life-turns-into-bad-jerry-bruckheimer-mov,220/). As one New York resident is quoted in the article on this point, " 'Terrorist hijackings, buildings blowing up, thousands of people dying—these are all things I'm accustomed to seeing,' said Dan Monahan, 32, who witnessed the fiery destruction of the Twin Towers firsthand from the window of his second-story apartment in Park Slope, Brooklyn. 'I've seen them all before—we all have—on TV and in movies.' " A little later, we read,

> For nearly two full weeks, Americans sat transfixed in front of their televisions, listening to shocked newscasters struggle to maintain their composure while describing events that would have been rejected by Hollywood producers as not believable enough for a Sylvester Stallone vehicle. All the familiar action-movie elements were there: terrorists taking over a plane, panicked crowds, huge fireball explosions, Secret Service agents ushering the president to a secret underground military base in Nebraska to plan the next move. A news report revealed that the terrorists had planned to strike Air Force One. At any moment, it seemed a squadron of alien warships would materialize and begin to menace Jeff Goldblum.

16. Žižek, *Welcome to the Desert of the Real!*, 19.

17. This disappointment is given a striking figure in the decontainment of the Afghanistan and Iraq wars and in the mounting desperation on the part of US political elites to put them in the rearview mirror. These adventures were sold initially, in the Bush administration's narrativization of 9/11, as part of the easy (and definitive) conclusion of that 9/11 narrative.

18. In the years following the attacks, blustery insistence by what Michael Bérubé has called the "Manichean Left" (see his *The Left at War* [New York: NYU Press, 2009]) that the US reaped on 9/11 what it had sowed for decades and nationalistic emblematizing by what I will call the "Moronic Right" depicting for one example I ambivalently admit I have seen a bald eagle with Osama bin Laden in its beak alike displayed a slack-witted demand that experience offer itself up in easily legible narratives.

19. Ilka Saal, "Regarding the Pain of Self and Other: Trauma Transfer and Narrative Framing in Jonathan Safran Foer's *Extremely Loud and Incredibly Close*," *MFS: Modern Fiction Studies* 57.3 (2011): 459; see also 457–458.

20. Saal, "Regarding the Pain of Self and Other," 454.

21. Saal, "Regarding the Pain of Self and Other," 456.

22. Cathy Caruth, "Unclaimed Experience: Trauma and the Possibility of History," *Yale French Studies* 79 (1991): 182, 187–188, 192.

23. In this context, it is not infrequently paired with Judith Butler's *Precarious Life: The Power of Mourning and Violence* (New York: Verso, 2006) in an effort to stage as well a critique of short-sighted nationalism.

24. Citing Caruth, Philippe Codde reads Foer's novel as a "traumatic history": if the novel represents a search for "a painful past that is by definition inaccessible," and if Oskar never finds what he searches for, his quest nonetheless reveals something that was unsought, namely, other people's trauma. Rather than representing the traumatic past or rendering it accessible, language in the form of traumatic history—as an open, constructed record of inscription and reinscription pursued with others rather than the closed, reconstructed record of a self-evident event—becomes for Codde the ethical space in which people are linked together, where "alternative forms of communication" can "fill the void left by traumatic experiences" ("Philomela Revisited," 241–243, 246). Benjamin Bird suggests a different focus on the ethics of trauma by emphasizing Judith Butler's recent argument that traumatic loss occasions a crisis of identification and self-relation (see Butler, *Precarious Life*, 21–22). Bird is interested in trauma's potential to serve as an occasion for greater self-understanding and therapeutic self-exploration pursued by a national subject. By bringing together a number of historical traumas—Dresden, Hiroshima, 9/11—Foer's novel focuses the "need to retrieve and examine memories of trauma that may illuminate present day tragedy"; his appeal to an archive of historical suffering further illustrates trauma theory's investment in an identitarian concept of history-as-ethics (Benjamin Bird, "History, Emotion, and the Body: Mourning in Post-9/11 Fiction," *Literature Compass* 4.3 [2007]: 562). Matthew Mullins comes to a similar conclusion, reading in Foer's novel an articulation of what he calls "traumatic solidarity." In opposition to the militantly hermetic nationalism that arose in the US after 9/11, Foer's novel "becomes a space in which to challenge the

effects of national solidarity and America's sense of being the lone victim . . . and to promote instead a connection between victimization and identity that breaches existing collective identities." Enacted in visions of "global community" suggested by the novel's rendering proximate of historically and geographically distanced events (such as Dresden, Hiroshima, and 9/11), "traumatic solidarity" stands as an "additional collective that works across" the numerous group identities that individuals already claim, such as class, gender, religion, occupation, nationality; rather than reinforcing such categories, "traumatic solidarity should breach identity borders" (Matthew Mullins, "Boroughs and Neighbors: Traumatic Solidarity in Jonathan Safran Foer's *Extremely Loud and Incredibly Close*," *Papers on Language and Literature* 43.3 [2009]: 304, 300, 299). Thus in the novel we witness a salubrious interdependency, as Oskar comes to greater self-consciousness only through the other, from the perspectives of other people, even as these others depend on him.

25. This is attested in Saal, Codde, Bird, and Mullins alike.

26. Michael Rothberg, *Traumatic Realism: The Demands of Holocaust Representation* (Minneapolis: University of Minnesota Press, 2000), 101, 103.

27. The impulse behind these invented but determinant scenes of death is repeated in Oskar's other inventions, such as a building that moves up and down around a stationary elevator, which "could be extremely useful, because if you're on the ninety-fifth floor, and a plane hits below you, the building could take you to the ground, and everyone could be safe" (3), or a birdseed shirt, whose appeal to avian desire might well save a life in the event of a jump from a burning skyscraper.

28. I should also say that I think this function keeps the book from being simply sentimental. Incidentally, I am not alone in noticing that Oskar does not delude himself in his imaginative conferral of determinacy. See, for, example, Elisabeth Siegel, "'Stuff That Happened to Me': Visual Memory in Jonathan Safran Foer's *Extremely Loud and Incredibly Close* (2005)," *COPAS* 10 (2009), http://copas.uni-regensburg.de/article/view/115/139; Codde, "Philomela Revisited," 250–251; and Stefanie Hoth, "From Individual Experience to Historical Event and Back Again: '9/11' in Jonathan Safran Foer's *Extremely Loud and Incredibly Close*," *Kulturelles Wissen und Intertextualität: Theoriekonzeptionen und Fallstudien zur Kontextualisierung von Literatur*, ed. Marion Gymnich, Birgit Neumann, and Ansgar Nünning (Trier, Germany: Wissenschaftlicher Verlag Trier, 2006), 296–297, though Hoth does not emphasize as much as I might like the fact that Oskar really appreciates that he cannot (in her words) "flee the harsh reality" in his "fantasy."

29. Saal, "Regarding the Pain of Self and Other," 456.

30. Saal, "Regarding the Pain of Self and Other," 455.

31. Saal, "Regarding the Pain of Self and Other," 468–469; see also Foer, *Extremely Loud and Incredibly Close*, 215.

32. Saal, "Regarding the Pain of Self and Other," 473.

33. Isaac Bashevis Singer, *Enemies, a Love Story* (New York: Farrar, Straus and Giroux, 1972), 242; further references to the book will be cited parenthetically in the text.

34. Žižek, *Welcome to the Desert of the Real!*, 16.

35. That said, it is doubtful that the name *is* Jewish, given the paternal Dresden history we are provided. Of course, we know precious little about Oskar's mother.

36. Incidentally—again—and not that this is either here or there, this fact can be seen to buttress the link between Foer's and Spiegelman's books: readers of the latter will recall that Vladek admits to Artie "I made in the States a living dealing diamonds" (Spiegelman, *And Here My Troubles Began*, 125).

37. There is some question whether grandmother's letters are in fact sent to—or even intended for—Oskar. Three narrators appear in Foer's book: Oskar, who guides us through much of the present action; grandfather Thomas, who writes the "Why I'm Not Where You Are" sections (that is, his letters); and grandmother, who authors the four "My Feelings" sections. (Incidentally, Saal points out that the three narratives appear "in an unchanging sequence of Oskar-Grandpa-Oskar-Grandma (repeated four times, with a final chapter by Oskar)" [Saal, "Regarding the Pain of Self and Other," 463].) The first of grandmother's sections is addressed "Dear Oskar" (75), but grandfather Thomas writes in one of his letters that when he looked at the memoir that grandmother had been writing, there was nothing but a collection of empty pages (120–123). Though she later writes in a "My Feelings" section, "I . . . pretended to write. I hit the space bar again and again and again" (176), it is possible that *none* of grandmother's "writing" in fact exists for others to see.

38. We will later learn enough to presume that he keeps so many animals because of the horrific night he spent euthanizing the suffering inhabitants of the Dresden zoo after the firebombing.

39. In the time since the attacks, Oskar has devoted a great deal of energy to writing letters to a variety of more or less famous people, a list that includes, as he in one scene tells his mother, "Kofi Annan, Siegfried, Roy, Jacques Chirac, E. O. Wilson, Weird Al Yankovic, Bill Gates, Vladimir Putin, and some other people" (106). Elsewhere, we learn of several others.

CONCLUSION

1. See the recent Pew study: Pew Research, Religion & Public Life Project, *A Portrait of Jewish Americans*, 1 October 2013, http://www.pewforum.org/2013/10/01/jewish-american-beliefs-attitudes-culture-survey/ (accessed 24 November 2013).

2. Daniel Boyarin and Jonathan Boyarin, "Introduction / So What's New?," in *Jews and Other Differences: The New Jewish Cultural Studies*, ed. Jonathan Boyarin and Daniel Boyarin (Minneapolis: University of Minnesota Press, 1997), xi.

BIBLIOGRAPHY

Alter, Robert. *After the Tradition: Essays on Modern Jewish Writing*. New York: Dutton, 1969.

"American Life Turns into Bad Jerry Bruckheimer Movie." *Onion*, September 26, 2001. http://www.theonion.com/articles/american-life-turns-into-bad-jerry-bruckheimer-mov,220/.

Anderson, Benedict. "Exodus." *Critical Inquiry* 20.2 (1994): 314–327.

Arac, Jonathan. *"Huckleberry Finn" as Idol and Target: The Functions of Criticism in Our Time*. Madison: University of Wisconsin Press, 1997.

———. "Toward a Genealogy of the U.S. Discourse of Identity: *Invisible Man* after Fifty Years." *Boundary 2* 30.2 (2003): 195–216.

Aviv, Caryn, and David Shneer. *New Jews: The End of the Jewish Diaspora*. New York: NYU Press, 2005.

Badiou, Alain. *Saint Paul: The Foundation of Universalism*. Stanford: Stanford University Press, 2003.

Barrish, Phillip. "'The Genuine Article': Ethnicity, Capital, and *The Rise of David Levinsky*." *American Literary History* 5.4 (1993): 643–662.

Bersani, Leo. "Is the Rectum a Grave?" *October* 43 (Winter 1987): 197–222.

Bérubé, Michael. *The Left at War*. New York: NYU Press, 2009.

Biale, David. "Confessions of an Historian of Jewish Culture." *Jewish Social Studies* 1.1 (1994): 40–51.

Biale, David, Michael Galchinsky, and Susannah Heschel, eds. *Insider/Outsider: American Jews and Multiculturalism*. Berkeley: University of California Press, 1998.

———. "Introduction: The Dialectic of Jewish Enlightenment." In *Insider/Outsider: American Jews and Multiculturalism*, edited by David Biale, Michael Galchinsky, and Susannah Heschel, 1–13. Berkeley: University of California Press, 1998.

Bird, Benjamin. "History, Emotion, and the Body: Mourning in Post-9/11 Fiction." *Literature Compass* 4.3 (2007): 561–575.

Blair, Sara. "Whose Modernism Is It? Abraham Cahan, Fictions of Yiddish, and the Contest of Modernity." *Modern Fiction Studies* 51.2 (2005): 258–284.

Bloom, Alexander. *Prodigal Sons: The New York Intellectuals and Their World*. New York: Oxford University Press, 1986.

Bové, Paul. *Mastering Discourse: The Politics of Intellectual Culture*. Durham: Duke University Press, 1992.

Boyarin, Daniel. *A Radical Jew: Paul and the Politics of Identity*. Berkeley: University of California Press, 1994.

Boyarin, Daniel, and Jonathan Boyarin. "Diaspora: Generation and the Ground of Jewish Identity." *Critical Inquiry* 19.4 (1993): 693–725.

———. "Introduction / So What's New?" In *Jews and Other Differences: The New Jewish Cultural Studies*, edited Jonathan Boyarin and Daniel Boyarin, vii–xxii. Minneapolis: University of Minnesota Press, 1997.

Boyarin, Daniel, Daniel Itzkovitz, and Ann Pellegrini, eds. *Queer Theory and the Jewish Question*. New York: Columbia University Press, 2003.

Boyarin, Jonathan. *Thinking in Jewish*. Chicago: University of Chicago Press, 1996.

Boyarin, Jonathan, and Daniel Boyarin, eds. *Jews and Other Differences: The New Jewish Cultural Studies*. Minneapolis: University of Minnesota Press, 1997.

Brook, Vincent, ed. *You Should See Yourself: Jewish Identity in Postmodern American Culture*. New Brunswick: Rutgers University Press, 2006.

Butler, Judith. *Bodies That Matter: On the Discursive Limits of "Sex."* New York: Routledge, 1993.

———. *Precarious Life: The Power of Mourning and Violence*. New York: Verso, 2006.

Cahan, Abraham. "The Late Rabbi Joseph, Hebrew Patriarch of New York." *American Monthly Review of Reviews* 26.3 (1902): 311–314.

———. *The Rise of David Levinsky*. 1917. Reprint, New York: Penguin, 1993.

———. "The Russian Jew in America." *Atlantic Monthly* 82 (July 1898): 128–139.

———. *"Yekl" and "The Imported Bridegroom" and Other Stories of the New York Ghetto*. New York: Dover, 1970.

Cammy, Justin, Dara Horn, Alyssa Quint, and Rachel Rubinstein, eds. *Arguing the Modern Jewish Canon: Essays on Literature and Culture in Honor of Ruth R. Wisse*. Cambridge: Harvard University Press, 2008.

Caruth, Cathy. "Unclaimed Experience: Trauma and the Possibility of History." *Yale French Studies* 79 (1991): 181–192.

Chametzky, Jules. *From the Ghetto: The Fiction of Abraham Cahan*. Amherst: University of Massachusetts Press, 1977.

Chiang, Mark. *The Cultural Capital of Asian American Studies: Autonomy and Representation in the University*. New York: NYU Press, 2009.

Chuh, Kandice. *Imagine Otherwise: On Asian Americanist Critique*. Durham: Duke University Press, 2003.

Codde, Philippe. "Philomela Revisited: Traumatic Iconicity in Jonathan Safran Foer's *Extremely Loud and Incredibly Close*." *Studies in American Fiction* 35.2 (2007): 241–254.

Cohen, Elliot E. "An Act of Affirmation: Editorial Statement." *Commentary* 1 (1945–1946): 1.

Cooney, Terry. *The Rise of the New York Intellectuals: "Partisan Review" and Its Circle, 1934–1945*. Madison: University of Wisconsin Press, 1986.

Cuddihy, John Murray. *The Ordeal of Civility: Freud, Marx, Lévi-Strauss, and the Jewish Struggle with Modernity*. 2nd ed. Boston: Beacon, 1987.

Cutter, Martha. "Introduction: Reading, Writing, and Recognition." *MELUS* 37.1 (2012): 5–13.

Deleuze, Gilles, and Félix Guattari. *Kafka: Toward a Minor Literature*. Translated by Dana Polan. Minneapolis: University of Minnesota Press, 1986.

Deutscher, Isaac. *The Non-Jewish Jew and Other Essays*. Edited by Tamara Deutscher. Oxford: Oxford University Press, 1968.

Dickstein, Morris. *Double Agent: The Critic and Society*. New York: Oxford University Press, 1992.

"Discussion" section to part 1, "Debate." In *The Identity in Question*, edited by John Rajchman, 129–144. New York: Routledge, 1995.

Douglas, Christopher. *A Genealogy of Literary Multiculturalism*. Ithaca: Cornell University Press, 2009.

Duvall, John N., and Robert P. Marzec. "Narrating 9/11." *MFS: Modern Fiction Studies* 57.3 (2011): 381–400.

"Editorial Statement." *Partisan Review* 4 (December 1937): 3–4.

Fiedler, Leslie. *Fiedler on the Roof: Essays on Literature and Jewish Identity*. Boston: David R. Godine, 1991.

———. "What Can We Do about Fagin? The Jew-Villain in Western Tradition." *Commentary* 7 (1949): 411–418.

Finkelstein, Norman. *The Ritual of New Creation: Jewish Tradition and Contemporary Literature*. Albany: SUNY Press, 1992.

Finkelstein, Norman G. *The Holocaust Industry: Reflections on the Exploitation of Jewish Suffering*. 2nd paperback ed. London: Verso, 2003.

Foer, Jonathan Safran. *Extremely Loud and Incredibly Close*. 2005. Reprint, Boston: Mariner, 2006.

———. *Everything Is Illuminated*. 2002. Reprint, New York: Harper Perennial, 2003.

Foote, Stephanie. "Marvels of Memory: Citizenship and Ethnic Identity in Abraham Cahan's 'The Imported Bridegroom.'" *MELUS* 25.1 (2000): 33–53.

Foucault, Michel. *The Birth of Biopolitics: Lectures at the Collège de France, 1978–1979*. Edited by Michel Snellart. Translated by Graham Burchell. New York: Picador, 2008.

———. "'*Omnes et Singulatum*': Toward a Critique of Political Reason." In *The Chomsky-Foucault Debate: On Human Nature*, edited by John Rajchman, 172–210. New York: New Press, 2006.

———. "Truth and Power." In *Power/Knowledge: Selected Interviews and Other Writings, 1972–1977*, edited by Colin Gordon, 109–133. New York: Pantheon, 1980.

Franco, Dean. *Ethnic American Literature: Comparing Chicano, Jewish, and African American Literature*. Charlottesville: University of Virginia Press, 2006.

———. "Portnoy's Complaint: It's about Race, Not Sex (Even the Sex Is about Race)." *Prooftexts* 29.1 (2009): 86–115.

———. *Race, Rights, and Recognition: Jewish American Literature since 1969*. Ithaca: Cornell University Press, 2012.

———. "Rereading Cynthia Ozick: Pluralism, Postmodernism, and the Multicultural Encounter." *Contemporary Literature* 49.1 (2008): 56–84.

Freedman, Jonathan. *Klezmer America: Jewishness, Ethnicity, Modernity*. New York: Columbia University Press, 2008.

Funkenstein, Amos. "The Dialectics of Assimilation." *Jewish Social Studies* 1.2 (1995): 1–14.

Garber, Marjorie. *Academic Instincts*. Princeton: Princeton University Press, 2001.

Gilman, Sander L. *Jewish Frontiers: Essays on Bodies, Histories, and Identities*. New York: Palgrave Macmillan, 2003.

Glass, Loren. *Counterculture Colophon: Grove Press, the Evergreen Review, and the Incorporation of the Avant-Garde*. Stanford: Stanford University Press, 2013.

Glazer, Nathan. "*Commentary*: The Early Years." In *"Commentary" in American Life*, edited by Murray Friedman, 38–51. Philadelphia: Temple University Press, 2005.

———. "Discussion Forum." In *The New York Public Intellectuals and Beyond: Exploring Liberal Humanism, Jewish Identity, and the American Protest Tradition*, edited by Ethan Goffman and Daniel Morris, 158–161. West Lafayette, IN: Purdue University Press, 2009.

Goffman, Ethan, and Daniel Morris, eds. *The New York Public Intellectuals and Beyond: Exploring Liberal Humanism, Jewish Identity, and the American Protest Tradition*. West Lafayette, IN: Purdue University Press, 2009.

Gold, Michael. *Jews without Money*. 1930. Reprint, New York: Carroll and Graf, 1984.

Guttmann, Allen. *The Jewish Writer in America: Assimilation and the Crisis of Identity*. New York: Oxford University Press, 1971.

Herzl, Theodor. *The Jewish State*. 1896. Reprint, Mineola, NY: Dover, 1988.

Hook, Sidney. "Anti-Semitism in the Academy: Some Pages of the Past." *Midstream*, January 1979, 49–54.

Horowitz, Sara R. "The Paradox of Jewish Studies in the New Academy." In *Insider/Outsider: American Jews and Multiculturalism*, edited by David Biale, Michael Galchinsky, and Susannah Heschel, 116–130. Berkeley: University of California Press, 1998.

Hoth, Stefanie. "From Individual Experience to Historical Event and Back Again: '9/11' in Jonathan Safran Foer's *Extremely Loud and Incredibly Close*." In *Kulturelles Wissen und Intertextualität: Theoriekonzeptionen und Fallstudien zur Kontextualisierung von Literatur*, edited by Marion Gymnich, Birgit Neumann, and Ansgar Nünning, 283–300. Trier, Germany: Wissenschaftlicher Verlag Trier.

Howe, Irving. "The New York Intellectuals: A Chronicle and A Critique." *Commentary* 46.4 (1968): 29–51.

———. "Philip Roth Reconsidered." *Commentary* 54.6 (1972): 69–77.

JanMohamed, Abdul R., and David Lloyd. "Introduction: Toward a Theory of Minority Discourse: What Is to Be Done?" In *The Nature and Context of Minority Discourse*, edited by Abdul R. JanMohamed and David Lloyd, 1–16. New York: Oxford University Press, 1990.

———, eds. *The Nature and Context of Minority Discourse*. New York: Oxford University Press, 1990.

"Jewishness and the Younger Intellectuals: A Symposium." *Commentary* 31.4 (1961): 306–359.

Joseph, Philip. "Literary Migration: Abraham Cahan's 'The Imported Bridegroom' and the Alternative of American Fiction." *MELUS* 27.4 (2002): 3–32.

Jumonville, Neil. Introduction to *The New York Intellectuals Reader*, edited by Neil Jumonville, 1–11. New York: Routledge, 2007.

———, ed. *The New York Intellectuals Reader*. New York: Routledge, 2007.

Klingenstein, Susanne. *Enlarging America: The Cultural Work of Jewish Literary Scholars, 1930–1990*. Syracuse: Syracuse University Press, 1998.

———. "'It's Splendid When the Town Whore Gets Religion and Joins the Church': The Rise of the Jewish Neoconservatives as Observed by the Paleoconservatives in the 1980s." *Shofar* 21.3 (2003): 83–98.

———. *Jews in the American Academy, 1900–1940: The Dynamics of Intellectual Assimilation*. 1991. Reprint, Syracuse: Syracuse University Press, 1998.

———. "Town Whores into Warmongers: The Ascent of the Neoconservatives and the Revival of Anti-Jewish Rhetoric in American Public Discourse, 1986–2006." In *The New York Public Intellectuals and Beyond: Exploring Liberal Humanism, Jewish Identity, and the American Protest Tradition*, edited by Ethan Goffman and Daniel Morris, 275–311. West Lafayette, IN: Purdue University Press, 2009.

Kramer, Michael P. "Beginnings and Ends: The Origins of Jewish American Literary History." In *The Cambridge Companion to Jewish American Literature*, edited by Michael P. Kramer and Hana Wirth-Nesher, 12–30. Cambridge: Cambridge University Press, 2003.

———. "Race, Literary History, and the 'Jewish' Question." *Prooftexts* 21.3 (2001): 287–349.

Kristol, Irving. *Neoconservatism: The Autobiography of an Idea*. 1995. Reprint, Chicago: Ivan R. Dee, 1999.

Kronfeld, Chana. "Beyond Deleuze and Guattari: Hebrew and Yiddish Modernism in the Age of Privileged Difference." In *Jews and Other Differences: The New Jewish Cultural Studies*, edited by Jonathan Boyarin and Daniel Boyarin, 257–278. Minneapolis: University of Minnesota Press, 1997.

Krupnick, Mark. "Lionel Trilling, 'Culture,' and Jewishness." *Denver Quarterly* 18 (Autumn 1983): 106–122.

Levinson, Julian. *Exiles on Main Street: Jewish American Writers and American Literary Culture*. Bloomington: Indiana University Press, 2008.

———. Review of *Singing in a Strange Land: A Jewish American Poetics*, by Maerra Y. Schreiber. *American Jewish History* 94.1–2 (2008): 135–137.

Malamud, Bernard. *The Assistant*. 1957. Reprint, New York: Farrar, Straus and Giroux, 2003.

———. *Conversations with Bernard Malamud*. Edited by Lawrence Lasher. Jackson: University Press of Mississippi, 1991.

———. *The Natural*. 1952. Reprint, New York: Farrar, Straus and Giroux, 2003.

McGurl, Mark. *The Program Era: Postwar Fiction and the Rise of Creative Writing*. Cambridge: Harvard University Press, 2009.

Mearsheimer, John J., and Stephen Walt. "The Israel Lobby and U.S. Foreign Policy." Kennedy School of Government Working Paper RWP06-011, March 13, 2006.

———. *The Israel Lobby and U.S. Foreign Policy.* New York: Farrar, Straus and Giroux, 2007.

Michaels, Walter Benn. *Our America: Nativism, Modernism, Pluralism.* Durham: Duke University Press, 1995.

———. *The Shape of the Signifier: 1967 to the End of History.* Princeton: Princeton University Press, 2004.

———. *The Trouble with Diversity: How We Learned to Love Identity and Ignore Inequality.* New York: Holt, 2006.

Miller, Joshua. *Accented America: The Cultural Politics of Multilingual Modernism.* Oxford: Oxford University Press, 2011.

Mouffe, Chantal. "Democratic Politics and the Question of Identity." In *The Identity in Question*, edited by John Rajchman, 33–46. New York: Routledge, 1995.

Mullins, Matthew. "Boroughs and Neighbors: Traumatic Solidarity in Jonathan Safran Foer's *Extremely Loud and Incredibly Close.*" *Papers on Language and Literature* 43.3 (2009): 298–324.

Newton, Adam Zachary. *Facing Black and Jews: Literature as Public Space in Twentieth-Century America.* Cambridge: Cambridge University Press, 1999.

———. "Incognito Ergo Sum: 'Ex' Marks the Spot in Cahan, Johnson, Larsen, and Yezierska." In *Race and the Modern Artist*, edited by Heather Hathaway, Josef Jařab, and Jeffrey Melnick, 140–183. Oxford: Oxford University Press, 2003.

O'Hara, Daniel. "'The Cry of Its Occasion': On the Subject of Truth; or, The Terror in Global Terrorism." *Boundary 2* 34.2 (2007): 55–69.

———. *Empire Burlesque: The Fate of Critical Culture in Global America.* Durham: Duke University Press, 2003.

———. *Lionel Trilling: The Work of Liberation.* Madison: University of Wisconsin Press, 1988.

———. *Radical Parody: American Culture and Critical Agency after Foucault.* New York: Columbia University Press, 1992.

Omer-Sherman, Ranen. *Diaspora and Zionism in Jewish American Literature: Lazarus, Syrkin, Reznikoff, Roth.* Hanover, NH: Brandeis University Press, 2000.

Omi, Michael, and Howard Winant. *Racial Formation in the United States: From the 1960s to the 1990s.* New York: Routledge, 1994.

"Our Country and Our Culture." *Partisan Review* 19.3–5 (1952): 282–326, 420–450, 562–597.

Ozick, Cynthia. "America: Toward Yavneh." In *What Is Jewish Literature?*, edited by Hana Wirth-Nesher, 20–35. Philadelphia: JPS, 1994.

Palumbo-Liu, David, ed. *The Ethnic Canon: Histories, Institutions, and Interventions.* Minneapolis: University of Minnesota Press, 1995.

———. "Multiculturalism Now: Civilization, National Identity, and Difference before and after September 11." *Boundary 2* 29.2 (2002): 109–127.

Partisan Review editors. "Editorial Statement (1934)." In *The New York Intellectuals Reader*, edited by Neil Jumonville, 56–57. New York: Routledge, 2007.

Pellegrini, Ann. *Performance Anxieties: Staging Psychoanalysis, Staging Race*. New York: Routledge, 1996.

Podhoretz, Norman. Introduction to "A Symposium: Jewishness and the Younger Intellectuals." *Commentary* 31.4 (1961): 306–310.

———. "Issues: Between Nixon and the New Politics." *Commentary* 54.3 (1972): 4–8.

———. "My Negro Problem—and Ours." *Commentary* 35.2 (1963): 93–101.

Polan, Dana. "Translator's Introduction." In *Kafka: Toward a Minor Literature*, by Gilles Deleuze and Félix Guattari, xxii–xxix. Minneapolis: University of Minnesota Press, 1986.

Rajchman, John, ed. *The Identity in Question*. New York: Routledge, 1995.

Rancière, Jacques. "Politics, Identification, and Subjectivization." In *The Identity in Question*, edited by John Rajchman, 63–72. New York: Routledge, 1995.

———. *The Politics of Aesthetics*. Translated by Gabriel Rockhill. London: Continuum, 2004.

Riddel, Joseph N. "To Perform—A Transitive Verb?" In *America's Modernisms: Revaluing the Canon, Essays in Honor of Joseph N. Riddel*, edited by Kathryne V. Lindberg and Joseph G. Kronick, 14–25. Baton Rouge: Louisiana State University Press, 1996.

Rody, Caroline. *The Interethnic Imagination: Roots and Passages in Contemporary Asian American Fiction*. Oxford: Oxford University Press, 2009.

Rosenfeld, Isaac. "The Fall of David Levinsky." In *Preserving the Hunger: An Isaac Rosenfeld Reader*. Edited by Mark Shechtner, 152–159. Detroit: Wayne State University Press, 1988.

Ross, Andrew. *No Respect: Intellectuals and Popular Culture*. New York: Routledge, 1989.

Roth, Henry. *Call It Sleep*. 1934. Reprint, New York: Picador, 2006.

Roth, Philip. *American Pastoral*. 1997. Reprint, New York: Vintage, 1998.

———. *The Counterlife*. 1986. Reprint, New York: Vintage, 1996.

———. *Operation Shylock: A Confession*. New York: Vintage, 1993.

———. *The Facts: A Novelist's Autobiography*. 1988. Reprint, New York: Vintage, 1997.

———. *Zuckerman Bound: A Trilogy and Epilogue, 1979–1985*. 1985. Reprint, New York: Library of America, 2007.

Rothberg, Michael. *Traumatic Realism: The Demands of Holocaust Representation*. Minneapolis: University of Minnesota Press, 2000.

Rutherford, Jonathan. "A Place Called Home: Identity and the Cultural Politics of Difference." In *Identity: Community, Culture, Difference*, ed. Jonathan Rutherford, 9–27. London: Lawrence and Wishart, 1990.

Saal, Ilka. "Regarding the Pain of Self and Other: Trauma Transfer and Narrative Framing in Jonathan Safran Foer's *Extremely Loud and Incredibly Close*." *MFS: Modern Fiction Studies* 57.3 (2011): 453–476.

Said, Edward W. *Beginnings: Intention and Method*. 1975. Reprint, New York: Columbia University Press, 1985.

———. *Representations of the Intellectual*. New York: Vintage, 1994.

Saldívar, José David. *Border Matters: Remapping American Cultural Studies*. Berkeley: University of California Press, 1997.

———. *Trans-Americanity: Subaltern Modernities, Global Coloniality, and the Cultures of Greater Mexico*. Durham: Duke University Press, 2011.

Salidívar, Ramon. "Historical Fantasy, Speculative Realism, and Postrace Aesthetics in Contemporary American Fiction." *American Literary History* 23.3 (2011): 574–599.

Santner, Eric. *The Royal Remains: Two People's Two Bodies and the Endgames of Sovereignty*. Chicago: University of Chicago Press, 2011.

Schreier, Benjamin. "The Failure of Identity: Toward a New Literary History of Philip Roth's Unrecognizable Jew." *Jewish Social Studies: History, Culture, Society* n.s. 17.2 (2011): 101–135.

———. "Jew Historicism: Delmore Schwartz and Overdetermination." *Prooftexts* 27.3 (2007): 500–530.

———. "Literary-Historical Zionism: Irving Kristol, Alexander Portnoy, and the State of the Jews." *Contemporary Literature* 55.4 (2014): 760–791.

Schwartz, Delmore. "The Duchess' Red Shoes." In *Selected Essays of Delmore Schwartz*, edited by Donald A. Dike and David H. Zucker, 203–222. Chicago: University of Chicago Press, 1970.

Siegel, Elisabeth. "'Stuff That Happened to Me': Visual Memory in Jonathan Safran Foer's *Extremely Loud and Incredibly Close* (2005)." *COPAS* 10 (2009). http://copas .uni-regensburg.de/article/view/115/139.

Singer, Isaac Bashevis. *Enemies, a Love Story*. New York: Farrar, Straus and Giroux, 1972.

Sollors, Werner. *Beyond Ethnicity: Consent and Descent in American Culture*. New York: Oxford University Press, 1986.

———. "A Critique of Pure Pluralism." In *Reconstructing American Literary History*, edited by Sacvan Bercovitch, 250–279. Cambridge: Harvard University Press, 1986.

Spanos, William V. *The Errant Art of Moby-Dick: The Canon, the Cold War, and the Struggle for American Studies*. Durham: Duke University Press, 1995.

Spiegelman, Art. *Maus: A Survivor's Tale*. Vol. 2, *And Here My Troubles Began*. New York: Pantheon-Random, 1991.

Spivak, Gayatri. "Criticism, Feminism, and the Institution." In *Intellectuals: Aesthetics, Politics, Academics*, edited by Bruce Robbins, 153–172. Minneapolis: University of Minnesota Press, 1990.

Suchoff, David. "The Rosenberg Case and the New York Intellectuals." In *Secret Agents: The Rosenberg Case, McCarthyism, and Fifties America*, edited by Marjorie Garber and Rebecca L. Walkowitz. New York: Routledge, 1995.

Teres, Harvey M. *Renewing the Left: Politics, Imagination, and the New York Intellectuals*. New York: Oxford University Press, 1996.

Trilling, Diana. "Lionel Trilling: A Jew at Columbia." *Commentary* 67.3 (1979): 40–46.

Trilling, Lionel. *Beyond Culture: Essays on Literature and Learning*. 1965. Reprint, New York: Harcourt, Brace, Jovanovich, 1978.

——. "Manners, Morals, and the Novel." In *The Liberal Imagination: Essays on Literature and Society*, 193–209. New York: Harcourt Brace Jovanovich, 1978.

"Under Forty: A Symposium on American Literature and the Younger Generation of American Jews." *Contemporary Jewish Record* 7.1 (1944): 3–36.

Wald, Alan. *The New York Intellectuals: The Rise and Decline of the Anti-Stalinist Left from the 1930s to the 1980s*. Chapel Hill: University of North Carolina Press, 1987.

Walkowitz, Rebecca L. "Introduction: Secret Agents." In *Secret Agents: The Rosenberg Case, McCarthyism, and Fifties America*, edited by Marjorie Garber and Rebecca Walkowitz, 1–8. New York: Routledge, 1995.

Warner, Michael. *The Trouble with Normal: Sex, Politics, and the Ethics of Queer Life*. Cambridge: Harvard University Press, 1999.

West, Nathanael. *"Miss Lonelyhearts" and "The Day of the Locust."* 1933–1939. Reprint, New York: New Directions, 1962.

Wirth-Nesher, Hana. *Call It English: The Languages of Jewish American Literature*. Princeton: Princeton University Press, 2006.

Wisse, Ruth R. "The Conscience of a Jewish Conservative." *Jewish Ideas Daily*, January 21, 2011. http://www.jewishideasdaily.com/content/module/2011/1/21/main-feature/1/the-conscience-of-a-jewish-conservative/.

——. "The Jewishness of *Commentary*." In *"Commentary" in American Life*, edited by Murray Friedman, 52–73. Philadelphia: Temple University Press, 2005.

——. *The Modern Jewish Canon: A Journey through Language and Culture*. New York: Free Press, 2000.

——. "The New York (Jewish) Intellectuals." *Commentary* 84.5 (1987): 28–38.

Žižek, Slavoj. *Welcome to the Desert of the Real!* New York: Verso, 2002.

INDEX

ABOUT THE AUTHOR

Benjamin Schreier is Associate Professor of English and Jewish Studies and Lea P. and Malvin E. Bank Early Career Professor in Jewish Studies at Penn State University. He is the author of *The Power of Negative Thinking: Cynicism and the History of Modern American Literature* (2009) and the editor of the journal *Studies in American Jewish Literature.*